Walk Your Way to
BETTER HEALTH

Happy Walking!
Michael Stut

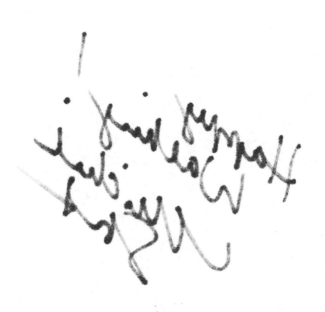

Walk Your Way to
BETTER HEALTH

THE WORLD'S EASIEST WAY TO DROP POUNDS, BOOST ENERGY, AND BEAT DISEASE

MICHELE STANTEN
and the editors of Prevention

RODALE

Rodale Inc. makes every effort to use acid-free ♾, recycled paper ♻.

Photographs by Mitch Mandel/Rodale Images and Matt Rainey/Rodale Images

Book design by Chris Gaugler

Library of Congress Cataloging-in-Publication Data is on file with the publisher.

ISBN 978-1-62336-922-4

2 4 6 8 10 9 7 5 3 1 Direct Mail hardcover

We inspire health, healing, happiness, and love in the world.
Starting with you.

Dedicated to my colleagues at America Walks and the Every Body Walk Collaborative, whose tireless efforts are helping to get more Americans walking more and ensure that all Americans have safe places to walk.

Contents

Stage 3: WEEKS 7 THROUGH 9

MEALS, RECIPES, AND MORE

Welcome

I'm so excited that you're joining me to walk your way to better health! This program is a follow-up to my earlier book *Walk Off Weight*, which helped thousands to get moving, walk off pounds and inches, and get healthy! The focus of that book was interval-walking workouts to boost results. *Walk Your Way to Better Health* builds on that program. There are many ways and reasons to walk. By offering even more comprehensive, customizable walking workout plans—including intervals—*Walk Your Way to Better Health* will help you use walking *your way* to achieve *your* personal goals—from creating an exercise habit or busting off a weight-loss plateau to lowering your risk of a host of diseases or coping with a specific diagnosis.

So, what is "better health?"

That's up to you to decide (maybe in consultation with your doctor). Each of our bodies is different. Each of our lives is different. Each of our genetics is different. Each of our experiences is different. Each of our tastes is different. We are all different in so many ways.

There is no one definition of better health. It means different things to different people: eating healthier and losing weight to get off diabetes medication, using healthier ways to cope with stress, or relieving knee pain without surgery. It could be building enough endurance to walk a marathon or to play with your grandchildren. Or, you may think of it as avoiding a second heart attack.

With all of these divergent goals (and many others), it's impossible for one specific plan to work well for all. That's why *Walk Your Way to Better Health* offers a multitude of options. Once you decide on your goal—what better health means to you—you'll find a variety of workouts and tools to help you succeed.

Whether you've walked for exercise in the past, are currently walking, or aren't moving much at all, this program is designed to get you the results *you* want by offering personalized walking workouts and showing you how to maximize your effort without spending hours exercising in some sweaty gym.

The program also includes a simple, flexible eating plan with delicious recipes to help support your journey to better health. You can exercise all you want, but if you have poor eating habits, it's going to hinder your progress. That's why the program offers a comprehensive eating plan designed to boost key nutrients, avoid junk foods, and curb overeating—all while keeping you satisfied and allowing you to personalize it to your lifestyle and tastes.

The program also includes mental strategies. Most people don't think about the mental aspect when they try to start exercising more or eating better, but this component is the foundation to success. If your mind isn't on board with what you want to do—for example, if negative self-talk keeps telling you that you're a failure—creating a regular walking routine will be an uphill battle. I have strategies that will help you to break through mental obstacles, boost your motivation, and stick with it, even when life happens!

And finally, there are strategies and tools you need to overcome any obstacles in your path to better health, which will help you maximize your overall results. No matter where you live, no matter how much free time you have in a day, walking can be the first step (pun intended) to leading a healthier, happier life.

THE POWER OF WALKING

You can walk your way to a slimmer figure, lower cholesterol and blood pressure, more energy, a flatter belly, better sleep, less pain, and a reduced risk of developing heart disease, diabetes, and even some types of cancer, just to name a few. If you already have a chronic condition like heart disease, diabetes, or arthritis, walking can help ease symptoms, slow disease progression, or help you cope emotionally.

The impact that walking has on your body also affects you mentally, emotionally, and spiritually. Walking can be a remedy for stress, anxiety, and depression. It can boost your mood, protect you from negativity, and help you manage difficult relationships—and it may even give you the confidence you need to get out of an unhealthy situation, if that's what you decide.

While we're all in this together, we each have our own unique needs, situations, and desires. That's what this whole program is about—figuring out what *you* want, selecting a plan that's right for *you*, and then tweaking it to make it *yours* for maximum success. Walk *your* way—to wherever or whatever you want! I'm here to help you every step of the way.

Happy walking!

Michele

THE BEAUTY OF WALKING *YOUR* WAY

Chapter 1

The Best (and Worst) Exercise

There are no perfect workouts, and that includes walking. Yes, walking has many attributes, but it's not perfect. Before you start, it's important to understand walking's potential downsides as well as its upsides. This knowledge will help you to get more out of your workouts and better results.

One of the reasons walking is considered the best exercise is because it's easy to do. You can do it anywhere. You don't need to learn complicated steps or buy expensive equipment. You don't need a gym membership. You can do it alone or with others.

Walking offers instant benefits. You'll feel happier and calmer. Worries and tension will ease. Cravings will vanish. Keep it up, and you'll fall asleep at bedtime—and stay asleep—more easily. Body aches and joint pain will subside.

You're probably thinking, "So, what's bad about walking?"

While the benefits certainly outweigh any negatives, walking can set you up for frustration and maybe even make that couch an all-too-enticing invitation.

Why? Because most people *just* walk. This observation is based on my 20-plus years of talking to, coaching, and walking with all levels of walkers, reading lots of research and surveys, talking to hundreds of experts, and being a walker myself.

Now, don't get me wrong, any walking is good—to a point. What I mean by "just" walking is doing the same thing day after day, which usually means a comfortable pace following the same route every time.

BODY BOREDOM

The result of all this sameness is that you get bored—both your mind and your body. You can avoid the mental boredom by walking with a friend or by walking while you watch TV, which many people do. But you probably don't even think of body boredom. This is when your body has gotten so efficient at what you're doing that you no longer see any results—the number on the scale or your blood pressure or cholesterol level isn't going down anymore.

Here's how it works (in a nonscientific way).

If you haven't been exercising at all, and you start walking, your body is like "Whoa! What is this?" and it starts to make some changes.

Your heart rate picks up a bit. Instead of directing most of your blood supply to organs like your stomach for everyday tasks, such as digesting food, your body redirects it, sending more to the working muscles in your buttocks and legs. Your lungs are busier. Mood-lifting hormones are being pumped out. If you've been sedentary, this is a shock to your system. In reality, our bodies were designed to work this way, but our drive-thru, online-ordering, desk-sitting, car-driving culture has made this a rare phenomenon for too many bodies in America.

The same thing happens the next day when you go out for a walk, and the next day, and the next. A few weeks into it, your body is now responding, "Walking time!" and knows exactly what to expect. Keep it up longer, and the response is more like, "Walking. Here we go again." The response is so automatic, like your body is on autopilot.

This is a good thing when it comes to your mind and creating a habit—you automatically go for a walk every day, no excuses. That's a great place to be! And I'll talk more about that later and help you get to that point. If you are looking for results like getting fitter and losing weight (which is probably why many of you are reading this), that is exactly what you *don't* want to happen.

Albert Einstein said it best: "Insanity is doing the same thing over and over again and expecting different results."

When your body is on autopilot and not being challenged, you stop seeing results. The scale gets stuck. You're taking less blood pressure medication, but can't get off it completely. You're not noticing the same kind of mood boost after a walk. You hit that dreaded plateau—no more improvements. That depletes your motivation. Then, without the mental stimulation from changing up your routine, it gets harder and harder to lace up your sneakers and get out the door for a walk. You start to skip walks, and, before you know it, you're on Facebook or Netflix instead of outside walking.

That's where *Walk Your Way to Better Health* comes in. It's going to help you get out of the all-too-common walking rut—and keep you out of it!

TOO EASY

One of walking's downsides is also one of its upsides—it's easy to do. That's a huge benefit when it comes to getting started. You already know how to do it. It's enjoyable, so you're more likely to do it. Walking is comfortable, not scary like other forms of exercise such as running (being breathless or knees hurting), Zumba (fancy footwork to follow), or CrossFit (intense instructors barking orders). Whether they are accurate perceptions or not, they impact your desire to do an activity. The availability, the approachability, and the comfort of walking make it an easier form of exercise, but it can still be an intense workout (more on that to come).

As you progress, however, those attributes can backfire. You get stuck in your comfort zone. It's particularly easy to do and can happen quickly with walking because, for most of us, it's comfortable from the start.

Now, if you're perfectly happy with the results that you've gotten and eagerly look forward to your daily walks, that comfort zone may seem fine. Sometimes, though, we don't know what we need or how much better walking could be. That was Marion's experience. Marion is a spunky 74-year-old who came to one of my walking classes with her daughters. Despite having Parkinson's disease, she's walked regularly for 12 years. During my classes, I have everyone do a timed lap in the beginning, so they can see how they improve after adding some technique to their walking. As Marion did her final lap, I noticed that she wasn't going to beat her time (I'd never had this happen before). As she approached the group at the finish line, she cheered with a smile, "I did better!" She began crying tears of joy as she explained that, for the first time in 3 years, she was able to walk and look at the trees. As the Parkinson's

had progressed, she had started to look down at her feet because she was fearful of falling. With the posture tips she learned (see pages 34 and 61), Marion became confident walking with her head up and enjoys walking even more.

You never know what amazing results may be waiting for you when you try something new.

Since you picked up this book, I'm guessing that you *want* to make some changes now! So, if you're currently walking and not happy with the results or need some motivation (like many of our test panelists, whose stories you'll read throughout this book), the solution is to get out of your comfort zone. If you

WALKER APPROVED

While I've used many of the strategies or individual plans in this book both personally or with clients, I wanted to make sure that, when put all together, they would deliver. To do that, I had 13 women and 2 men road test the plan to see what kind of results you can expect.

Most of the panelists wanted to lose weight or flatten their bellies, so they followed the plans that would help them achieve those goals. Others were interested in firming up, walking faster, or training for an event. I had appropriate plans for them, too.

After 9 weeks, the group lost weight and inches—7 pounds and 4 inches, on average. Those who were focused on weight loss dropped 9.5 pounds, slimmed down 5.5 inches overall, and whittled their waistlines by 1.5 inches, on average—with some of them losing up to 18 pounds, nearly 12 inches overall, and 4 inches off their waistlines.

Now remember, everybody is different. So, even if two people who weigh the same follow the exact same program, they will likely get different results. The same thing happens when people

take medications to lower their blood pressure or cholesterol levels. Some will lower their levels more than others, even if they are taking the same dosages. With the Walk Your Way to Better Health program, there are so many different plans to follow that results will definitely vary. But I will promise that if you follow your plan consistently, you will see results—just be aware that your plan may change along the way (and I'll help you navigate those finer tweaks, too).

While following the program, test panelist Janet Starner realized that it's okay to modify a plan. "I used to think that it was my fault if an exercise or diet regimen wasn't working," she said. "I must have done something wrong, not tried hard enough." But now, she acknowledges that not every plan is right for everyone, and what was right for you at one point in your life may not be right for you now or in the future. "The big change I made is to allow myself to listen to fitness prescriptions, but if they don't work for me, I alter or discontinue them. I no longer think of that letting go as weakness but rather as being smart."

want to see changes in your body and your health, the status quo just doesn't cut it. You need to challenge your body.

Unfortunately, most of us, myself included, aren't very good at pushing ourselves when it comes to exercise. Years ago, while working with a trainer, she asked me how much weight I wanted to use for bent-over rows. Before I could respond "12 pounds," which was my usual choice, she said, "15," and picked up a set of 15-pound dumbbells and handed them to me. And guess what? I did all my sets and reps with 15 pounds. But if she hadn't challenged me, I might still be lifting 12-pounders today.

Too often, you get into a lull with exercise that has become too easy. It feels good, or at least it's tolerable. You're afraid that pushing out of that comfort

MY WALKING JOURNEY

I may be a walker now, but it wasn't until an injury sidelined me that I came to appreciate all that walking has to offer. I grew up in the 1970s during the running boom. So, when I did a CROP Hunger Walk—not run—fund-raiser event with two of my best friends, Jodi and Linda, and Linda's mom, Flora, I ran. Being the cool sixth graders that we were, and thinking walking was for old people, Jodi and I took off running. But that didn't last very long, maybe a half mile. Despite taking an early lead, we soon had side stitches and were breathless, and Linda and her mom quickly caught up to us. We were pretty embarrassed, but we ended up having a lot more fun walking and chatting during the remaining 4 to 5 miles. At the end, Flora didn't complain about being tired like we did, and she looked strong crossing the finish line. That experience left an impression on me, but it would be decades until I'd appreciate walking like Flora did.

As a kid, walking was transportation. I grew up walking to school from kindergarten through 12th grade (except when I played on my mom's sympathy to drive me to early band rehearsals in high school). I'd walk two blocks to the corner store to get milk or bread for my mom. I'd walk to the park or to my friends' houses. We'd walk downtown to

the movies, to go shopping, or for pizza. We'd walk to the library.

In high school, walking became more of a social activity. My friend Karen's mom, Veronica, got it! She walked for exercise, and Karen often accompanied her. So, when we'd hang out, I'd join them. We usually walked at night, and we would talk (and gossip) up a storm—the latest guys we had crushes on, weekend plans, the boyfriends who broke our hearts, who was dating whom, what we were going to do with our lives, and where we were going to go to college. We worked out a lot of teenage issues on those 3- to 4-mile walks, and Veronica had a front-row seat to what was going on in her kid's life. (Hint to parents!) The faster we talked, the faster we walked. I still didn't consider it exercise, though. It was like a cooldown to the high-impact aerobics classes I'd taken.

It wasn't until my goal of running a marathon for my 30th birthday crashed and burned that I saw the real value and potential in walking. I worked for *Prevention* magazine, a sister publication of *Runner's World* magazine. At the time, walking was pretty much the only form of exercise we covered in the magazine. I was in my twenties, and running was definitely the cooler activity at Rodale. There were always races happening that

zone won't feel so good, so you often avoid it. Or, you underestimate your abilities.

In many cases, your body can do a lot more than you think it can. And the really cool thing is that when you start to push yourself physically, you discover how amazing you and your body are. The effect that can have on your psyche can be profound. I see this in women who I've trained for half- or full

marathons—walking them, of course. When they cross the finish line, they feel invincible! There is nothing they can't do and nothing they can't get through.

Walk Your Way to Better Health will nudge you out of that comfort zone so you not only get the benefits you want but also increase your enjoyment of walking.

employees could participate in—and the runners always looked like the fun, hip group. I was also a fitness instructor at the largest health club in the area, teaching high-impact aerobics classes several times a week. Running felt like a good fit for me. So, I did the beginner running class and started to do 5Ks.

Almost weekly at Rodale, someone was sharing their marathon experience. The idea of completing 26.2 miles seemed daunting for someone who had never participated in sports, yet the challenge was tempting. I started training for a half-marathon as I was turning 29, with the goal of doing a full marathon the following year. Unfortunately, my knees weren't on board with that decision. Despite resting, icing, and physical therapy, I just couldn't get past 6 to 8 miles without knee pain. So, no marathon for me.

I was bummed because I wanted to achieve some big fitness landmark. Shortly after my 31st birthday, I heard about the Avon 3-day walk for breast cancer. I didn't think of it as a fitness challenge but as a way to support a friend whose breast cancer had come back and to honor my three aunts who had all survived the disease. This time, I walked with my mom. The event was in May, so we were training in the middle of winter. I knew that I'd stick with it more if I had a walking

buddy. It turned out to be a great opportunity for us to reconnect. Although she lives only 20 minutes from me, we hadn't spent so much time together since I had lived at home about 10 years earlier. We walked through snow, ice, and downpours to prepare. And then, during the event, we walked through a heat wave. But that didn't matter. It was still one of the most amazing things I have ever done.

There were walkers of all shapes and sizes. Some of them extremely fit, others out of shape, and still others in the midst of or just having completed treatment for breast cancer. Unlike the running events I had previously done, we walked and talked, sharing our stories. Walking united all of us, and we were in it together. It was a very emotional experience.

It also showed me, once and for all, the potential of walking. Walking could be a fitness challenge, yet it is doable for just about anyone—even walking 20 miles a day for 3 days in a row. Tackling and achieving a big walking goal was inspiring and confidence boosting, and I wanted to share that amazing feeling with others. That's when I started coaching people to walk full and half-marathons—and I finally did my marathon—walking it, of course—for my 37th birthday, with 100 *Prevention* readers!

WALKING'S "BAD RAP"

As you can see, walking isn't really the "worst" exercise. Yes, it has some downsides—just like every other type of exercise. Running is high impact and can be hard on your joints. For spinning or yoga classes, getting to the gym to participate can be a hassle. But no one would argue that these activities don't count as exercise—unlike some who will say that about walking.

"Why Walking Is Not Exercise"[1] was a headline in a major newspaper in 2011. I was shocked! And one blog said walking is "a pale imitation of real exercise like running, swimming, rowing, or bicycling."[2] And then there's an online video entitled "Walking Is Not Exercise."[3]

They claim it's not strenuous enough. It doesn't challenge your cardiovascular system enough. Walking won't change your body, they say, or even help you maintain your weight. But, they do acknowledge its merit if you have a lot of weight to lose, or if you are really out of shape, elderly, injured, or just starting out.

Thankfully, the number of articles, books, and

WALKING VS. RUNNING

You've probably heard that when it comes to slimming down, running beats walking. When you look at pure numbers and even scientific studies, running certainly has an advantage—but the picture isn't black and white.

If a runner and walker, who each weigh 150 pounds, go out for a 30-minute run or walk, respectively, guess who's going to burn more calories? Not surprisingly, the runner will—by about 170, if she's running at a 10-minute-per-mile pace and the walker is striding along at a 15-minute-per-mile pace.

That's pretty black and white, but here's the gray.

Can you run at a 10-minute-per-mile pace for 30 minutes? Can you do this regularly without any joint problems? If so, great! Do it! Then, walk on days in between to allow your body to recover from the higher impact.

Walking is a great form of exercise, but it's not the only one! If you can run, run. If you love Zumba, do Zumba. If you're into yoga, get your om on regularly. But, if you love walking, don't stop doing it just because you hear that you'll lose

more weight running. If you want to burn as many calories (350) as the runner in the previous example, you'd have to go for almost an hour. If you pick up your pace to 4.5 mph (a 13:15-minute-per-mile pace), you can get it done in 42 minutes. Push it to 5 mph (a 12-minute-per-mile pace), and you just have to go 6 minutes longer than the runner. Yes, that is a speedy pace, but it's possible if you work at it.

Again, this comparison only matters if you can run that fast. I used to be around that speed in my twenties, but now, I'm closer to 5 mph when I run, and I can't do more than 5 minutes before my knees cry uncle. Even if I could go for 30 minutes, I'd burn the same number of calories as a walker at that pace (about 300). So, if I walk at my usual 4.5 mph, I'd need to go an extra 6 minutes to make up the difference. At 4 mph (a 15-minute-per-mile pace), an extra 20 minutes (a total of 50 minutes) would do it.

Yes, it requires more time to walk instead of run, but the amount of time—and sustaining the activity itself—is probably more doable and more enjoyable than running, at least for many of us.

videos that tout the benefits of walking seriously outweigh these. Our test panel results will dispute those bogus claims about the lack of results achievable with walking (see "Walker Approved" on page 5). The evidence is strong and clear that walking *is* exercise. In fact, it's so convincing that in 2015, the US Surgeon General issued a Call to Action to promote walking and walkable communities.[4]

They're not the only ones who believe you can walk off weight. The National Weight Control Registry is a database of more than 10,000 men and women who have lost at least 30 pounds and kept it off for at least a year—but on average, participants have lost 71 pounds and kept it off for 6 years,[5] with some losing as much as 300 pounds or maintaining their weight loss for up to 66 years.[6] When researchers investigated how these successful losers did it, they found that 94 percent of them increased physical activity. Guess what type of exercise was reported the most? Yup, walking!

So, let's get back to the Surgeon General's Call to Action. Why walking and not running, cycling, or Zumba? While all of them provide benefits, walking is the most accessible for the greatest number of people. That makes perfect sense, from a public health standpoint, to effect change in the largest number of people.

They are looking to activate couch potatoes or on-again-off-again exercisers, and walking is the most logical way to do that. But what happens then is we get the one-size-fits-all message. "Walk for 30 minutes a day" or "Take 10,000 steps a day."

You may even be following one of these recommendations—and they are great to begin with, but they don't take your individual body, desires, and circumstances into account. If you're successful at hitting those goals, over time, your mind and body are likely to get bored. With *Walk Your Way to Better Health,* you'll get a comprehensive walking plan—including strength training, an eating plan, and stick-with-it strategies—that is personalized to you, so you get the results you want.

STEPS TO SUCCESS

While customizing your plan is important, there are some concepts that apply to everyone and will increase your chances for success.

Walking *only* isn't enough. Walking is cardio exercise that makes your heart and lungs stronger, but it does very little, if anything, for your muscle strength. That's why strength training is a key part of the Walk Your Way to Better Health program. Physical activity guidelines from the US Department of Health and Human Services and the American College of Sports Medicine in Indianapolis recommend that all adults strength train, such as lifting weights, at least twice a week.

Somewhere in your midthirties, you start to lose muscle, if you're not doing some type of strength training. The loss accelerates as you get older, especially after menopause. Muscle loss also occurs when you lose weight. Less muscle means that your metabolism slows, so you burn fewer calories throughout the day. Over time, it can also contribute to developing diseases like diabetes. But strength training stems the loss of muscle so you avoid, or at least minimize, detrimental effects. It also boosts results. Strength training is the second most common activity of the successful losers from the National Weight Control Registry. And depending upon what your goals are, strength training may be just as important as walking, for example if you want to firm up or keep your metabolism revved up.

For your best shot at better health, you'll want to

combine walking with lifting weights, just don't carry weights while you walk. (See page 68 to find out why.)

Consistency is key. It's kind of common sense. The more regularly you walk, the more likely you will be to get results. But just to confirm it, scientists did a study.

French researchers[7] had 149 obese women, ages 50 to 65, participate in a 16-week walking program that recommended walking three times a week for 45 minutes each session. The researchers tracked adherence to the program to determine how it affected results. Not surprisingly, the women who walked the most, missing on average only 3 out of 48 sessions, lost a greater amount of weight and body fat and shrunk their waistlines more than those who walked inconsistently, averaging less than 2 walks a week. The more you do, the more you lose. Remember the successful losers from the National Weight Control Registry? They averaged 40 to 60 minutes of exercise a day[8]—gotta make it a habit!

Don't beat yourself up when you're not consistent, though—it happens to all of us! The women who didn't walk as much still lost weight. And all of the women had similar improvements in cholesterol levels. So, get out there and walk! It does a body good—even if you do it infrequently—but the more you do it, the more benefits you'll reap.

Planning ahead for your workouts will help you to be more consistent. That's what test panelist Rebecca (page 70) did. Every weekend, she'd schedule her workouts into her calendar. (For more strategies to improve consistency, see Get Mentally Strong (page 20) and Overcoming Obstacles (page 333).

You'll also be more consistent if you follow the 2-day rule from my fellow fitness instructor Chris Freytag. It's simple: Don't let more than 2 days go by between workouts. So, if you walk on Monday, but miss Tuesday and Wednesday, don't go to bed before working out on Thursday—even if you can't do a full workout, do something. If you follow this rule, it will guarantee that you get at least three workouts in a week. Not the best, but good enough—and, sometimes, that's the best we can do. And that's okay.

Chapter 2

Your Body on a Walk

Before you take that first step, let's look at what happens throughout your body as you walk, and the benefits it offers to each area. Being aware of all good things that walking (or any type of exercise) has to offer may help to internally motivate you. This is called intrinsic motivation, and, over the long haul, it is what you need to stay on track. Extrinsic, or external, motivation like losing 20 pounds for your high-school reunion doesn't have the staying power of internal motivators like the endorphin-initiated mood boost a walk can have. You're going to be racing to the door for a walk after you see all of the amazing things exercise does for your body.

When you're sitting at your desk, your body is primarily under the control of the parasympathetic nervous system. This command post is responsible for keeping things running smoothly—digesting food, storing energy, and promoting growth, all while keeping your heart rate, blood pressure, and metabolism low.

But as soon as you take your first steps, control shifts to your sympathetic nervous system—commonly referred to as your fight-or-flight system—to prepare your body for action. Here's what happens throughout your body and the benefits—both short- and long-term—you'll receive.

YOUR BRAIN

When you slip on your sneakers, the anticipation of going for a walk causes your brain to send get-ready signals out to other parts of your body. Without your realizing it, you start to breathe a little faster, and your heart starts to beat a little faster before you even take your first steps. Your brain is responsible for sending out messengers that trigger many of the changes in other parts of your body throughout your walk.

As you log more miles, your brain releases "happy" chemicals, like serotonin and dopamine. This combination of chemicals can lift your mood during and after your workout. If you push yourself harder, feel-good endorphins flood your body. These chemicals have an analgesic effect that counteracts discomfort or even pain from high-intensity activities. While it is commonly referred to as runner's high, walkers may experience it, too.

Our test panelist Janet Starner knows firsthand

how powerful a runner's high can be. "I was addicted to the endorphin rush and couldn't wait to run every day," says Janet, who started running at age 60. But when she switched to walking because of knee problems, Janet lost that lovin' feeling. "I never got the endorphin rush that I had had with running." That is, until she tweaked her walking technique and sped up to above 4 mph (a 15-minute-per-mile pace). "I just recently am able to walk fast enough, for short periods, to achieve the same runner's high I had when I could run," she reported about halfway through the Walk Your Way to Better Health program.

The good feeling can do more than just motivate you to walk more. An Australian study found that 200 minutes of walking a week (about 30 minutes a day) can alleviate symptoms in middle-age women with mild to moderate depression.[1] Other research has shown that brisk walking—sometimes as little as 30 to 45 minutes, three times a week—can be as effective as taking Zoloft.[2] And combined with medication, walking has even helped people with depression that doesn't respond to typical treatments.[3]

Walking releases a protein called BDNF, or brain-derived neurotrophic factor. Harvard psychiatrist John J. Ratey, MD, author of *Spark: The Revolutionary New Science of Exercise and the Brain*, has dubbed this protein Miracle-Gro for the brain because it encourages growth of new brain cells, which may explain some of the long-term cognitive benefits of exercise.

Unlike our waistlines, our brains usually shrink as we get older, and that means dying brain cells and memory problems. In particular, the hippocampus, a key area of the brain responsible for memory, normally shrinks by 1 to 2 percent a year in older adults without cognitive impairment. But when researchers had 60 sedentary adults (average age of 67) start walking at a moderate intensity for 40 minutes, three times a week, their brain volumes increased, with the hippocampus regions growing by 2 percent.[5] That may not sound like much, but it equates to a reversal of 1 to 2 years' worth of brain volume loss. Additional tests confirmed that these changes helped improve memory.

Along with a bigger hippocampus, a quicker walking pace and logging more miles may help to reduce your risk of developing dementia as you get older. For pace, aim to keep your normal walking speed faster than 2.2 miles per hour as you age.[6] (See page 73 to estimate your walking speed.) And for the amount of walking to do, 6 miles a week appears to be protective for healthy adults.[7] Even if you are experiencing some cognitive decline, walking may help. According to a 10-year University of Pittsburgh study, walking 5 miles a week helped people with mild cognitive impairment or Alzheimer's disease to maintain brain volume and reduce memory problems. Walking also appears to enhance brain connectivity, improving your ability to plan, prioritize, strategize, and multitask.

Beyond sharpening your thinking, the effects that exercise has on your brain may also help your waistline. Several studies have now found that a 15-minute walk can short-circuit cravings, especially for chocolate.[8] And walking may lower your risk of having a stroke. In one study, women who walked 3½ or more hours a week had a 43 percent lower risk of having a stroke than women who were inactive.[9]

YOUR HEART

As you start walking, your heart progressively beats faster, revving from a typical resting rate of 60 to 80 beats per minute up to 120 to 160 beats per minute, depending on your age and the intensity of your walk. Along with speeding up, your heart also pumps out more blood with each beat. This increase during a walking workout is four to five times the volume, from about 5 liters per minute when you're driving around town to 20 to 25 liters per minute when you're hoofing it. The harder you push yourself, the greater the increase. And that's a good thing!

Blood is the vehicle for delivering the oxygen that your muscles so desperately need to fuel you as you trek down the street. Your arteries, the blood vessels that carry blood away from your heart, are the roads the blood travels. To speed up delivery, blood flow shifts from a local route to the express lane. When you're going about your everyday activities, blood flow is making lots of deliveries, with working organs like your stomach and kidneys getting more service. But once you hit the pavement and start pumping your arms, the roads or arteries leading to your organs constrict, while those leading to your buttocks, quadriceps, and other working muscles dilate to fast-track oxygen-rich blood to your muscles for priority delivery. During high-intensity exercise, 80 to 85 percent of blood flow goes to your working muscles—about a four-fold increase compared to when you're logged on to Facebook.

Just like your arteries, your veins, the blood vessels that carry blood back to the heart, are like a circuit of roads. When you're out walking, your veins are transporting metabolic waste such as carbon dioxide and lactic acid that results from all of the energy production in your muscles. If these by-products aren't removed quickly, they can cause fatigue and impair

Did You Know?

Walking Boosts Your Self-Esteem. Taking an hour-long walk three times a week will leave you feeling better about yourself and liking the way you look more.

performance. Veins whisk them away from muscles to the lungs, liver, or kidneys for removal. As you become more fit, your body grows more capillaries in your muscles and lungs to speed the delivery of oxygen and the removal of waste products, so you can walk longer and harder.

All of this extra force and blood flow does cause a temporary rise in your blood pressure, but, over time, the effects of exercise result in lower blood pressure overall because a stronger heart can pump more blood with less effort. Postmenopausal women with borderline high blood pressure walked down their blood pressure levels 11 points in less than 6 months by taking an extra 4,000 steps (about 2 miles) daily, according to a University of Tennessee study.[10]

Challenging your heart like this also makes it stronger and capable of pumping out more blood with every contraction. But that's not the only heart benefits walking has to offer. Your blood vessels will remain more flexible. Your platelets will be less sticky and less likely to form a clot. Clot-dissolving enzymes in your blood will increase. Levels of C-reactive protein, a marker of whole-body inflammation, will decrease.

This is just a snapshot of improvements from walking that protect your heart. Walking can lower your risk of having a heart attack by up to 35 percent, according to an analysis of 18 studies.[11] If you do have a heart attack, a fit heart is more likely to survive the attack and recover more fully and quickly.

YOUR LUNGS

As your pace picks up, your lungs expand and contract more frequently, increasing your breathing rate from 12 to 15 breaths a minute at rest up to 35 to 45 at max-effort levels. Inside your lungs, oxygen-deficient blood is dumping carbon dioxide, a waste product of energy production that will be expelled with each exhalation. In its place, oxygen, the essential ingredient your muscles need to convert carbs and fat into energy to fuel muscle contractions, is picked up.

The harder you push yourself, the more oxygen you need. To satisfy this need, you unconsciously shift to breathing through your mouth instead of your nose and take deeper breaths to take in more air. Simultaneously, blood flows to an increased number of air sacs in your lungs to allow more oxygen to enter the blood.

As you become fitter, your lungs work more efficiently, so you'll be less winded or maybe not winded at all when you quickly climb a flight of stairs. Exercise also lowers your chances of developing lung cancer by up to 30 percent.[12] It can even offer some protection for smokers. For those with asthma or other lung diseases, walking may help improve lung function and reduce the severity of symptoms. In one study, walking about 2 miles a day reduced hospitalization in people with chronic obstructive pulmonary disease (COPD).[13]

Did You Know?

Walking Combats Breast Cancer. Strolling at a 2 to 3-mile-per-hour pace for about an hour a week—that's 8½ minutes a day—improved the survival rate of women with breast cancer, according to a Harvard study.[14] The risk of dying from the disease went down further if they hit the pavement for 3 to 5 miles a week.

YOUR BONES AND JOINTS

With every step, you are supporting your body weight, which is why walking is considered a weight-bearing activity. It's exactly the type of activity you need to keep or make your bones strong. Unlike swimming or riding a bike, where there is no impact, walking provides impact to stimulate bone strengthening.

As you warm up and really start cruising, impact increases for more bone strengthening, while still being low impact compared to activities such as running. Walking produces a force equivalent to one to one-and-a-half times your body weight, while running's impact is more like three times your body weight. The more impact, the stronger your bones will be, but you have to balance that with the potential for injuries while doing higher-impact activities.

Strong bones can protect you against osteoporosis and fractures. When researchers tracked more than 60,000 women ages 40 to 77, those who walked 4 hours a week—that's about 35 minutes a day—had a 40 percent lower risk of suffering a hip fracture during the 12-year study.[15]

The more you move, the more lubricating fluid your joints produce, so you'll feel less stiff on the second and third block of your walk than you did during the first. The majority of your joints get their nutrition from this synovial or joint fluid, so movement is critical. If you're not walking, your joints get less fluid and nutrition, which can speed deterioration.

Walking 5 to 6 miles a week may help stave off osteoarthritis, especially in the knees and hips, which are the most commonly affected joints. If you have osteoarthritis, as little as 45 minutes a week of walking can help ease pain and stiffness and maintain function over time, researchers found.[16]

YOUR MUSCLES

They flex and extend with every step you take and every arm swing you make. As blood flow and energy production revs, your muscles become warm and more pliable. During most walks, slow-twitch (aerobic) muscle fibers will be firing more than your fast-twitch (anaerobic) ones. That's because slow-twitch fibers have more stamina, thanks to higher concentrations of mitochondria and capillaries. They're like the tortoise—they contract slowly but keep going and going, while fast-twitch fibers are like the hare. They're quick and powerful, but they putter out just as rapidly. Fast-twitch fibers kick into action during vigorous activity such as very fast interval walking, but you never use only one type of muscle fiber exclusively. While your muscles are contracting, they are also plucking oxygen from all the blood that's flowing to them, making energy to fuel your activity, burning calories, and releasing waste products back into the blood for removal.

When you hit a hill or climb some stairs, 25 percent more muscle fibers in your buttocks start to fire, helping to tone your booty. Really push off of your toes and the balls of your feet as you step to activate more muscle fibers in your calves for shapelier legs. Want to tone your back or arms? Focus on your arm swing. Research shows that when you pay attention to a muscle you're working, you can activate more muscle fibers, which will help you firm up faster.

Walking also activates muscles to release a fat-burning hormone, called irisin, that was discovered in 2012. It appears to reprogram fat cells to burn energy instead of storing it, increase metabolic rate, and convert low-calorie-burning white fat cells to higher-calorie-burning brown fat cells—all changes that can make weight loss easier.

YOUR MITOCHONDRIA

These are the powerhouses of your cells that jump into action to fuel muscle contractions so your legs can move. Inside your muscles, they use carbohydrates and fats to make adenosine triphosphate (ATP), the energy source required for muscle contractions. Your body relies on fat for longer, lower-intensity workouts, while its primary source of fuel for shorter, more-intense workouts is carbohydrates.

Along with the revved-up production of ATP, your metabolic rate rises from burning about 1 calorie a minute at rest to 3 or 4 calories a minute as you warm up. As you settle in at a good brisk pace, it will crank up to burn 5 or 6 calories a minute. If you kick it up for some speed walking or intervals, you could spike it to nearly 10 calories a minute, depending on how fast you can walk and how much you weigh. (These estimates are based on a 150-pound person.)

Walk regularly, and mitochondria increase in number and activity, by up to 50 percent,[18] to improve your endurance and fat-burning ability. In one study, these types of changes in mitochondrial activity following interval training resulted in a 36 percent increase in fat burning,[19] which means you'll be able to go longer, and slimming down will be easier.

YOUR PANCREAS

This gland, located in your abdomen, produces digestive enzymes and hormones involved in regulating blood sugar. As you're racking up the steps, your pancreas slows production of insulin (the hormone that promotes fat storage), while increasing levels of the hormone glucagon. Glucagon pulls sugar out of storage so it can be used as fuel by muscles.

Because the pancreas produces insulin, it plays an important role in diabetes, which walking can protect you against. Follow the standard 30-minutes-a-day recommendation, and you could lower your risk of developing diabetes by 30 percent, according to a review of 10 studies.[20] If you have diabetes, keep walking, because it improves blood sugar control, which can minimize some of the serious side effects of diabetes, like increased rates of heart disease.

And, walk—don't run—to avoid diabetes. Walkers who logged 2 miles five times a week were less likely to develop diabetes than runners, who tallied nearly twice as many miles, according to one study.[21] Because fat is the primary fuel for moderate exercise, walking may better improve the body's ability to release insulin and control blood sugar.

YOUR SKIN

As your muscles work to speed you down the street, your muscles produce heat, which triggers the blood vessels in your skin to dilate. The increased blood flow can give you a flushed look, and your skin will feel warmer. As your body's thermostat rises, your two million–plus sweat glands start to work overtime, especially if it's a sunny, hot day. As the sweat on your skin evaporates, it removes heat and cools

your body—like having your own built-in air conditioner. This evaporation of sweat also removes fluids from your body, which is why it's important to be hydrated before you start exercising, sip (don't chug) water during exercise, and drink up afterward, especially if you're sweating a lot.

But exercise does more than just make your skin sweat. It appears to keep your skin looking younger. When researchers[23] from McMaster University in Ontario took skin samples from young and old exercisers and couch potatoes, they found that the old exercisers' skin didn't exhibit the same age-related changes as their peer couch potatoes. Instead, it looked closer to the samples from the younger group. Next, the researchers had sedentary seniors start exercising and found that after 3 months, some of the age-related changes had been reversed and the collagen levels had increased.

So, yeah, walking may make you look more youthful, too.

YOUR ADRENAL GLANDS

These small-yet-powerful hormone producers lie on top of your kidneys and release epinephrine and norepinephrine (adrenaline and noradrenaline) as part of the fight-or-flight response that kicks in when you start walking. The hormones signal the heart to beat faster and stronger.

As exercise continues and intensity rises, these glands release cortisol. While cortisol has been implicated in the storage of fat when you're stressed out, under exercise conditions, it prompts the breakdown and release of fat from fat cells.

YOUR PITUITARY GLAND

This pea-size gland sits at the base of the brain. It is referred to as the master gland because it produces a variety of hormones that signal other glands to

Did You Know?

Walking Improves Your Balance. Walking actually trumps balance training. When it comes to preventing falls, older adults who walked reduced their risk of falling more than peers who practiced standing on one foot and other balance exercises.[22]

PROFILE: Kim Bray, 62

Lost 18 pounds & 11.75 inches

While Kim had time to walk and a beautiful area to walk in, she still wasn't able to get out three times a week for 30 minutes at first—"the bare minimum that I felt would keep me healthy." Her list of excuses: bunion surgery (but her doctor had cleared her to walk), crime in her neighborhood (but her police detective son told her not to worry), too many hills, no one to walk with, and "I've tried this before."

Kim didn't really believe that walking would help her to achieve her weight-loss goal. She thought that she was "too old, too fat, and too out of shape to excel or benefit from walking."

Despite her beliefs, being a part of the test panel held Kim accountable, so she started getting out for walks regularly. Things really started to change once Kim began paying attention to her walking technique. Instead of just putting one foot in front of the other, she focused on maintaining good posture, taking shorter steps, and bending her arms. Within the first week, Kim was surprised at how much farther she was walking. "I never pushed myself before. At that point, nothing had physically changed for me to go farther. It was a mental change." She had a goal for each walk, and when she achieved it, she felt a sense

of accomplishment and was encouraged to do more.

The physical changes quickly followed. Kim was down about 8 pounds midway through the program, and she was climbing hills more easily and fitting into some of her smaller-size clothes. "It has been years since I could get into my smaller jeans, and it feels awesome," she said. "I am tucking in my shirts and wearing belts again." By the end of the program, she had shed 18 pounds, $3\frac{1}{2}$ inches off her waist, and nearly 3 inches off her hips, and she reported that even some of her smaller clothes were getting too big.

"This program has proved me wrong. I can lose weight by walking. I love walking now that I have learned techniques to make it more productive." In fact, you could say Kim is addicted to walking! "I used to wake up thinking about breakfast, especially toast. I love toast. Not anymore. I wake up thinking about where I am going to walk today. Walking makes me feel better physically and mentally—much better than toast ever could—which I stopped eating along with sweets, and my cravings went away."

And remember those excuses? They're gone, too! Kim doesn't mind walking alone, and rain, cold temperatures, and even snow don't slow her down. "I walk through most weather and don't want to stop."

BEFORE

AFTER

release their hormones. One of those hormones is human growth hormone (HGH), which is released when you exercise.

HGH can be thought of as a youth hormone since it is produced at high amounts when you are young, peaking in puberty, and then declining as you get older. But exercise can boost levels of HGH, which increases protein production to build muscle and decreases fat, making you look and feel younger.

The harder you push yourself when you're out walking, the bigger the boost in HGH you'll get. Lifting weights is also a good way to increase levels, so don't skip your strength workouts. But even moderate-intensity walks are beneficial. A study from the Nicolaus Copernicus University in Torun, Poland, found that a 10-week Nordic walking program (walking with poles) produced a 47 percent increase in HGH in postmenopausal women.[24]

HGH isn't the only pituitary hormone influenced by exercise. When you start to sweat, the antidiuretic hormone vasopressin, which targets your kidneys, is released to decrease urine production in an effort to stave off dehydration, if you're not drinking enough as you exercise.

YOUR DNA

While you inherit your DNA from your parents, the latest science shows that you may be able to influence your genes rather than just being stuck with them, and exercise is one way you can do so.

Every cell in your body packs a tremendous amount of coiled DNA—about 6 feet if you stretched it all out. Scientists have discovered small molecules that sometimes attach to DNA, which tightens the coil and represses, or switches off, the influence of certain genes. However, if those molecules are released, the coil loosens, which instead activates certain genes. The activation or deactiva-

tion of our genes is part of what determines which traits we develop, influencing everything from our appearance to our health. This is why, for example, some women with a breast cancer gene might develop the disease, while others won't.

In one study, researchers tested DNA in muscle cells before a bout of exercise and then 20 minutes afterward. They found that more methyl groups—a particular type of the small molecules mentioned—were released from genes involved in metabolism, thanks to the workout. In other words, the exercise prompted the methyl group to release from the DNA coil, thereby activating the metabolism genes and suggesting a possible improvement in the body's ability to burn fat. The effect was short-lived, so it's not a magic bullet. But, researchers are looking into whether these kinds of externally prompted genetic changes may become permanent over time.[25]

Another group of researchers looked at the fat cells of 23 healthy-but-sedentary men in their mid- to late thirties before they started an exercise program. On average, the men did two cardio exercise classes a week for 6 months. When the researchers checked out their fat cells again, they found that nearly 200 genes, including ones linked to obesity and type 2 diabetes, had been turned off.[26] They don't know how long the effects will last if exercise is stopped, but it shows that your genes aren't necessarily your destiny.

When Harvard researchers analyzed data from more than 12,000 men and women, they discovered that whether you have a high genetic propensity for obesity or a low one, exercise can inhibit the activity of weight-promoting genes. People who walked briskly for about an hour a day had a 50 percent reduction.[27] And according to other research, exercise may have up to a 75 percent effect on some genes.[28] Conversely, watching TV was found to increase the activity of these weight-promoting genes, according to the Harvard study. And the effects of each are independent, meaning even long walks won't override hours in front of the TV or computer. So, if your goal is to lose weight, get out and walk, *and* reduce the amount of time on your butt for best results.

The effects that exercise has on your DNA may also help you live longer. At the ends of DNA, there are telomeres. As you age, telomeres shorten, and their length has been associated with mortality.[29] But taking vigorous walks for 42 minutes over 3 days— 14 minutes a day—protects telomeres and may even help them to grow longer, effectively turning back the clock.

RECOVERY

When you stop your workout, all systems settle back down to normal and command reverts back to the parasympathetic nervous system. But this doesn't happen instantaneously. During the transition, your metabolism remains elevated, so you're burning bonus calories even when you're not exercising. The longer or harder you work out, the more time it will take your body to return to normal. As it downshifts, you'll continue to burn calories at an accelerated rate for as little as 20 minutes or possibly as long as up to 24 hours. This afterburn can help with weight loss, which is why the Lose Weight walking plans (see pages 75 and 152) are designed to maximize it.

Chapter 3

Get Mentally Strong

Before you jump into the walking plans and start working your leg and butt muscles, let's work your mental muscles. From Chapter 2, you know what your brain does when you're walking, but equally important is what it's doing when you're not walking.

Your brain can be your biggest ally for success, or your biggest barrier. Over several decades, neuroscientists have made some remarkable discoveries into how adaptable our brains are. The belief once held was that our brains develop during childhood and then stop, remaining unchanged throughout adulthood. The idea was that you were basically set in your ways, but new research shows that your brain has the capacity to change well into old age. And that's good news!

This is called neuroplasticity, the brain's ability to transform and create new neural pathways throughout your life. It explains how someone who has difficulty walking after a stroke can regain his or her ability to walk through rehabilitation. If you've picked up this book, I'm assuming that your neuropathways for the physical act of walking are firing just fine.

But injuries, disease, and rehabilitation aren't the only ways you form new neuropathways. Thoughts and experiences also affect your brain in this very physical way. You've probably heard the phrase "change your mind, change your life." In fact, there was a book published with that title more than 20 years ago. While it may sound like one of those woo-woo self-help mantras, there's now plenty of science to back it up.

If you constantly bombard your brain with negative messages and self-talk, your brain rewires itself so that when presented with new situations or experiences, your immediate response is as you've practiced—in other words, your response is negative.

And this is where your brain can have a big, even life-threatening, influence on your walking ability.

Numerous studies have proven that walking speed is an important indicator of health, especially as you get older. Research has shown that as walking speed declines as you age, your chance of being disabled or hospitalized increases. In one study,[1] people who had the greatest declines in walking speed over 8 years had a 90 percent increased risk of dying during that time compared to those who had smaller declines or maintained their walking speed. (Another reason to get out there and walk regularly! And strength train!)

But here's the really fascinating part: *Thinking that you're going to slow down as you age becomes a self-fulfilling prophecy.*

Researchers assessed the walking speeds and attitudes about aging of nearly 5,000 adults with an average age of 63. Two years later, they retested everyone and found that those who had negative thoughts about aging, feeling like they have little control over what will happen to them, slowed down more than twice as much as those who felt more in control as they age. This was particularly surprising since both groups were healthy at the time, and the results were independent of age, baseline physical ability, and other conditions that might have affected walking speed.[2]

So, just like physical factors, such as extended bed rest or too much muscle loss, can affect your ability to walk as you age, so, too, can mental or psychological ones, like thinking you are going to be frail when you get older.

That is pretty mind-blowing!

In the past, the idea of training your brain was more about setting goals and sticking to them, but now we know there is other mental work to be done. The right mental attitude is just as important as a good pair of sneakers, if you want to succeed. And in this chapter, you're going to find strategies to build your mental muscle. Now, keep in mind that we are all different, so some strategies may not apply to you—this is all about your way! However, it's worth reading about them because knowledge is power, and one day in the future, you might have to navigate that particular danger zone. Use the strategies

that address your needs and learn from the others so that once you get your physical muscles moving, you'll be more likely to keep them going!

FIND THE JOY IN YOUR WALK

If you think of going out for a walk as something you "have to do," another task on your to-do list, or an activity that's taking you away from something else that you'd rather do, then your fantastic neuroplastic brain will create a pathway of firing neurons that ensures that you will always respond to walking negatively.

Instead, train your brain to come up with positive ways to frame walking. One of the easiest strategies that I've found is to change "I have to take a walk" or "I need to take a walk" to "I get to take a walk." Then it sounds and feels more like a privilege or something desirable. "Have to" sounds more like a duty and can have a negative connotation. For some, simply changing the words is enough. If you need more, think about all of the people in the world with physical limitations that prevent them from taking a walk in the park, or others whose life circumstances don't allow them the freedom, safety, or time to enjoy a leisurely walk. Consider that the very concept of walking for fun is a luxury we humans have only enjoyed since the industrial revolution gave us free time. It wasn't very long ago that our exercise was restricted to grueling manual labor!

Even if you have to walk on your lunch hour, early in the morning, or late at night to fit it in, you are fortunate that you get to take a walk. And if you don't now, it may seriously impair your ability to do so as you get older.

Walk with pleasure. You can also make walking more desirable by associating it with other things you enjoy, like spending time with a friend or family member. Listen to music or an audiobook (just be alert to your surroundings, and use only one earbud for safety reasons). Take in the beautiful scenery either mentally or by snapping photos of a brilliant sunrise or sunset, blossoming trees and flowers throughout the seasons, or even wildlife that you may spot. Several of our test panelists shared photos of deer and fox they saw on their walks.

Relish "me" time. If you walk solo, think of your walks as me time. It's a chance to escape your obligations, clear your head, and reset both your body and your mind. It's a chance to do something good for you, to rejuvenate, so when you go back to your house, office, or your next errand, you're calmer and more productive. Instead of Calgon bubble baths taking you away, let your walks take you away—and you'll get even more benefits than a soak in the tub.

Dress the part. For some, comfy or hip walking clothes or accessories can make walking more desirable. When avid walkers were surveyed, 45 percent said that clothing and gear helped to keep them motivated.[3] For others, the idea of not having to change clothes to go for a walk may be more likely to get them going. So, do what works for you.

Find your happy walk. Depending upon where, when, or how you walk, different treks can have different effects on how you feel. Figure out the location and type of walking that makes you the happiest. Maybe it's strolling through a park, walking and talking with a close friend, or maybe it's a heart-pumping race to complete a particular route faster than before. It could even be strolling through a museum. Whatever it is, make sure you take your happy walk regularly, and more often if you need a mood boost or are struggling to get out the door. If your happy walk isn't convenient for every day—for instance, a beautiful hiking trail in the mountains—

make a plan to get there every few months (or sooner) for inspiration, and come up with another happy walk closer to home.

SPEAK KINDLY

If most of us recorded the voices in our heads and then played it back, we'd be appalled at what we hear. "I can't do this." "I'm such a failure." "I look terrible." And that's probably the mild stuff.

Remember all the negative thoughts are building pathways in your brain that just lead to more negativity. To change this, you have to start by being aware of it. Pay attention to your thoughts. As soon as they head down the negative pathway, cut them off at the pass! Immediately counter a negative thought with "stop it." You can even say it out loud for more impact. I do this if just thinking it doesn't work. Then, talk yourself out of the negative. Here's an example.

It's 10:00 p.m. and you see that you've gotten only 4,359 steps in today. Your immediate thought is "I'm such a failure. I never stick to my resolutions. Why even bother?" and so on, until you plop on the couch with a bowl (or a whole container) of ice cream.

Instead, what if you did this?

It's 10:00 p.m. and you see that you've gotten only 4,359 steps in today. Your immediate thought is "I'm such a failure. I never . . . Wait a minute, STOP IT! Okay, I didn't do so well today, but I hit my goal the past 3 days and came really close the other days of the week. That's so much better than I used to do. I'm not going to let one bad day ruin it. I still have an hour before bedtime, so I'll hop on my treadmill (march in place, walk around the house, or climb some stairs) and get some more steps in."

Then, while you're walking, you think back over your day and look for opportunities where you could have gotten some extra walking in. Learn from your mistake, and then plan accordingly for tomorrow, so you don't end up in the same situation.

Think about how you'd talk to a friend. You'd never chastise her for a mistake like missing a workout or eating piece of cake. Unless you're her frenemy, you'd do exactly the opposite, wouldn't you? You'd console her. You'd stop her from beating herself up. You'd remind her of how amazing she is, and you'd offer her solutions. That's what you need to do for yourself, too. You owe it to yourself to be nicer to you! Plus, the more you do it, the more nice-to-yourself

neuropathways you'll create, so it will get easier.

Even before you develop new, positive neuropathways, language has an immediate impact on your psyche and actions. Take the words "don't" and "can't." They sound similar and their meanings are similar, but they can have very different effects. In a study from the *Journal of Consumer Research*,[4] nearly 80 percent of the women who used an "I don't" phrase, such as "I don't skip exercise" or "I don't drink soda" stuck with their goal for 10 days compared to only 10 percent of women who used the "I can't" phrase. Experts say the word "don't" is

WALK YOUR WAY TO
WALK WHENEVER YOU CAN!

Phone time is walk time. Today, a friend called me just as I was pulling into the bank. Instead of sitting in the car and chatting with her, I walked around the block as we caught up. Every minute, every step, counts!

Cut wait time. If I arrive early to an appointment, I'll take a quick walk before heading in. Or, I'll walk while waiting for my kids at practice or a lesson. Test panelist Jackie (see page 341) walked while her car got an oil change one day.

Walk in whatever you're wearing. If I only have 10 to 15 minutes, I don't want to waste precious walking time changing clothes. As long as they are comfortable, and I don't mind if they get a little sweaty, I go!

Get a spare pair. Keep an extra pair of walking shoes in your car or office so that you're ready anytime you have a few minutes.

Coulda, woulda, shoulda. You don't want to feel this way. Regret sucks. So, use it to your advantage the next time you're feeling unmotivated. Think about how much worse you'll feel if you *don't* go for a walk.

Follow the 10-minute rule. On days when you're just not feeling it, compromise. Walk for just 10 minutes. Don't change your clothes. Simply set a timer for 10 minutes, and start walking. When the timer goes off, you're off the hook. You can stop without feeling guilty!

But here's what usually happens: Once you start walking, you usually keep going. Because you're already out there, or you start feeling good. I did it on an icy, windy winter day, when all I wanted to do was stay in my pj's and curl up on the couch with a latte and a good book. I put my sneakers on with my pj's (I wasn't planning on walking fast) and hopped on my treadmill with my iPad to catch up on some reading. Next thing I knew, I was reading another article and walking faster. I hopped off the treadmill 63 minutes later feeling really good about myself.

And if you stop at 10 minutes, no sweat! Some walking is always better than none, and tomorrow is another day to do more.

motivating because it signals control, determination, and empowerment.

Saying "I can't" feels and sounds like you really want to but someone or something is preventing you from doing it. When you say "I don't," it comes across like you're in control and you are making the decision.

Language can even affect your actions after a workout. How do you describe the walks you take? Are they walking workouts or are you walking for fitness? Or, are you taking a walk in the park or walking with a friend? If you describe or think of your walks as exercise, you may need to be extra-vigilant when you chow down postworkout. Cornell researchers[5] found that people who were told to walk for exercise ate 35 percent more dessert at their next meals than those who were told to go on nature walks. Despite the different descriptions of the walks, both groups followed the same route at the same intensity. Yet, the exercise walkers were less happy and more fatigued than the nature walkers. In a second study, another group of people did the same thing, but this time, they were given a snack after their walks. And once again, exercise walkers consumed more than twice as many calories worth of M&M's as the nature walkers.

Researchers speculate that when physical activity is viewed as effort, you may be more likely to reward yourself afterward, often with food. Instead, think of your walks as fun adventures or as opportunities to escape, so it feels more like a treat in and of itself. Keep this in mind, too, if you're putting walking on your calendar: Instead of writing "workout," "exercise," or even just "walking," try "nature walk," "fun walk," "walk outside," or "walk with a friend." It may just entice you more so you don't skip that walking appointment.

SOME IS BETTER THAN NONE

How many times have you thought about taking a walk, but didn't because you didn't have time for your usual 45-minute route or even a 30-minute one? I admit it . . . I've done that! I used to do it a lot back before I had kids. If I couldn't do a full, killer workout, I often did nothing. But after having kids and adding on all of those responsibilities on top of a more-than-full-time job, plus other stuff, I didn't have an hour-plus to drive to the gym and do an hour or an hour-and-a-half workout. Even my walking was "go big or go home" before I had kids—like a 3-day, 60-mile breast cancer walk. But now, I'm all about the 10- to 15-minute walk, because it's often easier to find multiple small chunks of time instead of one big one.

You don't have to do all or nothing! Some is better than none!

The research backs up that these short bouts of exercise throughout the day offer similar benefits as one longer session. In fact, the shorter bouts may offer some additional benefits. For instance, shorter 15-minute walks after meals have been shown to better regulate blood sugar than doing one 45-minute walk in people at risk of developing diabetes, according to a George Washington University study.[6]

Just last week, I had planned to have 30 to 45 minutes in between dropping my son off at the gym and picking my daughter up at school. With work calls and traffic, 25 minutes quickly vanished. I was ready to keep driving right past the park and figured I'd be 10 to 15 minutes early picking up my daughter, so I'd just catch up on e-mail or make a phone call. But then, I decided, forget that! I need some fresh air and movement before I'm back in the car chauffeuring the kids to evening activities. So, I made a left into the park, and even though I didn't have my favorite walking sneakers on, I hopped out of the car and got two brisk laps around the park in before I had to get my daughter.

It wasn't a long walk, nor was it perfect, but it energized me for the rest of my day. The next time work, kids, or just plain excuses or procrastination eat into your walking time, just do it anyway.

HAVE YOUR OWN BACK

One of the best strategies for walking regularly is to do it with someone else. Why? Because we show up. We don't want to let our friend, family member, or coworker down. So, we do it for them, even when we don't feel like it or have other pressing things to do.

This kind of accountability can be really useful. Similarly, taking actions like announcing your goals to all your Facebook friends, joining online groups, or just keeping in mind all the people who rely on you to be healthy and present can be powerful motivators.

But let's think about it for a moment. Would you walk if no one was waiting for you at the park or street corner? If you didn't have to report your number of steps online? Be honest. Some days, I will, but some, I won't. I get too busy with work, taking care of the house, chauffeuring my kids to their various activities, or volunteering. I'm not telling you anything you don't already know. Even some of the test panelists who were retired and had time to walk still didn't show up some days.

In the long run, you'll find success becomes a permanent state when you start showing up for *you*—not just for others.

In the beginning, it will probably be the accountability to others that will push you, but over time, making yourself part of the accountability process will strengthen the influence you have on yourself. You are the most important part here and no matter what, you're not going anywhere, so you need to have your back in those situations when there might not be someone else nudging you along.

As Ralph Waldo Emerson said, "Make the most of yourself, for that is all there is of you."

You deserve to take a walk. You deserve to eat healthy, delicious food. Look in the mirror, and tell yourself that you deserve to be healthy. Or, write about it in a journal. Or, talk to friends about it (they could probably use the pep talk, too). Heck, do all of the above, and take advantage of any opportunity to tell yourself how amazing and deserving you are. The next time you're buying a birthday card for someone, pick up one of those "thinking of you" cards that you'd send to a friend who's having a tough time. Sign it, maybe even writing a note to yourself, address it, put a stamp on it, and ask friend to mail it to you in a week or so or drop it in a mailbox somewhere. I know it sounds silly, but remember those neuropathways? You need to build ones that appreciate you, that support you, and that celebrate you!

CHANGE YOUR VIEW OF WALKING

What comes to mind when you think of taking a walk? Probably strolling around your neighborhood or development, or maybe walking in a nearby park or on a local trail. While those are great options, the more locations that you can associate with walking, the more steps you're likely to take.

Think about the places you go on a regular basis. Work. Your kid's school. The grocery store. Fields where your kids (or grandkids) play sports. Places where your kids take art, dance, or music lessons. The nail salon. Doctors' offices. The homes of good

WALKING ESSENTIALS

Besides getting your brain on board, there are few other must-haves for walking success. When it comes to gear, though, walking is low maintenance. You don't need a lot of expensive gear. The only essentials are a comfortable pair of walking shoes and socks.

People always ask me, "What's the best walking shoe?" Unfortunately, I can't tell them, because no two pairs of feet are the same. There are so many factors that affect the fit and feel of a shoe that it's impossible to recommend a specific shoe for everyone. The most important consideration when choosing a walking shoe is comfort. If the shoe doesn't feel good as soon as you slip it on, try on the next one and the next one until you find one that feels great right away. To find the best shoe for you, and to get a good fit, follow these tips.

Shop at a specialty running/walking store. The staff is more knowledgeable than if you go to a large chain retailer, so you'll get more personal, expert advice. The staff at specialty stores will ask you about your activity and watch you walk to help you find the right shoe for your feet and your activity level. You can even bring in a pair of old shoes so they can observe the wear pattern, which tells them a lot about how you walk.

Be a p.m. shopper. Throughout the day, your feet swell. Trying on shoes when your feet are at their largest will ensure a comfortable fit for walking any time of the day.

Start with socks. They are an essential piece of gear because they keep your feet dry and blister-free, and they can even reduce impact up to 20 percent. You want to select your socks first because they come in a variety of thicknesses, which can affect how your shoes fit. The thickness is a personal preference, but you definitely want to avoid cotton because they won't keep your feet dry from sweat or weather. Instead, choose socks made of synthetic fabrics that wick away moisture.

Consider running shoes. Yes, you can wear a running shoe for walking because they are both designed for forward motion. (But don't wear walking shoes for running. They aren't designed for the higher impact.) Most of the walkers I've coached wear running shoes, and I do, too. There are simply more options, making it easier to find a good fit. The shoes to skip: cross-trainers, tennis, and basketball. They are designed for lateral, not forward, action.

Bend it. Grab the toe and heel of a shoe and pull them toward each other. The shoe should bend easily at the ball of the foot. If it doesn't, look for another style that is more flexible, for greater range of motion and an easier push-off.

Look for a low heel. Big, bulky heels can impede the natural rolling foot motion of walking. They may also make you more susceptible to tripping.

Find some wiggle room. The right fit means that your toes should be able to move around inside the shoe. You should have at least a thumb's-width between your longest toe and the front of your shoe. Don't try to squeeze into a smaller size. Your feet swell during walks, especially long ones, and the wrong size shoes can result in pain.

Take a test walk. Specialty stores understand the need for this, so they are more likely to let you go outside or provide a treadmill for a test walk. At the very least, take a few laps around the inside of the store to get a feel for the shoes. Try on several brands for comparison. If you notice any rubbing, discomfort, or hot spots, move on to the next pair.

Replace sneakers every 300 to 500 miles. They may not look worn out, but materials inside sneakers that provide support and cushioning usually break down more quickly than the exterior. If you're overweight or wear very lightweight shoes, aim for the lower end of the range.

friends or family members. The next time you're at one of your regular haunts, scout out walking options. See if there's a park or trail to walk on. Or, simply start down the street (assuming it's safe to walk there), and go out for 10 to 15 minutes, turn around, and walk back—even 5 minutes is better than nothing. Don't make it more complicated by thinking that you need the perfect location and 30 or more minutes to make it worthwhile. (Remember, we're going to stop that all-or-nothing thinking!)

Today, I was 20 minutes early to pick up my son at baseball practice. So, I did a quick loop on the nearby walking path instead of just waiting in the car or sitting on the bleachers. Keeping a pair of sneakers in your car comes in handy for impromptu walks like this.

Also, look for opportunities when you can leave your car parked right where it is. Just about everyone can walk a mile, and according to the League of American Bicyclists, about 30 percent of all trips we make are 1 mile or less. If you're like me and live farther than a mile from any destinations, drive and park once whenever possible. I leave my car in the school parking lot after dropping off my daughter, and from there, I can walk to the bank, pharmacy, grocery store, post office, or nail salon. I'm all for making a walk do double-duty—a good workout *and* a way to get an errand done. Or, in large shopping centers, don't move your car. Instead, walk between stores, even if they are at opposite ends—in fact, it's even better for you when they are! If you have too many bags, simply put them in your car before going to the next store—you're getting extra steps!

It takes a little more effort to walk to destinations, but it's worth it. Along with doing something good for your body and your health, you'll be doing something good for the environment and save a little gas and wear and tear on your car. If walking to places from your home isn't practical, is it something you can do when you're at work? Look for lunch spots or places to do errands that are within about ½ mile. Or, drive partway there and park a half mile or so away from your destination, and walk the rest of the way. We all have errands to run and places to go—see how many of them or parts of those trips you can do on foot.

BELIEVE THAT YOU CAN DO IT

You may not have heard of it, but self-efficacy, a theory used in health psychology, can have a big effect on whether you achieve a goal or not.

Efficacy is effectiveness, or the ability to produce a desired outcome or result. So, self-efficacy is *your* being able to produce that desired outcome or result. High self-efficacy means that you have a strong belief or lots of confidence in your ability to do this. Low self-efficacy, not so much. It's possible to have different levels of self-efficacy for different tasks or goals. For example, you might be really confident in your ability to walk 5 days a week, but you're not so sure of yourself when it comes to cutting added sugars out of your diet.

Research shows that people with high self-efficacy are more successful at making behavioral changes, such as exercising or eating healthier. So, by believing that you can start and stick to a walking program, you'll be more likely to succeed. Now, that may be easier said than done. Unfortunately, failed attempts to stick with exercise in the past or bad experiences in gym class when you were a kid can have a serious effect on your self-efficacy, but there are strategies to build it up.

Create success. If you're really questioning your ability to follow this program, I strongly encourage you to start with "The Just Getting Started Plan" on page 34. It is the easiest, least time-consuming plan. All you have to do is walk for 10 to 15 minutes a day. You can do that! One of the best ways to build self-efficacy is by getting some early wins. Success breeds success.

No matter which plan you start with, track your eating and exercising, and review your progress each week. Then, celebrate your success. It doesn't have to be anything elaborate. Share it on Facebook, or have a sparkling water toast with your family at dinner. You can even do it daily. Acknowledging that you're following through on your walking plan helps to build your self-efficacy, which will come in handy when obstacles arise down the road.

For the eating plan, it might be helpful to set some specific small goals, such as swapping seltzer for soda or not using sugar in your tea or coffee. Track your progress, celebrate your successes, and then set another small goal.

And when you're not perfect, that's okay! Instead of beating yourself up (remember, we need to be nicer to ourselves), use the experience as a learning opportunity. Did you miss your morning walk because you felt like the Walking Dead after a late-night binge watch? If so, limit the number of episodes you watch at a time (besides, being planted on the sofa for that long can make it tougher to achieve all the healthy changes you want). Or, save binge watching for nights when you know you can sleep in.

Check out others. Seeing other people like you who've succeeded will boost your self-efficacy. You can start by checking out the profiles of our test panelists throughout the book. They were right where you were not too long ago. Let their stories inspire you! Or, read other stories about people who've overcome adversity to be walkers, runners, or other athletes.

I invite you to join me and other walkers on my Facebook page MyWalkingCoach or look for other online groups where you can meet people who are on a journey similar to yours. I also encourage my clients to hang out at the finish line of a half- or full marathon. Look for walker-friendly ones: half-marathons with 3½-hour or longer time limits or marathons with 7-hour or longer time limits. Or, distance charity walks. You will see people of all ages (some in their seventies, eighties, even nineties), shapes, and sizes crossing the finish line. Some will be cancer survivors or may still be getting treatment. Some may have multiple sclerosis, arthritis, diabetes, Parkinson's, or other diseases. But they are still putting one foot in front of the other and doing it. Witnessing them doing it will reinforce your belief in yourself to follow in their footsteps (you don't have to do a half- or full marathon—although once you get hooked on walking, you may want to!).

Get support. Having others encourage you can increase your self-efficacy. The best way to get this type of support is to ask for it. Choose someone you can count on and whose style matches with what you need—remember this is all about you—*your* way! You might prefer someone who is more empathetic and encouraging, or you might want someone who will be tough and push you to follow through. You can have more than one person. Once you decide on your supporters, ask for their help and tell them specifically what you need. It might be as simple as calling or texting you every Monday with some encouraging words. Or, you might want them to be your walking buddy two or three times a week. The clearer you are on what you need, the more likely you are to get it.

Plan ahead for obstacles. You'll boost your self-efficacy by being prepared. Think about obstacles that may come up. It's kind of like having a plan B.

PROFILE: Jenny Hughes, 43

Lost 7.6 pounds & 2.5 inches

Jenny Hughes went from feeling fearful and self-conscious when she walked to feeling confident and "standing taller." Since losing more than 7½ pounds and firming up, especially her legs, she's comfortably wearing her smaller-size jeans and even bought a pair of LuLaRoe leggings. "It's something simple, but a big step for me to wear leggings in public, and I feel darn good in them!"

But Jenny was a reluctant walker when she started the program. Due to abdominal surgery in 2011 and a knee injury, she was restricted from doing high-impact activities, but she longed to join her friends who were losing weight by running or doing exercise challenges. Instead, she followed her doctor's recommendation to walk. "I would leisurely walk, but I was fearful of aggravating my knee. I felt that I wasn't experiencing any true health benefits, and I was discouraged."

Things started to pick up once Jenny learned some walking techniques and became stronger. She had done some of the program's strength-training moves during physical therapy in the past. At the time, they helped to alleviate her knee pain. Knowing this helped motivate Jenny to start lifting weights, and she began to speed up her walks.

As a mom, wife, preschool director, teacher, and volunteer, Jenny was worried that walking would add another task to her to-do list and make her feel more stressed. Surprisingly, she discovered the opposite. Instead of feeling sluggish in the morning, her morning walks (after she got everyone off to work or school) left her feeling energized both physically and emotionally. When tested after the program, Jenny reported a 33 percent increase in her energy levels compared to the beginning of the program. And she found the fresh morning air and quiet time refreshing.

It still wasn't easy. "Some mornings, I would get overwhelmed," she said. On days like that, she'd either walk after work, or she'd break up her walks throughout the day. And she discovered a benefit to not always doing it perfectly. "Spacing out my walks alleviated stress at appropriate times," she explained. That encouraged her to add more walking to her day by parking farther away from entrances and taking the stairs.

"I realized that it was my responsibility to take charge of my day and my health for the benefit of myself and for my family! It was then that I realized that I was ready to face the responsibility of taking care of me and what was ahead."

BEFORE

AFTER

For instance, if your plan is to walk in the morning before anyone gets up, what is your plan when you oversleep? Pack your clothes and sneakers so you can take a lunchtime walk? Walk around the shopping complex before you hit the grocery store? Or, head straight to the park after work before you get caught up in evening activities? The more options you have, the more confident you'll feel in your ability to make it happen.

GIVE YOUR BRAIN A BREAK

The easier you can make a behavior—like walking wherever you are without changing clothes—the more likely you will be to do it. The harder it is to do something—say, drive 20 minutes to the gym to walk on the treadmill—the less likely you will be to do it.

The effort it takes for you to do something is what distinguished professor of psychology and management at Claremont University and author of *Flow: The Psychology of Optimal Experience* Mihaly Csikszentmihalyi calls activation energy.

The more activation energy a behavior requires, the less likely you will be to do it. For behaviors you want to adopt, like walking, you want to decrease the activation energy—make it as easy as possible to do. For example, keep a pair of sneakers in your office, another one in your car, and a third at home. (If you haven't noticed by now, this is one of my favorite tips.) Running up to your bedroom to get sneakers may not sound like much, but it increases the activation energy necessary, which may be just enough to make you skip your walk. I keep my sneakers on a shelf in the garage so I go out the door, slip them on, and go—no excuses!

What other ways can you make walking easier? What other behaviors do you want to adopt? How can you make them easier?

For behaviors that you want to stop, like eating added sugar, you should make it as hard as possible to do. For example, instead of leaving the sugar bowl on the counter, tuck it away in a high cabinet or even out of the kitchen. The extra effort to go get it may be enough to prevent you from adding sugar to your coffee or tea.

What behaviors do you want to stop doing? How can you make them harder?

You have a lot to think about, so the easier you can make some tasks for your brain, the better.

Wow, with all of this, you're probably wondering when in the world will you have time to walk! Actually, while you're out walking may be some of the best time to think about the strategies. I'm going to encourage you to focus on just one area for the first 3 weeks, then choose another for the next 3 weeks, and so on, until you've covered the ones that you need. You can start with one that you think will have the biggest impact on you, or choose one that you feel very confident in implementing. Remember, every little success you have will spur you on to more.

Chapter 4

Create Your Personal Walking Plan

Did you know that there's more than one way to walk? Most people go out and walk at a steady pace for a set distance. But there's also interval walking—speeding up and slowing down—and there are dozens, maybe even hundreds, of different ways to do intervals. There are leisurely walks, fast walks, body-toning walks, and meditative or stress-busting walks.

There are also different types of walks. Family walks. Nature walks. Sightseeing walks. After-dinner walks. And don't forget hiking. You can walk for transportation, like to work. You can walk for a purpose, like doing errands or walking the kids to the bus or to school. You can walk for no purpose at all. You can walk for a charity. You can walk around a track, on a treadmill, or in a mall. You can even walk a marathon!

When you start to think about it, it's pretty amazing how many different ways walking can be a part of your life. *Walk Your Way to Better Health* will help you take advantage of the many opportunities and ways of walking. With all of these possibilities in mind, in this chapter, I'll help you build a walking plan based on your goals and your lifestyle, so you'll be more likely to stick with it and get the results you want.

You can start this 9-week program now, and then repeat it for life. The program is broken into three stages, each 3 weeks long and each focusing on a different result. While the parts build on each other, after the initial 9 weeks, you can switch from one to another for fun or to achieve as varied results as you like. That's a heck of a lot of combinations to choose from—too many for me to count up.

You can extend any of the 3-week stages up to as many as 12 weeks. Each week in a stage builds upon the previous one. If you don't feel ready to step it up to the next week, simply repeat the current week, up to four times total. Or, move through all 3 weeks, and then repeat the final week in the stage three more times, if you want additional results, are still working on mastering some of the workouts, or timing isn't right to take on a new routine. Remember, do what's right for *you*, because that's what matters.

When you're satisfied with your results and are ready to move into maintenance, you can follow any plan or even a specific week of a plan for as long as you like—though I do encourage you to mix it up every couple of months, just to keep it interesting.

HOW TO WALK YOUR WAY TO BETTER HEALTH

Stage 1 (Weeks 1 through 3) is the Basic Walking Plan that will build a solid walking foundation, increasing your mileage and your endurance so you'll be ready to tackle more challenging workouts, if you desire, in Stage 2. Everyone will follow this plan to start, unless you opt for "The Just Getting Started Plan" (see page 34). I know you're probably thinking, wait a minute! I've been saying over and over again that this is all about you, and now I'm giving you a one-size-fits-all plan. I'm doing this so you can build a strong foundation for your journey to better health. (And anyway, it's just for the first 3 weeks! We'll get fancier in the next stage.)

Stage 2 (Weeks 4 through 6) customizes your walking workout to meet a specific goal or result. Some of them may be more challenging than others. Here are the goals you can choose from.

- Lose Weight
- Flatten Your Belly
- Maximize Your Health (prevent disease)
- Firm Up
- Get Faster
- Train for a 5K
- Train for a 10K (Weeks 4 through 9)

TAKE A WALK TEST

One of the best ways to stay motivated is to see your progress. To do that, you need a baseline. So, before you start any program, clock yourself to see how quickly you are currently walking. Then, you can retest yourself every 3 weeks to see your progress and celebrate your achievement.

You can use any distance that you are currently comfortable walking. You'll just want to make sure that you use the same distance for follow-up tests. The test panelists did a 1-mile test (four times around a standard track). A school track is the best place to test yourself because it's flat, and you don't have to worry about traffic. You can also use a path at a park or even walk around an empty parking lot. Just avoid testing yourself on streets where you might have to start and stop, which will keep you from getting an accurate measurement.

You'll want to spend about 5 minutes warming up. Then, get at your starting point, with your timer ready to go. You want to walk the mile (or whatever distance you selected) as quickly as possible, while still being able to talk. You should not be gasping for air. Don't start out so fast that you're dragging at the end. Aim for a pace that you feel you can maintain for the entire distance. Remember, this is a baseline to see where you are now. You don't want to push yourself beyond your ability and risk an injury before you've even started. When you've completed the distance, note your time. Save it so you can compare it to future walk tests. Finish by walking for another 3 to 5 minutes to cool down.

Stage 3 (Weeks 7 through 9) changes things up yet again to prevent your body from plateauing and your mind from getting bored. You can stick with the goal you picked in Stage 2, and you'll get 3 weeks' worth of new walking plans to keep the results coming. Or, you can pick a new goal from the same list to challenge your body in a new way and pursue different results.

In addition to walking, all of the plans include strength-training workouts. You can't get maximum results without strong muscles. Don't worry: All you'll need for most of the routines are some dumbbells and your own body weight, and you can do them in your living room.

So, let's get going!

WHERE TO START

In addition to the Basic Walking Plan (see Chapter 5), there is another option called "The Just Getting Started Plan" (see page 34). This is a stepped-down approach that eases you into the Basic Walking Plan with shorter walks and no strength training. While this is a good plan if you are very sedentary, very overweight, or have lots of health issues that impact your ability to walk, it can also be a great place to start for someone who's in good shape but struggles to stick with it or doesn't have a lot of time for exercise. Once you complete the 3-week starter plan, you'll be ready to tackle the basic plan and likely be more successful.

Answer the following questions to help you decide which plan is right for you.

On a scale of 1 to 4, rate how much you agree with each statement, with 1 being "strongly disagree," 2 being "disagree," 3 being "agree," and 4 being "strongly agree."

1. If my TV were powered by my treadmill, I could walk on it long enough to watch my favorite ½-hour sitcom.   1 2 3 4

2. People are amazed at how I get so much done in a day.   1 2 3 4

3. One big shake-up is the way to go instead of making small changes a little at a time. 1 2 3 4

4. I'd bet a week's pay or more that I can follow this program.   1 2 3 4

5. My friends, family, or others will have my back and cheer me on.   1 2 3 4

6. I try to do something new and challenging at least once a month.   1 2 3 4

If you scored . . .

- 1–12: Your best approach for success is to begin with "Just Getting Started" on page 34.

- 13–18: You could go either way. Review both plans, and then consider what else is going on in your life right now. Choose the plan that will best fit into your lifestyle today.

- 19–24: You can jump right into the basic walking plan on page 43.

THE JUST GETTING STARTED PLAN

This is the plan for you if:

- You're not sure that you can walk for 30 minutes straight.

- You struggle to stick with consistent exercise.

- You don't have a lot of time.

- You prefer to make changes slowly.

This plan will build your endurance, your walking muscles, and your confidence, while setting the stage to make walking a regular part of your life. You'll walk daily, which will help to establish it as a habit, but you'll start with just 10 minutes. Who can't find 10 minutes to walk? Then, you'll gradually increase your walking time. If you need a day off, there is an optional rest day each week.

You'll also notice that strength training isn't part of this plan. I want you to get started without feeling overwhelmed by lots of changes. However, if you want to start strength training now instead of waiting 3 weeks, then you can follow the Strength Workout on page 56.

The goal of the plan is to simply get out and walk at a speed that's comfortable to you. You don't have to worry about walking technique at this point; however, you'll feel a lot more comfortable as you walk if you maintain good posture (see right).

Here's what to do:

Walk the recommended amount of time all at once, unless otherwise noted.

Week 1

4 days: Walk at a comfortable pace for 10 minutes.*

3 days: Walk at a comfortable pace for 15 minutes.

Week 2

4 days: Walk at a comfortable pace for 15 minutes.*

3 days: Walk at a comfortable pace for 20 minutes.

Week 3

4 days: Walk at a comfortable pace for 20 minutes* (you can split these walks into two 10-minute bouts, if you like).

3 days: Walk at a comfortable pace for 30 minutes.

*If you need a rest day, you can skip one of these walks.

Posture Basics

- Stand tall. Imagine that you're trying to reach the top of your head toward the sky.

- Keep your eyes up. Look 10 to 20 feet in front of you instead of down at your feet.

- Swing your arms freely. Just let them move naturally from your shoulders.

Before you jump to your plan, finish reading this chapter, because there are some important steps to complete that could impact your success.

If you're not happy with beginning with "The Just Getting Started Plan" (opposite), I want you to repeat after me (worth reading for all! These strategies may come in handy any time you start to doubt yourself):

- "This is what's right for *me* right now."

- "This is about *me*, no one else."

- "I'm not going to worry about or compare myself to others."

- "Starting here is going to help *me* to be more successful."

Say it out loud. Look in a mirror and tell yourself these things. I know it seems silly, but what would be really silly—and a big waste of time—is if you beat yourself up or put yourself down over this. We are all at different points in our journeys to be healthier. Starting where you are right now will help you avoid doing too much, too soon, which can often undermine your efforts before you've even started!

You want to finish, and finish strong, so if you need more of a foundation, give yourself the extra 3 weeks for "The Just Getting Started Plan" and get over it! Remember, this program is for life, so what's another 3 weeks?

SET YOURSELF UP FOR SUCCESS

Walk Your Way to Better Health is not about working your butt off for 9 weeks and then going back to your old habits. It's about making changes that stick! It's about taking walking from a task on your to-do list to making it a part of your life, a habit, just like brushing your teeth and buckling your seatbelt. (I do hope you do both of these!) Don't you wish exercising happened just as naturally?

Without the struggle: "I should go to the gym, but I'd rather crash on the couch after work" or "I don't have time to go to Zumba."

Without the negotiation: "I don't want to get up; I'll work out at lunch" or "I'll just run longer tomorrow."

Without the guilt: "I blew it because I didn't work out today" or "I'm such a failure; I never stick with anything" or "I should spend time with my kids instead of going to the gym."

Life would be easier and more enjoyable if you just did it, right? No more wasted time debating with yourself. Isn't it about time you cross "exercise" permanently off your to-do list? The pre-program steps that follow will help.

Over the past 25 years, I've observed hundreds of people trying to make lifestyle changes to improve their diets and become more physically active. Most of the time, they follow a one-size-fits-all plan. They usually do pretty well during the official program time, but when the accountability is gone, they slip back into their old habits, regaining weight and becoming less active.

One of the reasons that this may be happening is that they're trying to fit their life into a program, when it should be the other way around. For success, you want to instead fit the program into your life!

The main focus of the exercise below is self-awareness. It's the foundation of self-improvement. You need to be aware of who you are and what you are doing *now* so you can make informed choices. Then, you need to be conscious of the changes that you're making—you don't want to just blindly follow some plan. This is about getting to know yourself better so you can better yourself.

My approach:

Record → Review → Revise → Results

Record—Before starting the program, record what you eat and how active you are for at least 3 typical days. Don't change anything! This should be an honest review of where you are right now. You can write the information down in a journal or a notebook, on your computer or phone, or make a copy of the sample logs on the next page. It doesn't matter how you record it, it just matters that you do it.

Review—Once you have this data, review it to make an honest assessment of where you are right now. How active are you really? How many fruits and veggies are you really eating during the day? How much time do you actually spend sitting? Are you drinking enough water? Be critical as you look over your days.

Revise—Now look for opportunities to tweak your days so you can be more active—where can you find pockets of time, or create them, for walking? Figure out what your biggest diet downfalls are and start to make changes according to the eating guidelines in Chapter 21. Combine this knowledge along with the Walk Your Way to Better Health program and come up with a plan for fitting the program into your life as seamlessly as possible. For example, instead of taking an afternoon work break in the cafeteria with coworkers, head outside for a walk. Better yet, invite your coworkers! You'll be able to catch up with them calorie-free. An added benefit is that doing it with someone else will keep you more accountable.

And the **Results** will naturally follow!

FOOD LOG

Write down everything you eat or drink, including how much of each item (measure, when possible). Don't forget to include condiments such as ketchup, butter, or additions to coffee or tea. The more specific you can be, the more opportunities you'll have to make your diet healthier and lose more weight.

Please do this for 3 days—2 typical weekdays and 1 typical weekend day—to get an accurate assessment. If you don't typically eat all three meals or this many snacks, just skip those entries. If you eat multiple times between meals, you can list it all in the same snack column.

Please also assess your hunger before you eat and after you are finished eating. Use the 1 to 10 scale below to rate your hunger before and after your meals.

1–2	Ravenous
3–4	Hungry
5–6	Comfortable
7–9	Full
10	Stuffed

Finally, jot down your moods or thoughts at mealtime. For example, you might be stressed if you're having a crazy workday, or tired, or maybe you had a fight with your spouse.

WALK WITH MICHELE

To help you get the most out of your walks, I've created audio workouts to accompany most of the walking routines throughout the program. All you have to do is pop in an earbud (only use one or keep the volume low) and walk to the beat. I'll offer you encouragement and technique reminders along the way. If you're doing an interval walk, you won't have to worry about tracking your time. I'll tell you when to speed up, when to slow down, and keep you pumped as you push yourself. It's like having me there coaching you every step of the way.

If you don't already have the MP3 loaded with the audio workouts or downloads of them, you can still get them at RodaleStore.com.

Food Log

DAY: DATE:

Meal/Snack (include serving size/brand names, when appropriate)	Time/Place	Hunger Level (before/after)	Moods/Thoughts
Breakfast: Steel-cut oatmeal (³/₄ cup) w/skim milk (¹/₂ cup) Banana Coffee (8 oz.) w/half & half (1 oz.)	6:30 a.m./at home	2 / 5	Really tired from going to bed late the night before & frustrated that I was running late for work.
Breakfast:		/	
After-breakfast snacks/bites/nibbles:		/	
Lunch:		/	
After-lunch snacks/bites/nibbles:		/	
Dinner:		/	
After-dinner snacks/bites/nibbles:		/	

Physical Activity Log

Record your activity from the time you get up in the morning until you go to bed at night. Write down what you are doing and where. In particular, you are trying to capture how much of your time is spent doing sedentary or active activities. You should be looking at ½-hour time periods, so feel free to round up or down. For activities lasting more than ½ hour, you can bracket multiple time slots to make recording easier.

   Please do this for 3 days—2 typical weekdays and 1 typical weekend day—to get an accurate assessment. Don't change your routine. Go about your day as you normally would, just record what you're doing.

Sample

	Time	Activity	Location
A.M.	5:00	Sleep	Home
	5:30		
	6:00		
	6:30	Shower	
	7:00	Eat breakfast	
	7:30	Get kids ready & fed	
	8:00	Walk kids to bus stop & walk back home	Neighborhood
	8:30	Grocery shopping	Store
	9:00		
	9:30	Gardening	Home
	10:00	Drive to work	Car
	10:30	Work at desk	Office
	11:00		
	11:30		
P.M.	12:00	Walk to get lunch	Outside
	12:30	Run errands on foot	Office park area

Physical Activity Log

DAY: DATE:

Time	Activity	Location
12:00		
12:30		
1:00		
1:30		
2:00		
2:30		
3:00		
3:30		
4:00		
4:30		
5:00		
5:30		
6:00		
6:30		
7:00		
7:30		
8:00		
8:30		
9:00		
9:30		
10:00		
10:30		
11:00		
11:30		

A.M.

Physical Activity Log

Time	Activity	Location
12:00		
12:30		
1:00		
1:30		
2:00		
2:30		
3:00		
3:30		
4:00		
4:30		
5:00		
5:30		
6:00		
6:30		
7:00		
7:30		
8:00		
8:30		
9:00		
9:30		
10:00		
10:30		
11:00		
11:30		

P.M.

WEEKS 1 THROUGH 3

Chapter 5

Basic Walking Plan

Stage 1 of Walk Your Way to Better Health creates a foundation of walking with longer durations but lower intensities.

For each walk, begin with easy walking to warm up, and then cool down at the end with easy walking, followed by stretching (see page 52). I have also included an optional Dynamic Warmup routine that you can do before you start walking or after your easy walking warmup. The Dynamic Warmup provides more moves and time to get your muscles, joints, tendons, and ligaments (and mind!) prepared to walk.

You're not going to be ambling during these walks, and your muscles need more blood flow and oxygen when you pick up the pace. A warmup eases your body into more energetic walking. Think of it like gradually accelerating your car as you get on the highway versus going from 0 to 60 in 5 seconds flat. The slower acceleration offers a smoother ride, and for your body, that means less discomfort as you place more demands on it. The more prepped your body is, the more enjoyable your walk will be and the less susceptible to injury you will be.

Three days a week, you'll be doing a moderate walk, which means you'll be going at a purposeful pace, exerting some effort, but still able to talk in complete sentences. Two days of the week, you'll pick up your pace to a brisk level, exerting a little more effort, so it's harder to speak in complete sentences. (See "How Hard Should You Push?" on page 62 and "How Exercise Should Feel" on page 61 for more information on finding the right intensity for your walks.)

You will also be strength training two days a week (see page 56 for the strength-training routine). You can do strength-training workouts on a day when you walk, but do not strength train on consecutive days. Your body gets stronger if you allow a rest day in between strength workouts. It is okay, though, to walk on the in-between day.

On nonwalking days, you don't have to take a formal walk (you can if you'd like), but you should remain active, simply moving more throughout your day and sitting less. Each week, your walks will increase in length to build your endurance and burn more fat.

THE BEST TIME OF DAY TO WALK

There is research showing that a.m. exercisers are more likely to stick with an exercise program compared with those who exercise at other times of the day. That's not surprising when you consider that there are fewer distractions early in the day to derail your best intentions. But what if you are *not* a morning person?

I'm not a morning person. In fact, I'm a full-fledged night owl. I find that I am more productive and do some of my best work between 10 p.m. and 2:00 a.m. It's hard for me to get to bed before midnight. So, to walk before anyone is up and asking for Mom, I'd have to get up at about 5:00 a.m.—not happening! But, when I do manage to wake up before everyone (or, more accurately, when everyone else sleeps in), I really enjoy an early-morning walk and feel such a sense of accomplishment, like bragging rights! My workout for the day is done, and no matter what happens the rest of the day, I did something good for me!

Not long ago, I snuck out for an early a.m. walk. I didn't get up earlier, but I immediately put in my contacts and put on my walking clothes instead of hanging out in my glasses and pj's. Then I got my high-schooler out the door. I gave him a head start (10th graders don't want to be seen walking to the bus stop with their moms) before I headed out. I had ½ hour to myself before my husband would be awake and I'd have to wake up my daughter.

The world felt so peaceful and refreshing, like anything was possible—like maybe I could become a morning walker. With every step, the sky brightened as the sun peeked out from behind the trees. I wondered if I'd be more productive since I was walking first thing. When I walked in the door, I felt energized and ready to tackle my day. I definitely had an easier time focusing on one task at a time. I was also calmer and less likely to snap at my daughter when she lingered instead of hustling as she got ready for school. One day, I hope to slow down all of our hustling, but then again, I'm much more the go-go-go type than the laid-back type. And just like my desire to be a morning person, we have to recognize who we are, our personal tendencies, and our current situations, and then work with that—do it our way. Trying to force your life to fit someone else's ideals—even if it's a scientific study—doesn't happen, or at least not for the long term.

With kids and my work schedule, I don't see early-morning walks becoming a regular thing for me right now—despite all of the research supporting morning exercise. Instead, I follow the advice that I give to others: The best time of the day to exercise is the time when you're most likely to do it. For some, that will be early morning, others may opt for lunchtime, while others will do best in the evening. For me, it depends on the day, but I make sure that I plan ahead. And remember, the best time to walk may change for you as your life transitions. I used to walk at 9:30 p.m. with neighbors when my oldest was a toddler and I worked full-time in an office. Now that he's a teenager, I want to be around at night.

To figure out the best time for you, review your Physical Activity Log from Chapter 4 (see page 38). This can help you to find pockets of time that are best for you to schedule your walks.

Now that you have an idea of when your best pockets of time appear in your schedule, here's the plan for Stage 1 (you can select any day of the week to do your walks).

YOUR BASIC WALKING TRAINING PLAN

WEEK 1

- *3 days a week:* Moderate Walk—3-minute warmup, 35-minute moderate pace, 2-minute cooldown (40 minutes total)

- *2 days a week:* Brisk Walk—3-minute warmup, 25-minute brisk pace, 2-minute cooldown (30 minutes total)

- *2 days a week:* Strength training (10 to 20 minutes total; see page 56)

WEEK 2

- *3 days a week:* Moderate Walk—3-minute warmup, 45-minute moderate pace, 2-minute cooldown (50 minutes total)

- *2 days a week:* Brisk Walk—3-minute warmup, 35-minute brisk pace, 2-minute cooldown (40 minutes total)

- *2 days a week:* Strength training (10 to 20 minutes total; see page 56)

WEEK 3

- *3 days a week:* Moderate Walk—3-minute warmup, 55-minute moderate pace, 2-minute cooldown (60 minutes total)

- *2 days a week:* Brisk Walk—3-minute warmup, 45-minute brisk pace, 2-minute cooldown (50 minutes total)

- *2 days a week:* strength training (10 to 20 minutes total; page 56)

Moderate walk

TIME	DURATION	ACTIVITY	INTENSITY
0:00	3 minutes	Warmup, easy walk	3
3:00	35 minutes*	Moderate walk	5–6
38:00	2 minutes	Cooldown	3
40:00	TOTAL: 40 minutes		

* For Week 2, increase to 45 minutes; for Week 3, to 55 minutes.

Brisk walk

TIME	DURATION	ACTIVITY	INTENSITY
0:00	3 minutes	Warmup, easy walk	3
3:00	25 minutes*	Brisk walk	6–7
28:00	2 minutes	Cooldown	3
30:00	TOTAL: 30 minutes		

* For Week 2, increase to 35 minutes; for Week 3, to 45 minutes.

DO YOUR BEST

By Week 3, walking will require a significant amount of time, but don't get discouraged if you can't do it all. Remember, no all-or-nothing thinking here. Instead, modify the plan so it works for you—walk *your* way!

- You can break up the walks into smaller 10- to 15-minute bouts and do them throughout the day. Even if you end up not doing enough sessions to total that day's goal, it's okay. You did more than you would have done if you had skipped the entire walk because you couldn't fit it in all at once.

- You can split the walks up over more days. For example, three 60-minute moderate walks is 180 minutes. You could do that over 4 days (45 minutes each) or 5 days (36 minutes each).

You'd have 2 more days of brisk walks—for 6 or 7 days of walking a week. That would mean you'd have to do both strength training and walking on at least one day a week, which is fine.

Most important, don't give up! This program is about progress, not perfection, which brings me to the 80-20 rule. If you follow the workout and eating plans 80 percent of the time, you are doing great! Let the other 20 percent go. No guilt! No beating yourself up. Just move on. Get back on track with your next day's workout or your next meal. Test panelist Rebecca said the 80-20 rule saved her. "In the past, if I thought I failed, I'd give up too easily. But with the 80-20 rule, I never felt like a failure if, every once in a while, I missed a workout or had dessert. It was just a part of the planned and allowable 20 percent." See? It's doable. Do what you can. Do *your* best!

Sample Schedules

At the bottom of the page, you'll find just two options for how to organize your workouts. Arrange them as you wish to fit within your schedule using the following guidelines.

1. Don't do two complete walks on the same day. For example, don't do a full-length moderate and a full-length brisk walk on the same day. It is, however, fine to break up one of those walks to do over the course of a day instead of all at one time.

2. Don't do strength workouts on consecutive days.

	Sunday	Monday	Tuesday	Wednesday	Thursday	Friday	Saturday
Option 1: No rest days	Moderate walk	Strength train	Brisk walk	Moderate walk	Strength train	Brisk walk	Moderate walk
Option 2: Rest days	Brisk walk	Rest day	Moderate walk and strength training	Moderate walk	Rest day	Brisk walk and strength training	Moderate walk

Prep Steps

You can just lace up your sneakers and go. If you're bouncing-out-of-your-seat eager to do that, then take a walk right now! But, when you return, I want you to do this initial prep work to ensure that you maintain your enthusiasm and keep walking in the weeks to come. If you can wait a minute, do the prep work first.

1. **Come up with at least three places or routes where you can walk.** Two of them should start from locations you frequent such as your work, your kid's school, or your home. For ideas, see "Change Your View of Walking" on page 25. There are no prerequisites for where to walk, but here are a few things to keep in mind.

   - Safety should be your number-one priority, so choose your locations and routes accordingly.

   - Hills will increase the intensity of your walks. Until you've built up your endurance, you'll enjoy your walks more if you stick to level terrain whenever possible. If you can't avoid hills, count them as a Brisk Walk and go for the shorter time. You may want to shorten your walks by 5 to 15 minutes to adjust for the increased intensity, if there are a lot of hills or if the hills are particularly steep. Pay attention to your body and your level of exertion (see "How Hard Should You Push?" on page 62). If you are having difficulty speaking as you're walking, it's too intense.

   - The more locations you have to walk, the more likely you will be to do it!

2. **Open your calendar, and schedule your walks.** This is especially important for Week 1. Review your Physical Activity Log you did from Chapter 4 (see page 38) to help you find openings in your schedule to fit in your walks. Then, put your walks in your calendar and treat them like other important appointments. Finally, make any arrangements needed to ensure that you keep your walking appointments. For example, confirm with your spouse which days they will cook dinner so you can walk. Or, set up a carpool with other parents to pick up your kids on certain days of the week so you can get your workout in. Or, meet a friend at the coffee shop near a park so you can log some miles after your get-together, or invite your friend to join you. (Check out "The Best Time of Day to Walk" on page 43 for more advice on scheduling your walks.)

3. **Do a walk test.** If you haven't already taken the walk test in Chapter 4 (see "Take a Walk Test" on page 32), head to the track. Having a baseline of how fast you currently walk will allow you to monitor your progress over the 9 weeks. Seeing the improvements can help to keep you motivated as well.

Walk Your Way to Better Knees

When 43-year-old test panelist Jenny Hughes's knee pain would act up due to damp weather conditions, walking wasn't an option. But instead of missing a day of working out, she substituted her walk with strength training and stretching. Bonus: The strength and flexibility gains in her legs have helped to reduce the frequency of knee pain.

DYNAMIC WARMUP

You should start every walk with at least 3 minutes of easy walking to warm up your body. This is an optional warmup routine. You can do it before you start walking as an addition to the walking warmups that are part of the moderate and brisk walks (see page 45) or instead of them. It's a great practice if you are feeling particularly stiff or stressed. It's also a great way to warm up before a strength workout.

- Shoulder rotation
- Torso pull
- Standing cat cow
- Toe pointer
- Ankle circle
- Foot rocker
- Leg swing

SHOULDER ROTATION

Stand tall with your feet slightly apart and your arms relaxed at your sides. (A) Without raising your arm, lift your right shoulder forward and up toward your ear. Then circle it back and down, making the movement smooth. Repeat with your left shoulder. Alternate shoulders, doing 5 rotations on each side. (B) Repeat, but this time raise your arm and let your elbow lead as if it is drawing circles. Alternate arms, doing 5 rotations on each side. (C) For the final set, extend your arm and rotate it to make large circles. Alternate arms, doing 5 rotations on each side. You can circle both shoulders at the same time for any of the variations if you prefer.

A   B   C

TORSO PULL

(A) Stand with your feet about hip-width apart and your arms extended straight out in front of you with your palms touching. (B) Bend your right elbow and pull your hand back toward your right hip as you rotate your torso to the right. Return to the starting position, and then repeat on the left side. Alternate, doing 5 pulls on each side.

STANDING CAT COW

Stand with your feet about hip-width apart and sit back into a partial squat with your hands on your thighs. (A) Lift your chest and your tailbone to arch your back. Hold for a second. (B) Round your back, bringing your chin toward your chest and tucking your tailbone. Hold for a second. Repeat 4 more times.

TOE POINTER

Balance on your left leg and extend your right leg with your right foot off the floor. Hold on to a chair or other sturdy object, if needed. (A) Point your foot, and then (B) flex your foot, pulling your toes up toward your shin. Do 10 times, and then repeat with your left foot.

ANKLE CIRCLE

Balancing on your left leg, extend your right leg. Hold on to a chair or other sturdy object, if needed. (A) Slowly rotate your right foot in a counterclockwise direction, drawing circles with your toes. Do 10 counterclockwise circles and (B) 10 clockwise circles, then repeat with your left foot.

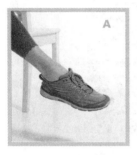 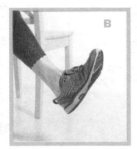 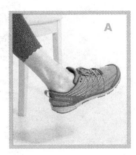 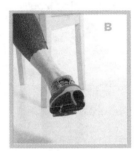

FOOT ROCKER

Stand with your feet slightly apart, arms relaxed at your sides. Hold on to a chair or other sturdy object, if needed. (A) Slowly roll up onto your toes, lifting your heels off the floor as high as possible. (B) Then, slowly roll back onto your heels, lifting your toes and the balls of your feet off of the floor. Do 10 forward-and-backward rolls.

 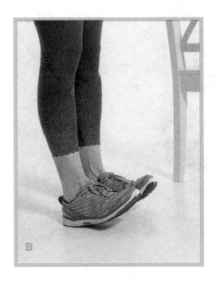

LEG SWING

Stand tall with your feet together. Hold on to a chair or other sturdy object, if needed. Shift your weight onto your left leg and hike your right hip up so your right foot is slightly off the floor. (A) With your foot flexed, swing your right leg forward and (B) back, keeping your foot pointing forward. Do 10 swings forward and back, then repeat with your left leg.

STRETCHING ROUTINE

As we get older, we lose flexibility. This makes it more difficult to do everyday tasks, increases our risk of injuries, and possibly even slows us down when we walk. A regular stretching routine is key to feeling younger and staying up to speed. The best time to stretch to improve or maintain your flexibility is after a workout, when your muscles are at their maximum warmth and most pliable. Stretching before exercise, which people typically think is the norm, offers little to no benefits and may even increase your risk of injury—so save it for afterward.

Aim to do this routine after all of your walks. It's also a good way to wrap up your Strength Workout (see page 56) or any other type of exercise you do.

For maximum results, you should hold each stretch for 30 seconds all at once—or break it up doing 3 reps for 10 seconds or 2 reps for 15 seconds.

- ■ Cross and reach
- ■ Heel drop
- ■ Low lunge
- ■ Leg up
- ■ Kickback
- ■ Sit back

CROSS AND REACH

Stand tall and hold on to a chair or other sturdy object, if needed. (A) Cross your right foot in front of your left foot. Reach your left arm up to the ceiling, lifting your rib cage, and then lean to the right. You should feel a stretch along the left side of your body down through the side of your left leg. Hold for 30 seconds total. (B) Cross your left foot in front of your right foot and repeat with your right arm. Do 2 or 3 times on each side.

A

B

HEEL DROP

Stand on a curb or step with your entire left foot flat on it. Place your right foot on the edge of the step so only your toes and the ball of your foot are on it, with your heel hanging off. Keeping your right leg straight, but not locked, lower your heel until you feel a stretch up your calf. Hold for a total of 30 seconds. Switch feet and repeat with your left leg. Do 2 or 3 times on each side.

LOW LUNGE

Kneel on the floor and place your right foot flat on the floor in front of you with your knee directly over your ankle. Place your hands on your right thigh. Shift your hips forward until you feel a stretch in the top of your left thigh. Make sure that your hips remain squared and facing forward and your left toes are pointing behind you. You may need to move your right foot forward slightly to prevent your knee from being out past your toes. Hold for a total of 30 seconds. Switch legs and repeat with your left leg forward. Do 2 or 3 times on each side.

LEG UP

Stand tall and place your left heel (toes pointing up) on a curb, step, or low bench. Place your hands on your right thigh. Slowly bend your right knee and hinge forward at your hips, sticking your butt out as if you are sitting back into a chair. Keep your chest lifted and lengthen your spine as you lean forward until you feel a stretch down the back of your left leg. Hold for a count of 10 to 15. Repeat with your right leg. Do 2 or 3 times on each side.

KICKBACK

Stand with your feet together and place your left hand on a wall, chair, or bench for balance. Bend your right knee, bringing your heel up toward your buttocks. Grasp your right foot with your right hand to gently bring your foot closer to your buttocks until you feel a stretch in the front of your right thigh. Tuck your tailbone under to feel more of a stretch. Hold for a count of 10 to 15. Repeat with your left leg. Do 2 or 3 times on each side.

SIT BACK

Stand with your feet together and place your left hand on a wall, chair, or bench for balance. Bend your left leg and place your left ankle on your right thigh. Slowly bend your right knee and hinge forward at your hips, sticking your butt out as if you are sitting back into a chair. Keep your chest lifted and lengthen your spine as you lower until you feel a stretch in your left hip and buttocks. Hold for a count of 10 to 15. Repeat with your right leg. Do 2 or 3 times on each side.

STRENGTH WORKOUT

Building strength and muscles is key if you want to keep moving—and be at your best—as you get older. Strength and muscle mass peak in your twenties, start to decline in your forties (sometimes even in your thirties), and progressively get worse as you age, making seemingly simple tasks like getting up from a chair or climbing stairs more difficult. I'm sure you've seen this in elderly friends or family members. Many people think that it's an inevitable part of getting old, but it doesn't have to be. That's why it's important that you strength train. In addition, building muscle will help you with weight loss, and it will power up your walks so you burn more calories.

- Squat and lift
- Bent-over row
- Bridge
- Plank

Do this routine twice a week, allowing at least 1 day between workouts. Recovery is key to building strength and muscles. Don't worry, ladies, you won't get big and bulky (you don't have the time or the hormones needed), so go ahead and pick up those heavier weights—you'll firm up faster!

Here's how to progress.

If a move is *too difficult*, you can do fewer reps or try the "Back it off" modification.

If a move is *too easy*, you can do more reps (up to 15 total) or more sets (up to 3 total). Or, try the "Pump it up" modification.

- Week 1: Do the routine one time through for 1 set of each exercise.

- Week 2: Do the routine one time through, and then repeat it one more time for a total of 2 sets.

- Week 3: Do the routine one time through, and then repeat it two more times for a total of 3 sets.

SQUAT AND LIFT

(A) Stand with your feet about shoulder-width apart, toes pointing straight ahead or slightly out, and arms relaxed at your sides. (B) Bend your knees and hinge forward from your hips, lowering yourself as if you are sitting back into a chair. Stick your butt out, shift your weight into your heels, and raise your arms out in front of you as you bend your knees and lower as far as possible, while maintaining good form. Stop before your hips are in line with your knees. Hold for a second. (C) Press into your heels, squeeze your buttocks, and stand back up. As you come up, rise up onto your toes, lifting your heels as high as possible. Hold for a second. Lower back to the starting position. Do 8 to 12 reps for a set.

Back it off: Do the squat only (without raising up onto your toes).

Pump it up: Hold dumbbells at your sides as you do the move.

BENT-OVER ROW

Place your left hand and left knee on a chair or bench. (A) Hold a dumbbell in your right hand with your arm hanging straight beneath your shoulder. (B) Bend your elbow and pull the dumbbell up toward your chest, keeping your arm in toward your body and your elbow pointing toward the ceiling. Hold for a second. Slowly lower the dumbbell. Do 8 to 12 reps with each arm for a set.

Back it off: Holding a dumbbell in your right hand, stand behind a chair with your left foot in front of your right. Lean forward slightly from your hips and place your left hand on the back of a chair. Either perform the move in this position and/or use a lighter weight.

Pump it up: Hold dumbbells in both hands and hinge forward from your hips so your arms are hanging beneath your shoulders. Keeping your abs tight, do rows with both arms at the same time in this position. (Do not do this if you have back problems.) Or do one-arm rows with heavier weights.

BRIDGE

(A) Lie on the floor on your back with your legs bent and your feet flat on the floor. Place your arms at your sides. Contract your abdominals and butt, and lift your hips and back off the floor so your body is in line from your shoulders to your knees. Hold for a second. Slowly lower. Do 8 to 12 reps for a set.

Back it off: Instead of doing reps, hold the bridge position for as long as possible, up to 1 minute.

Pump it up: Raise one leg off the floor, and perform one-leg bridges, repeating with the opposite leg.

PLANK

Lie facedown on the floor with your arms bent and your elbows under your shoulders. Tuck your toes under and lift your body off the floor so you are balancing on your fists, forearms, elbows, balls of your feet, and toes. Hold for up to 1 minute. If you're not able to hold for that long, hold for as long as possible, then lower and repeat. Keep your body in line from your head to your heels. Continue until you've held the plank for a total of 1 minute.

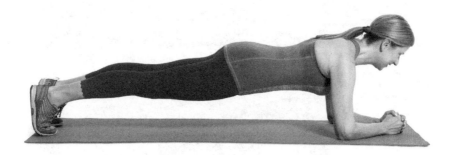

Back it off: Keep your knees on the floor.

Pump it up: After you push up into the plank, lift one foot off the floor and hold. Work up to holding for 1 minute on each leg, resting in between.

BASIC WALKING POSTURE

Walking generally feels pretty good. But as you pick up your pace or go for longer walks, if you're not maintaining good posture, you might notice some achiness or tension in certain areas of your body, like your neck or lower back. The more you walk and the faster you walk, the more important posture becomes. Here are the basics to get you started and set you up for success in the next stage.

- Stand tall. Imagine that you're trying to reach the top of your head toward the sky.

- Keep your eyes up. Look 10 to 20 feet in front of you instead of down at your feet. Your chin should be level to the ground.

- Bend your arms 90 degrees. The swinging movement should come from your shoulders, not your elbows. Imagine that your arm is in a cast so you don't straighten your arms as you swing.

- Swing your arms forward and back. Keep your arms close to your body. Bring your hand back to your hip on the back swing and no higher than chest height on the front swing. Don't let your arms go across your body or let your elbows wing out to the sides.

Walk Your Way to Make It a Family Affair

Invite your family to join you for some or all of your moderate walks. Walk with your kids before school—studies show that it helps them to perform better in class. Walk with your spouse after dinner—it encourages conversation and is a great way to catch up without any distractions. To entice your loved ones to join you, search for creatures with Pokemon Go, race to stay alive with Zombies, Run! (you can walk!), or save the world in The Walk. Please be careful of traffic and stay alert to your surroundings when playing games while walking.

HOW EXERCISE SHOULD FEEL

Anytime you're doing something that's out of your comfort zone—which is the intention of exercise in order for your body to change—it's going to be uncomfortable. It's normal, but some symptoms aren't normal and shouldn't be ignored. Here are guidelines on how exercise should feel, what's abnormal, and what to do if you experience any abnormal symptoms.

Normal	Abnormal	What to Do
Heart pumping rhythmically harder and faster	Chest pain, pressure, or tightness; skipped heartbeats or palpitations	Stop immediately and call 911.
Breathing faster and harder	Shortness of breath	Stop immediately and call your doctor or 911.
Muscle soreness or burning	Sharp, shooting pain in a muscle or any pain in a joint	Stop, rest, and ice the area. If the pain persists, or worsens, see your doctor.
General fatigue	Lightheadedness, dizziness, numbness, paralysis, speech difficulty, vision problems, or mental confusion	Stop immediately and call 911.

How Hard Should You Push?

Here are the intensity levels that you'll be aiming for throughout the various walking routines. The levels are based on a 1 to 10 scale, with 1 being equivalent to sitting and 10 feeling like you're sprinting for your life.

Intensity levels are very subjective and affected by your current fitness level. If you are a beginner, you will not have to go as fast to hit the same intensity level as someone fitter than you, but you will still get similar benefits. As you become more fit, you will find that you need to speed up to be working out at that same level. That's a good sign, showing that your heart and body are becoming better conditioned. Most important, listen to your body, and walk at a pace that's appropriate for you. (For guidelines, see "How Exercise Should Feel" on page 61.)

Activity	Intensity Level	Pace	How It Feels	Speed Estimates**
Inactive	1–2	Barely moving	Easy, could do it for very long periods of time	<2.0 mph
Easy*	3–5	Leisurely stroll	Light effort, rhythmic breathing; you can sing	2.0–3.5 mph
Moderate	5–6	Purposeful	Some effort, breathing some-what hard; you can talk in full sentences	3.0–4.0 mph
Brisk	6–7	In a bit of a hurry	Hard effort, slightly breathless; you can only talk in brief phrases	3.5–4.5 mph
Fast	7–8	You're late for an appointment	Very hard effort, breathless; yes/no responses are all you can manage	4.0–5.0 mph
Very Fast	8–9	You're trying to catch a bus as it's pulling away	Maximum effort, no breath for any talking	4.5–5.5 mph
Sprint	10	You're running for your life	All-out effort; can't maintain it for more than a minute	5.5+ mph

Use this for a warmup and a cooldown.

**These are only rough estimates, with the midpoint based on someone who is moderately fit. If you're just starting out, you'll probably hit each intensity level at a slower pace, closer to the lower end of (or even below) the speed range. If you've been walking regularly and are very fit, you may have to walk faster, aiming toward the higher end of the range, to achieve the recommended effort levels. Pay attention to your body, and do what feels right to you.*

PROFILE: Eileen Gradwell, 52

Lost 7.4 pounds & 5.2 inches

Walking helped Eileen power through some of the most challenging times in her life—a divorce and breast cancer. "Walking has always been a therapeutic and achievable activity for me."

It all started when Eileen signed up and trained to walk a marathon (26.2 miles) to help her cope with her divorce 15 years ago. "It gave me a focus and relief from the stress," she said. "It helped to give me back the power to understand that I could achieve anything that I set my mind to." She went on to walk two more marathons before settling into her new life as a single mom, in which she didn't find as much time to walk, but it remained her go-to activity. "It helped me survive a very sad time in my life."

Then, when Eileen was diagnosed with breast cancer a few years later, it became even tougher to get out for walks, but she pushed herself and even went to the gym and lifted weights. "It was a mental game to ensure that I was committed to living and not letting cancer take away anything other than my breast," she explained.

Before starting the Walk Your Way to Better Health test panel, Eileen was still dealing with some of the side effects from her treatment almost 10 years prior, including early menopause, belly fat, fatigue, and joint pain. "When I walked, I would feel tired, out of breath on the easiest incline, and my feet would feel like lead weights," she said.

When she started walking more on the program, her mood improved almost immediately. Her back no longer hurt once she started practicing good walking posture. And when she stopped looking at her feet, she discovered a whole new world. "It opened my mind up to the beauty all around. I loved watching the birds, seeing deer or fox, or just looking at the colors of the earth as the sun would rise."

Within 2 weeks, she noticed that she was having less joint pain. It continued to lessen as she mastered squats, lunges, and planks. At first, she held on to a chair for balance as she did squats, but soon, she was confident doing them with no support, and then started to add more reps. It took a little more determination and practice with the plank. "My arms would be quaking," she said. By following the modifications, though, she gradually worked up to doing three planks and holding each for a minute. "Small achievements are so empowering."

As she built up her stamina and got stronger, her walks "became energizing, instead of exhausting."

BEFORE

AFTER

UP THE HAPPINESS FACTOR

We've known for a long time that walking can elevate your mood, but the latest research shows just how powerful a dose can be.

- All you need is 12 minutes, even at an ambling pace.

- You don't have to expect any benefits.

- Even if you're bored or dread walking, your mood will lift compared to just sitting.

That's what researchers from Iowa State University found in a trio of experiments.[1] So, walking around the grocery store may leave you feeling pretty good, assuming you don't end up in the slowest checkout line.

For an even more robust boost, here are some strategies that you can use while doing most of the walks in the upcoming plans—or any walk at all!

Stroll outdoors. Treadmills or malls are great options when bad weather threatens your walks, but if you need to let off some steam or pump up your mood, head for the door. While all types of walks provide a mental pick-me-up, you'll get a bigger bump strolling outdoors, according to an Ohio State University study.[2] (Bonus: When something feels good, you'll be more likely to do it again.) Head for a park or other natural setting for an even greater uptick in your mood, according to a British study.[3] For possibly the biggest boost, choose a walking route that passes water. Looks like John Muir, a naturalist, conservationist, and founder of the Sierra Club, was right when he said, "In every walk with nature, one receives far more than he seeks."

Turn your walk into a meditation. Focus on your breath during the warmup and cooldown, matching your inhalations and exhalations to your steps. For example, inhale for four steps and exhale for four steps. As your breathing deepens, you should be able to take more steps for each inhalation and exhalation. During the rest of your walk, aim to stay focused on the present. Observe your surroundings, using all of your senses. Feel the wind in your hair or the sun on your face. Listen to the leaves rustling or the birds chirping. Look at the sky and see what images appear in the clouds, or focus on an object ahead of you and notice all the detail that comes into view as you get closer. If you notice your mind returning to your to-do list, worrying about something, or replaying a negative situation that happened, go back to paying attention to your breath and matching it to your steps.

Do a happy walk. Putting a little spring in your step (no, not the Prancercise kind) can leave you feeling happier, while walking with a slumped posture brings you down. How you carry yourself as you walk affects your mood, according to a German study.[4] When subjects adopted a depressed walking posture, their moods were more negative afterward compared to when they walked with a happy walking posture. So, stand tall with your shoulders back and your head held high. Give a little extra oomph with every step (just don't bounce—it slows you down and is harder on your joints). And smile!

WEEKS 4 THROUGH 6

Chapter 6

Customize for Your Goals

Congratulations on completing Stage 1 of the Walk Your Way to Better Health program! Woo-hoo! That's 3 weeks of walking under your belt (or 6 weeks, if you did "The Just Getting Started Plan"). Walking habit, here you come.

Now, you have a serious solid base for walking. You've increased the amount of walking you're doing by about 50 percent (even higher if you did the "The Just Getting Started Plan"). With all of those miles racked up, your walking posture should be improving. You should hopefully be finding it a little easier to fit your walks in, and maybe even feeling more desire to walk. Let's not forget all of the changes you've been making in your diet. By eating more nutritious foods, you should feel well fueled and have more energy for your workouts. And you should be noticing some benefits. Feeling happier? Got more energy? Clothes fitting better? Walking faster? Do another walk test (see page 32) to measure your progress.

This is just the beginning. During the next 3 weeks, you are going to shift your walking routine to focus on a specific goal of your choice. In addition to customizing your walks to get your desired results, this change also helps to prevent your body from going on autopilot and hitting a plateau.

The workout plans in this section are Stage 2. You'll have the opportunity to build on them, with more challenging plans during Stage 3 (Weeks 7 through 9), or pursue another goal. The goal options are the same for both stages (except for "Train for a 5K," which has only one 3-week plan, and "Train for a 10K," which is a 6-week plan that you'll stick with in both stages if you choose it), but the workouts are different. You'll learn more about that in Chapter 14 (see page 149). Right now, let's get started on those personal goals you want to achieve.

Here are the goals you can choose from.

- **Lose Weight**—interval walks for overall weight loss

- **Flatten Your Belly**—longer, faster walks for weight loss, with a focus on shrinking your midsection

- **Maximize Your Health**—build a walking habit with flexible walking goals to feel good and prevent diseases

- **Firm Up**—walking workouts with extra strength training to tone your body from head to toe, along with losing weight

- **Get Faster**—pick up your speed so you can maximize the benefits of walking in less time

- **Train for a 5K** (3-week plan only)—practice walking 3.1 miles at a constant speedy pace; signing up for an event can boost motivation

- **Train for a 10K** (6-week plan)—twice the length of a 5K; requires more training time; long walks will build your endurance to cover 6.2 miles; signing up for a more challenging event can boost motivation even more

You may want to achieve all of the above, but remember, one step at a time. The good news is that most of the programs will provide overlapping results. And in 3 weeks, you'll be switching up your routine again, so you'll have an opportunity to walk toward another goal at that time, if you'd like. Or, you can stick with your current goal and get new workouts to amplify your results.

GET UP TO SPEED

A common thread throughout almost all of the Stage 2 plans is that you will be picking up your pace. In some plans, it will be short bursts of speed. In others, you'll be cruising for the entire workout. Some plans will include both. The one plan that doesn't require fast walking is Maximize Your Health (see page 93), but if you choose that plan, you can certainly take it up a few notches—and you may want to when you hear some of the benefits of picking up speed.

Back in the early 1990s, researchers at the world-famous Cooper Institute of Aerobics Research in Dallas had 102 healthy-weight, sedentary women, ages 20 to 40, walk 3 miles, 5 days a week for 24 weeks. One group strolled at a 3-mph pace, another walked briskly at 4 mph, a third group built up to walking 5 mph, and one group did no exercise.[1] Despite

(continued on page 72)

THE WRONG WAY TO UP THE INTENSITY

Walking with hand or ankle weights will definitely increase the intensity of your walk, but they probably won't help you to get the results you want. Most people think about carrying weights in an effort to burn more calories or to tone up their arms or legs. The reality is that you probably can't manage enough weight on a walk to get visible results. How much weight are you really going to carry for a walk? Two pounds? Three? Maybe a few people could manage 5 pounds for a half-hour walk. Now, think about all the things you pick up on a typical day. Bags of groceries, 30 pounds of dog food, and maybe little kids. All are well over 5 pounds. You have to challenge your muscles, if you want to see results.

As for any bonus calorie burn, it's pretty wimpy, too. It's maybe 12 calories or so for a half-hour walk, and that is if you are able to maintain your usual speed, which becomes harder when you're carrying weights. Your arms act like a pendulum, and a weighted pendulum swings more slowly. If your arms slow down, then your feet slow down, too, and you burn fewer calories.

Most important, you're putting yourself at more risk for an injury. Swinging extra weight at the end of each arm puts a lot of stress on your shoulders, elbows, and wrists, and that could lead to strained muscles, ligaments, or tendons in the area. And it can throw off your gait, which may make you more susceptible to lower-body injuries, too.

For the best results, leave your weights at home, and walk faster!

DO IT YOUR WAY: Which Plan Is Right for You Right Now?

To decide on the best plan for you, consider the results that you want, along with your current fitness level. Here are some guidelines to help find the plan that suits you. Don't fret too much about it; remember, you get to pick another plan in 3 weeks.

1. **Is weight loss your number-one priority?**

   If no, jump to question 4. If yes, continue to the next question.

2. **Do you want to push yourself?**

   If no, then you should consider the following plans: Maximize Your Health (see page 93) or Train for a 5K (see page 126).

   If yes, continue to the next question.

3. **Do you have an hour to devote to walking most days of the week?**

   If no, then you should consider the following plans, which include shorter but higher intensity walks: Lose Weight (see page 75) or Get Faster (see page 118).

   If yes, then you should consider the following plans (Flatten Your Belly takes the most time): Lose Weight (see page 75), Flatten Your Belly (see page 85), or Firm Up (see page 100).

4. **Is getting healthy your number-one priority?**

   If no, jump to question 6.

   If yes, continue to the next question.

5. **Do you want to push yourself?**

   If no, then you should consider the following plans: Maximize Your Health (see page 93) or Train for a 5K (see page 126).

   If yes, then you should consider the following plans: Get Faster (see page 118) or Train for a 10K (see page 136).

6. **Is mental health (like stress reduction) your number-one priority?**

   If no, continue to the next question.

   If yes, then you can follow any of the plans and incorporate some of the mood-elevating strategies on page 64 for a bigger lift and greater stress reduction.

7. **Is looking better your number-one priority?**

   If no, continue to the next question.

   If yes, then you should consider the following plans: Flatten Your Belly (see page 85) or Firm Up (see page 100).

8. **Is feeling better your number-one priority?**

   If no, continue to the next question.

   If yes, then choose the plan that looks the most enjoyable to you.

9. **Not sure of your priority or can't just pick one?**

   If yes, then just pick a plan that looks interesting, and start walking.

   If no, then what the heck are you doing here?! No, seriously, look through all of the plans and choose the one the appeals to you the most. You can always switch plans later, if one is not right for you.

Remember, these are only guidelines. Review all of the plans before selecting one, and it's okay to go with your gut.

PROFILE: Rebecca Owens, 43

Lost 11.4 pounds & 6.25 inches

As a working, single mom, Rebecca's keys to success were planning and preparation. She couldn't commit to walk at a specific time every day because, with a 15-year-old son and 12-year-old daughter and working as a church musician and teacher, her schedule was always changing. But, when Rebecca started to use her weekends to prepare for the week ahead, she began changing her habits for the better.

Every weekend, Rebecca reviewed the meals and recipes, created her personal menu for the week, went shopping, and prepped food. She'd make quiche, soups, salads, and any other meals that would keep in the refrigerator for a few days. She'd prep fruits and veggies so they were easy to eat. "Every night, I would pack my snacks and lunch for work so I wouldn't skip meals like I used to and then be ravenously hungry and binge eat when I'd get home."

Rebecca also created a "calendar of walking appointments." She'd review her upcoming schedule and look for windows of time to slot in her walks. By scheduling them like work meetings, kids' activities, and other events, "I'd make them an equal priority," she said.

"Otherwise, it's too easy to find other things to fill up the time.

The more Rebecca walked, the more she wanted to walk. In fact, she called it her new hobby. "It's something I look forward to," she said. "I bought new sneakers, clothing for walking in bad weather, and headphones for my phone. I programmed music I love. I enjoy the process of walking." She also found that inviting her kids one at a time to walk with her provided an opportunity for them to talk and connect.

Not only was Rebecca walking more, but she was walking better and faster. Her fiancé says it looks "as though I'm running without leaving the ground." Not surprising, considering Rebecca was able to walk a mile in 13 minutes and 12 seconds (4.6 mph)—more than 3 minutes faster than before she started doing the program.

Along with the physical changes, Rebecca feels better. Thanks to the changes in her diet, she no longer experiences sugar crashes that would leave her feeling faint, moody, and jittery. The combination of exercise and a healthier diet were probably responsible for her 33 percent boost in energy as well.

BEFORE   AFTER

WALK YOUR WAY TO BETTER POSTURE

Let's take a closer look at the best walking posture for best results.

Ears in line with shoulders; don't jut your head forward

Eyes up; look out 10 to 20 feet in front of you

Chin level; don't look down at your feet

Shoulders relaxed, down, and back; don't pull them up toward your ears

Chest lifted; don't collapse and round your shoulders forward

Arms bent 90 degrees; don't let them swing down at your sides

Hands cupped loosely (or open)

Hips under shoulders

Abdominals tight; pull them in and up like you're zipping a snug pair of jeans

Pelvis neutral; don't tuck your tailbone or overarch your back

Knees pointing forward, not in or out to sides

Push off with your toes and ball of your foot

Toes forward, not pointing in or out

Land on your heel

having to work harder, the fast walkers were no more likely to drop out of the program than the other groups, and they didn't sustain any injuries. The results were worth the extra effort, too. The brisk walkers improved their cardio fitness levels more than twice as much as the strollers, while the fast walkers' gains were four times as much. Even better, the fast walkers completed their workouts in nearly half the time—36 minutes versus an hour for the strollers. Faster results in less time—who can argue with that?

The faster you go, the more calories you burn, too. That may seem like common sense, but what you may not know is that calorie burn increases exponentially, not linearly, when you crank up your pace. Speeding up from 2.5 mph (24-minute-per-mile pace) to 3.0 mph (20-minute-per-mile pace) nets you an extra 36 calories an hour. But a 0.5 mph increase at faster speeds results in bigger jumps in calorie burn. Going from 3 mph (20-minute-per-mile pace) to 3.5 mph (17-minute-per-mile pace) blasts an extra 57 calories an hour. You get the greatest calorie bumps when you rev up to above 4.0 mph (15-minute-per-mile pace). Going from 4.0 mph to 4.5 mph (13:15-minute-per-mile pace) incinerates nearly an extra 150 calories an hour. If weight loss is your goal, that should get your booty moving.

There are also more health benefits to be gained by speeding up—lower cholesterol, lower blood pressure, better blood sugar control, and reduced risk of several diseases. With all of those healthy benefits, it's really no surprise that faster walkers also tend to live longer than strollers.

Hopefully, I've enticed you to push yourself out of your speed comfort zone over the next 3 weeks and beyond. Here's how to get faster.

Elongate your spine. During the Basic Walking Plan (see page 43), you should have been focusing on

standing tall, by imagining the top of your head reaching toward the sky. Now, you're going to focus on your torso. You want to lift up out of your pelvis. Stand normally and place your fingertips of each hand on each hip bone and your thumbs on your rib cage. Stand up tall, elongating your spine, and feel how you gain more distance in between your hips and rib cage. This will allow your legs to swing more freely than when you slump into your pelvis.

Keep your eyes up and shoulders back. Look 10 to 20 feet in front of you instead of down at your feet. Your chin should be level and parallel to the ground. Keep practicing this to prevent upper-back tension. In addition, pay attention to keeping your shoulders back and down. It'll open up your chest, so you can take deeper breaths.

Swing your arms faster. From the Basic Walking Plan (see page 43), your arms should be bent at 90 degrees, as if they are in casts, as you swing them forward and back—not across your body or swinging out to the side. Now, pick up the pace of your arm swing. Your nervous system is wired in a way that your arms and legs want to be in sync. So, the faster your arms go, the faster your legs will go.

Roll and push off. Let's power up your feet. You want to land on your heel, roll through your foot, and then push off your toes and the ball of your foot to propel yourself forward. As you start to practice this technique or pick up your pace, you may notice that your shins start screaming. Don't worry! It's usually just from your shins being out of shape. If you do experience shin pain, see page 333.

Stop taking big steps. This is the most common mistake that people make when they try to walk faster, but it actually slows you down. When your front leg is far out in front of your body, it acts like a brake. In this position, your center of mass is behind your foot so you have to work really hard to pull

How Fast Are You Walking?

Count the number of steps you take in 1 minute. If you count your steps for 30 seconds, multiply by 2 to determine your 1-minute step count. Or, multiply by 4 if you count for a 15-second interval. Then, find the height that is closest to your own on the chart below and move across the chart to the right until you find the number closest to your 1-minute step count. Then follow that column up to the top of the chart to determine about how fast you're walking. These are estimates based on research from Boise State University.[2] You can also use an activity monitor with GPS like Garmin or an app like MapMyWalk or Runkeeper for more accurate speed checks.

Minutes per mile					
24 minutes	20 minutes	17 minutes	15 minutes	13 minutes	12 minutes
Speed					
2.5 mph	3.0 mph	3.5 mph	4.0 mph	4.6 mph	5.0 mph

Height

	2.5 mph	3.0 mph	3.5 mph	4.0 mph	4.6 mph	5.0 mph
5 ft 0 in	109	119	128	137	148	155
5 ft 2 in	108	117	127	135	146	153
5 ft 4 in	107	116	125	133	144	151
5 ft 6 in	106	114	123	131	142	148
5 ft 8 in	105	113	122	129	140	146

yourself over your front leg in order to step forward with your opposite leg. Instead, think short, quick steps. Your foot should land almost underneath you so you roll right over it. To get an idea of how short your step should be, raise one knee to hip height so your foot is hanging below your knee, like you're marching. Then, extend your leg, bringing your heel down to the ground. It should be just a few inches in front of your other foot.

If you want to know how fast you're going, you can invest in an activity monitor with GPS, or use an app like MapMyWalk. Or, you can estimate it by counting the number of steps you take in a minute, and then refer above to the chart "How Fast Are You Walking?"

Find a fast friend. Walking with someone who's a bit beyond your ability can help push you out of your comfort zone, according to test panelist Jenny (see page 29). "It encourages you to keep moving, or it gives you more of a challenge," she says. Just don't pick someone too much faster than you, otherwise you may both end up frustrated.

Now it's time to walk your way to whichever goal you've selected. In the following chapters, you'll find programs for the next 3 weeks, tailored to the goals I've listed. Make your choice, turn to that chapter, and get walking!

- **Lose Weight,** opposite
- **Flatten Your Belly,** page 85
- **Maximize Your Health,** page 93
- **Firm Up,** page 100
- **Get Faster,** page 118
- **Train for a 5K,** page 126
- **Train for a 10K,** page 136

Chapter 7

Lose Weight

For the next 3 weeks, you'll turn up your fat-burning by adding interval walks to your routine Interval walking alternates short bursts of fast walking with longer recovery bouts of moderate to brisk walking.

And they work. There's scientific research to back up the benefits of turning some of your steady-paced walks into intervals. When people with diabetes tried interval walking for 4 months, they lost six times more weight—9.5 versus 1.5 pounds—and shed more belly fat than people with diabetes who didn't vary their walking speeds, according to a Danish study.[1] The interval exercisers also had better blood sugar levels and increased their cardio fitness levels (meaning less huffing and puffing when they climb stairs), while steady-paced walkers showed no such improvements.

In addition to intervals you're going to change up your strength routine. Strength training enhances weight loss by building muscle, which cranks up your metabolism—the number of calories your body burns just to stay alive. Having more muscle also elevates your calorie burn whenever you do an activity. As you get stronger, you may also naturally become more active, because everyday activities become easier. Not to mention, strength training will help you develop shapelier arms, a firmer butt, and more toned legs.

The strength routine for this phase involves compound exercises that work multiple muscle groups at the same time. That means along with strength- and muscle-building benefits, these moves also burn more calories than doing strength exercises that isolate single muscle groups or individual muscles.

So, get ready to step up your benefits. Here's your personal walking plan to lose weight for Weeks 4 to 6.

Walk Your Way to More Motivation

Count the number of steps you take during your fast intervals. Try to beat that number on subsequent intervals. The challenge can make your walks more fun and effective, and seeing that number increase over time helps to keep you motivated.

YOUR LOSE-WEIGHT TRAINING PLAN

WEEK 4

- *2 days a week:* Moderate Walk—3-minute warmup, 55-minute moderate pace, 2-minute cooldown (60 minutes total)

- *3 days a week:* Interval Walk—3-minute warmup, 20-minute intervals (20 seconds fast, 1 minute brisk), 2-minute cooldown (25 minutes total)

- *2 or 3 days a week:* Strength training

WEEK 5

- *2 days a week:* Moderate Walk—3-minute warmup, 55-minute moderate pace, 2-minute cooldown (60 minutes total)

- *3 days a week:* Interval Walk—3-minute warmup, 20-minute intervals (40 seconds fast, 1 minute brisk), 2-minute cooldown (25 minutes total)

- *2 or 3 days a week:* Strength training

WEEK 6

- *2 days a week:* Moderate Walk—3-minute warmup, 55-minute moderate pace, 2-minute cooldown (60 minutes total)

- *3 days a week:* Interval Walk—3-minute warmup, 20-minute intervals (1 minute fast, 1 minute brisk), 2-minute cooldown (25 minutes total)

- *2 or 3 days a week:* Strength training

Walk Your Way to Fewer Cravings

Take a 15-minute walk when cravings or hunger strikes. Research shows that it can curb cravings and squelch hunger.[2]

Moderate walk

TIME	DURATION	ACTIVITY	INTENSITY
0:00	3 minutes	Warmup	3
3:00	55 minutes	Moderate	5–6
58:00	2 minutes	Cooldown	3
60:00	TOTAL: 60 minutes		

Fat-Burning Interval

Walk #1 (Week 4)

TIME	DURATION	ACTIVITY	INTENSITY
0:00	3 minutes	Warmup	3
3:00	1 minute	Moderate	5
4:00	1 minute	Brisk	6
5:00	20 seconds	Fast	8
5:20	1 minute	Brisk	6
6:20	20 seconds	Fast	8
6:40	1 minute	Brisk	6
7:40	20 seconds	Fast	8
8:00	1 minute	Brisk	6
9:00	20 seconds	Fast	8
9:20	1 minute	Brisk	6
10:20	20 seconds	Fast	8
10:40	1 minute	Brisk	6
11:40	20 seconds	Fast	8
12:00	1 minute	Brisk	6
13:00	20 seconds	Fast	8
13:20	1 minute	Brisk	6
14:20	20 seconds	Fast	8
14:40	1 minute	Brisk	6
15:40	20 seconds	Fast	8
16:00	1 minute	Brisk	6
17:00	20 seconds	Fast	8
17:20	1 minute	Brisk	6
18:20	20 seconds	Fast	8
18:40	1 minute	Brisk	6
19:40	20 seconds	Fast	8
20:00	1 minute	Brisk	6
21:00	20 seconds	Fast	8
21:20	1 minute	Brisk	6
22:20	20 seconds	Fast	8
22:40	20 seconds	Brisk	6
23:00	2 minutes	Cooldown	3
25:00	TOTAL: 25 minutes		

Fat-Burning Interval

Walk #2 (Week 5)

TIME	DURATION	ACTIVITY	INTENSITY
0:00	3 minutes	Warmup	3
3:00	1 minute	Moderate	5
4:00	1 minute	Brisk	6
5:00	40 seconds	Fast	8
5:40	1 minute	Brisk	6
6:40	40 seconds	Fast	8
7:20	1 minute	Brisk	6
8:20	40 seconds	Fast	8
9:00	1 minute	Brisk	6
10:00	40 seconds	Fast	8
10:40	1 minute	Brisk	6
11:40	40 seconds	Fast	8
12:20	1 minute	Brisk	6
13:20	40 seconds	Fast	8
14:00	1 minute	Brisk	6
15:00	40 seconds	Fast	8
15:40	1 minute	Brisk	6
16:40	40 seconds	Fast	8
17:20	1 minute	Brisk	6
18:20	40 seconds	Fast	8
19:00	1 minute	Brisk	6
20:00	40 seconds	Fast	8
20:40	1 minute	Brisk	6
21:40	40 seconds	Fast	8
22:20	1 minute	Brisk	6
23:20	2 minutes	Cooldown	3
25:20	TOTAL: 25:20 minutes		

Fat-Burning Interval

Walk #3 (Week 6)

TIME	DURATION	ACTIVITY	INTENSITY
0:00	3 minutes	Warmup	3
3:00	1 minute	Moderate	5
4:00	1 minute	Brisk	6
5:00	1 minute	Fast	8
6:00	1 minute	Brisk	6
7:00	1 minute	Fast	8
8:00	1 minute	Brisk	6
9:00	1 minute	Fast	8
10:00	1 minute	Brisk	6
11:00	1 minute	Fast	8
12:00	1 minute	Brisk	6
13:00	1 minute	Fast	8
14:00	1 minute	Brisk	6
15:00	1 minute	Fast	8
16:00	1 minute	Brisk	6
17:00	1 minute	Fast	8
18:00	1 minute	Brisk	6
19:00	1 minute	Fast	8
20:00	1 minute	Brisk	6
21:00	1 minute	Fast	8
22:00	1 minute	Brisk	6
23:00	2 minutes	Cooldown	3
25:00	TOTAL: 25 minutes		

Sample Schedules

Here you'll find two options for how to organize your workouts. Feel free to arrange them as you wish to fit within your schedule using the following guidelines.

1. Don't do two walking workouts on the same day. However, you can break up a walk over the course of a day. For example, you could do 10 minutes of intervals in the morning and another 10 minutes in the evening. Just remember to warm up and cool down for each one.

2. Don't do strength workouts on consecutive days.

3. If you walk and do strength training on the same day, you can do them at different times (make sure you warm up and stretch before and after each) or consecutively. When doing them consecutively, do the workout that offers you the benefits you most desire first. So, if burning fat is what you want, walk first. But, if you're more interested in firming up, then do the strength workout first. You get more benefits from a workout when you are fresh.

	Sunday	Monday	Tuesday	Wednesday	Thursday	Friday	Saturday
Option 1: No rest days	Interval walk	Strength train	Interval walk	Strength train	Moderate walk	Interval Walk	Moderate walk and strength train
Option 2: Rest days	Interval walk and strength train	Rest day	Interval walk	Rest day	Moderate walk and strength train	Interval walk	Moderate walk and strength train

YOUR LOSE-WEIGHT STRENGTH ROUTINE

Each combo move targets the entire body to boost your calorie burn. Do 1 to 3 sets of 8 to 12 reps of each exercise. Do 1 set of each exercise, and then repeat the exercises for a second set and again for a third set.

- Squat with overhead press
- Bridge with pullover
- Row with deadlift
- Pushup

SQUAT WITH OVERHEAD PRESS

(A) Stand with your feet about shoulder-width apart, toes pointing forward or slightly out to the sides. Hold a dumbbell in each hand, with your arms bent so the dumbbells are by your shoulders, palms facing forward. (B) Sit back into a squat, hinging forward at your hips and bending your knees. Keep your knees behind your toes as you lower.

(C) Hold for a second, and then stand back up, pressing the dumbbells straight up overhead. Hold for a second. Then, lower the dumbbells to shoulder height as you sit back into a squat. Do 8 to 12 reps.

A   B   C

Back it off: Use lighter weights. Don't lower as far into the squat.

Pump it up: Use heavier weights. Add a heel lift when you press the dumbbells overhead.

BRIDGE WITH PULLOVER

(A) Lie on your back, with your legs bent and your feet flat on the floor. Hold a dumbbell with both hands and extend your arms over your head, resting the dumbbell on the floor. (B) Contract your abdominals and buttocks, and press your feet into the floor to lift your butt and back off of the floor. Your body should be in line from your knees to your shoulders. As you do that, also raise the dumbbell up over your chest and toward your knees, without lifting your head off the floor. Hold for a second, then slowly return to the starting position. Do 8 to 12 reps.

Back it off: Use a lighter weight. Hold the bridge position and do reps for the pullover only.

Pump it up: Use heavier weights. Lift one foot off the floor to perform one-legged bridges.

ROW WITH DEADLIFT

(A) Stand with your feet about shoulder-width apart and hold a dumbbell in each hand with your arms extended down in front of your thighs, your knees slightly bent, and your palms facing your thighs. (B) Slowly lean forward, bending at the hips, and lower your torso until almost parallel with the floor. Keep the weights close to your body, your back straight, and your abdominals tight, to protect your back as you lower. (C) Then, bend your elbows up and out to the sides and pull the dumbbells toward your chest. Hold for a second. Slowly lower the dumbbells and stand back up, pressing your feet into the floor and squeezing your buttocks. Do 8 to 12 reps. (If you have back problems, replace this move with the Bent-Over Row in the workout on page 58.)

A   B   C

Back it off: Use lighter weights. Just do rows without doing the deadlift in between.

Pump it up: Use heavier weights.

PUSHUP

(A) Kneel on the floor and walk your hands out so you are balancing on your hands with your fingers forward, and on your knees with your feet in the air. (B) Bend your elbows out to the sides and lower your chest toward the floor. Your body should be in line from your head to your knees; don't bend at your hips or round your upper back. Hold for a second, then push back up. Do 8 to 12 reps.

Back it off: Do pushups while you are standing with your hands placed on a desk, table, or counter.

Pump it up: Lift your knees off the floor and do pushups, balancing on your hands and toes.

Chapter 8

Flatten Your Belly

To blast fat, you're going to kick up the intensity of your walks by going faster for the next 3 weeks. Research shows that the more vigorously you work out, the more belly fat you burn. Even if you burn the same number of calories while doing a moderate walk, you just won't get the same belly fat-blasting effect.

In a study from the University of Virginia, overweight, middle-aged women followed a low-intensity exercise routine or a high-intensity exercise routine. A third group did not have an exercise routine to follow, but all the groups maintained their current eating habits. The low-intensity group walked at a moderate rate 5 days a week. The high-intensity group did only two moderate-paced walks, along with three shorter-but-faster-paced walks a week. Both groups burned exactly the same number of calories per workout—400. To do that, the women had to walk longer at the moderate pace. They averaged 3.4 mph (a 17:40-minute-per-mile pace), and it took an average of 59 minutes to hit the calorie-burn goal. During the faster, high-intensity walks, the women averaged 3.7 mph (a 16:15-minute-per-mile pace), and it took an average of 53 minutes to burn 400 calories. The difference in speed was a

mere 9 percent—but the results were exponentially greater.[1]

Both groups lost weight, body fat, and belly fat, but replacing some moderate-intensity walks with shorter, faster-paced walks cranked up the results. Those power walkers lost almost 8 pounds during the 16-week study—70 percent more than the moderate walkers, who lost about 4½ pounds. The power walkers also shrunk their waistlines by about 2¼ inches—four times more than the moderate walkers. The differences were even greater for fat loss. Power walkers shed twice as much body fat and five times as much belly fat than the moderate walkers.

Now, that should get you pumped to pick up the pace! (If you experience any shin pain as you speed up, see Excuse Buster #1: Survive Shin Pain, page 333.) In addition, you'll start a new strength-training routine that specifically targets your midsection for a firmer, flatter look.

So let's get to it! Here's your plan for Weeks 4 through 6. Reminder: You can break up your walks throughout the day. Even if you aren't able to do the total recommended amount, remember that doing some is better than none!

YOUR FLATTEN-YOUR-BELLY TRAINING PLAN

WEEK 4

- *2 days a week:* Moderate Walk—3-minute warmup, 55-minute moderate pace, 2-minute cooldown (60 minutes total)

- *3 days a week:* Fast Walk—3-minute warmup, 30-minute fast pace, 2-minute cooldown (35 minutes total)

- *2 or 3 days a week:* Strength training

WEEK 5

- *2 days a week:* Moderate Walk—3-minute warmup, 55-minute moderate pace, 2-minute cooldown (60 minutes total)

- *3 days a week:* 3-minute warmup, 35-minute fast pace, 2-minute cooldown (40 minutes total)

- *2 or 3 days a week:* Strength training

WEEK 6

- *2 days a week:* Moderate Walk—3-minute warmup, 55-minute moderate pace, 2-minute cooldown (60 minutes total)

- *3 days a week:* 3-minute warmup, 40-minute fast pace, 2-minute cooldown (45 minutes total)

- *2 or 3 days a week:* Strength training

Moderate walk

TIME	DURATION	ACTIVITY	INTENSITY
0:00	3 minutes	Warmup	3
3:00	55 minutes	Moderate	5–6
58:00	2 minutes	Cooldown	3
60:00	TOTAL: 60 minutes		

Fast walk

TIME	DURATION	ACTIVITY	INTENSITY
0:00	3 minutes	Warmup	3
3:00	30–40 minutes*	Fast	7–8
33:00–43:00	2 minutes	Cooldown	3
35:00–45:00	TOTAL: 35, 40, or 45 minutes (increases each week)		

*For Week 5, increase to 35 minutes. For Week 6, to 40 minutes.

Sample Schedules

Here are just two options for how to organize your workouts. Feel free to organize them as you wish to fit within your schedule using the following guidelines.

1. Don't do two complete walks on the same day. For example, don't do a full-length moderate and a full-length fast walk on the same day. It is, however, fine to break up one of those walks to do over the course of a day instead of all at one time.

2. Don't do strength workouts on consecutive days.

3. If you walk and do strength training on the same day, you can do them at different times (make sure you warm up and stretch before and after each) or consecutively. When doing them consecutively, do the workout that offers you the benefits you most desire first. So, if burning fat is what you want, walk first. But, if you're more interested in firming up, then do the strength workout first. You get more benefits from a workout when you are fresh.

	Sunday	Monday	Tuesday	Wednesday	Thursday	Friday	Saturday
Option 1: No rest days	Fast walk	Strength train	Fast walk	Strength train	Moderate walk	Fast walk	Moderate walk and strength train
Option 2: Rest days	Fast walk and strength train	Rest day	Fast walk and strength train	Rest day	Moderate walk and strength train	Fast walk	Moderate walk

YOUR FLATTEN-YOUR-BELLY STRENGTH ROUTINE

These moves will cinch your waistline and tone your tummy.
Do 1 to 3 sets of each exercise, 2 or 3 nonconsecutive days a
week.

- Balance twist
- Plank curl
- Lunge with a twist
- Crunch
- Twisting side plank

BALANCE TWIST

(A) Sit on the floor with your legs bent and your feet flat on the
floor. Shift your weight back and raise your feet into the air with your knees bent, so you are balancing
on your sits bones. Bend your arms, and hold your hands in front of your chest. (B) With your abdominals
contracted, slowly twist to the right as far as possible. Hold for a second.
Rotate back to center, and then twist to the left. That's 1 rep. Hold for a
second, and then repeat twisting to alternate sides. Do 8 to 12 reps.

Back it off: Rest your heels on the floor
as you twist.

Pump it up: Hold a weight as you twist.

PLANK CURL

(A) Balance on your hands and toes, like for a pushup. (B) Contract your abdominals and pull your right knee in toward your chest. Hold for a second, and then extend your leg back down to the floor. Repeat with your left leg. Do 8 to 12 reps with each leg.

Back it off: Skip pulling your knees into your chest. Instead, lift one foot off the floor at a time. Hold for a second, then lower. Alternate legs.

Pump it up: Pull each knee in toward the opposite elbow for a twist.

LUNGE WITH A TWIST

(A) Stand with your feet together and hold a dumbbell with both hands in front of you at waist height.
(B) Step your right leg forward and lower into a lunge, keeping your right knee directly over your ankle and your left knee pointing down toward the floor. As you lunge, rotate your torso to the right. Hold for a second, and then press into your right foot to stand back up, rotating to the center as you do. Repeat to the opposite side. Do 8 to 12 reps to each side.

A   B

Back it off: Do the move without holding any weight.

Pump it up: Press into your right foot to stand back up, bringing your left knee up in front of you. Balance on your right leg for a second before lowering your left foot to the starting position.

CRUNCH

(A) Lie on your back with your legs bent and your feet flat on the floor. Place your hands gently behind your head. (B) Contract your abdominals and slowly raise your head, shoulders, and upper back off the floor. Don't pull on your neck. Hold for a second, and then slowly lower. Do 8 to 12 reps.

Back it off: Extend your arms in front of you on either side of your knees.

Pump it up: Extend your arms above your head.

TWISTING SIDE PLANK

(A) Lie on your left side with your feet stacked. Press yourself up onto your left hand to balance with your right arm extended toward the ceiling. Don't roll forward or back. Imagine your body is between two panes of glass. (B) Slowly swoop your right arm down, across, and under your body. Hold for a second, and then return to the starting position. Do 8 to 12 reps, then repeat on the opposite side.

Back it off: Bend your knees and rest your bottom knee on the floor.

Pump it up: Before twisting, raise your top leg toward the ceiling and lower it as you balance. Then twist. That's 1 rep.

Chapter 9

Maximize Your Health

Just getting up and moving helps to make you healthier and to reduce your risk for developing diseases such as heart disease, diabetes, and even some types of cancer. For the most benefit, consistency is key. So, by choosing to maximize your health, you're going to focus on moving more by making walking a daily habit over the next 3 weeks.

You already have started to develop a walking habit from the Basic Walking Plan (page 43), so you just need to add some walking 2 more days a week. Don't panic at the thought of doing it every day, though. This plan is still very flexible. You can break up your walking sessions and/or count walking that you do throughout your day to meet your daily goals.

Another feature of this plan is that you should walk at a comfortable pace. A comfortable pace is whatever you feel like doing that day. Some days, you might be up for a challenge or just want to work up a good sweat, so you go faster. Other days, a leisurely stroll is what feels good for you. Research shows that self-selecting your pace helps you to walk more consistently—and that's the key to long-term, health-maximizing results.

In the following pages, you'll find a plan to build you up to walking at least 30 minutes every day of the week, but you can do as many as 60 minutes each day. Based on research, there is a "dose response" to exercise. It means that as you increase the amount of walking you do, the benefits increase, too. In a British study, researchers found that the more walking men did, the lower their risk of having a stroke.[1] Those who did some walking (4 to 7 hours a week) reduced their risk by 11 percent, while the ones walking the most (22-plus hours a week) were 64 percent less likely to have a stroke. And it didn't matter what pace they were going. Other research has shown similar findings for other health problems such as heart disease, hypertension, and even cancer.

So, there's a lot to be gained by walking more. Part of the reason more walking may be so beneficial is because it reduces the amount of time you sit. Sitting is a sedentary activity has been touted as the

Walk Your Way to 2,000 Steps

You can rack up more than 2,000 steps and burn about 150 calories while you watch an episode of *This Is Us* with this easy trick: Simply stand up and walk in place every time a commercial comes on—no treadmill required.

"new smoking," as more studies show detrimental—and potentially fatal—effects of logging too much on-your-butt time.

This plan will get you up and moving, so you have less time to sit. In addition to the plan below, there are two additional goals that you can aim for to boost your health benefits during Stage 2.

- **Get 10,000 steps in each day.** You'll need an activity monitor such as a pedometer, FitBit type of device, or an app on your phone. All of your steps throughout the day count, including your scheduled walks. Pedometer users increase their physical activity by nearly 27 percent, adding about 2,500 steps a day, on average, according to an analysis of 26 studies that was published in the *Journal of the American Medical Association*.[2]

- **Don't sit for more than 2 hours at a time.** Set a timer for 2 hours (or less) when you sit down. When it goes off, get up and move for at least 5 minutes. Simply marching in place or stretching can help. If you can get up every hour, that's even better. Getting up and moving more often will help you to increase your daily step count too.

Walk Your Way to Consistency

Aim to create "streaks." A streak is where you do something every day, and you're motivated to keep doing it because you don't want to break the streak. Creating a visual representation of your streak, such as making a construction paper chain or string of beads, adding to it each time you walk, can be a powerful motivator to help you reach your goal. If you don't walk one day, you break your streak, and you have to start a new chain or string. You can also do this electronically with apps such as chains.cc or streaksapp.com.

YOUR MAXIMIZE-YOUR-HEALTH TRAINING PLAN

WEEK 4

- *5 days a week:* Walk a total of 30 to 60 minutes at a comfortable pace (you can split it up, or do it all at one time)

- *2 days a week:* Walk 10 minutes at a comfortable pace

- *2 or 3 days a week:* Strength training

WEEK 5

- *5 days a week:* Walk a total of 30 to 60 minutes at a comfortable pace (you can split it up, or do it all at one time)

- *2 days a week:* Walk 20 minutes at a comfortable pace (you can split it up, or do it all at one time)

- *2 or 3 days a week:* Strength training

WEEK 6

- *5 days a week:* Walk a total of 30 to 60 minutes at a comfortable pace (you can split it up, or do it all at one time)

- *2 days a week:* Walk 30 minutes at a comfortable pace (you can split it up, or do it all at one time)

- *2 or 3 days a week:* Strength training

Sample Schedule

TIME	ACTIVITY
7 a.m.	20-min. walk around the block
Noon	15-min. walk during lunch break
3 p.m.	10-min. walk during work break
6 p.m.	10-min. walk around the shopping center before grocery shopping for dinner

YOUR MAXIMIZE-YOUR-HEALTH STRENGTH ROUTINE

You'll be following the Strength Workout from Stage 1 (page 56) again for the next 3 weeks. You can continue at the level you were doing during the Basic Walking Plan (page 43), but pay attention to *how* you are doing. Probably, within the next 3 weeks, you will need to change things up in order to continue to challenge your muscles. When you feel like you could do more after you've completed all sets and reps, that's a signal that you need a new challenge. You can do that by using

- Squat and lift
- Bent-over row
- Bridge
- Plank

heavier weights or trying a harder modification of one of the moves. For example, if you were doing the "Back it off" variation for the plank, try doing the main move this time around. If you can't complete all of the reps at the more challenging level, do as many as possible, then step down to the level you had been doing to finish. Within a few weeks, you'll be pumping out full sets of the harder variation.

Do this routine 2 or 3 days a week, allowing at least 1 day between workouts. Complete the routine one time through, then repeat it two more times, for a total of 3 sets. You'll do 3 sets (if you're able) each week of this Stage 2 plan.

SQUAT AND LIFT

(A) Stand with your feet about shoulder-width apart, toes pointing straight ahead or slightly out, and arms relaxed at your sides. (B) Bend your knees and hinge forward from your hips, lowering yourself as if you are sitting back into a chair. Stick your butt out, shift your weight into your heels, and raise your arms out in front of you as you bend your knees and lower as far as possible, while maintaining good form. Stop before your hips are in line with your knees. Hold for a second. (C) Press into your heels, squeeze your buttocks, and stand back up. As you come up, rise up onto your toes, lifting your heels as high as possible. Hold for a second. Lower back to the starting position. Do 8 to 12 reps for a set.

Back it off: Do the squat only (without raising up onto your toes).

Pump it up: Hold dumbbells at your sides as you do the move.

BENT-OVER ROW

Place your left hand and left knee on a chair or bench. (A) Hold a dumbbell in your right hand with your arm hanging straight beneath your shoulder. (B) Bend your elbow and pull the dumbbell up toward your chest, keeping your arm in toward your body and your elbow pointing toward the ceiling. Hold for a second. Slowly lower the dumbbell. Do 8 to 12 reps with each arm for a set.

Back it off: Holding a dumbbell in your right hand, stand behind a chair with your left foot in front of your right. Lean forward slightly from your hips and place your left hand on the back of a chair. Either perform the move in this position and/or use a lighter weight.

Pump it up: Hold dumbbells in both hands and hinge forward from your hips so your arms are hanging beneath your shoulders. Keeping your abdominals tight, do rows with both arms at the same time in this position. (Do not do this if you have back problems.) Or do one-arm rows with heavier weights.

BRIDGE

(A) Lie on the floor on your back with your legs bent and your feet flat on the floor. Place your arms at your sides with your palms facing down. (B) Contract your abdominals and buttocks, and lift your hips and back off the floor so your body is in line from your shoulders to your knees. Hold for a second. Slowly lower. Do 8 to 12 reps for a set.

Back it off: Instead of doing reps, hold the bridge position for as long as possible, up to 1 minute.

Pump it up: Raise one leg off the floor, and perform one-leg bridges, repeating with the opposite leg.

PLANK

Lie facedown on the floor with your arms bent and your elbows under your shoulders. Tuck your toes under and lift your body off the floor so you are balancing on your fists, forearms, elbows, balls of your feet, and toes. Hold for up to 1 minute. If you're not able to hold for that long, hold for as long as possible, then lower and repeat. Keep your body in line from your head to your heels. Continue until you've held the plank for a total of 1 minute.

Back it off: Keep your knees on the floor.

Pump it up: After you push up into the plank, lift one foot off the floor and hold. Work up to holding for 1 minute on each leg, resting in between.

Chapter 10

Firm Up

With this plan, you'll maximize muscle building, so you'll look firmer and your whole body will get stronger. By adding a powerful arm swing to your walk during the Basic Walking Plan in Stage 1 (page 43), you've already turned walking from a typically lower-body workout into both an upper- and lower-body workout. You'll add to that by practicing some of the techniques listed here.

To really challenge your muscles, you'll be doing different strength workouts on alternate weeks in this stage.

One week, you'll be doing traditional strength workouts, but at higher intensities. Instead of working your entire body in one session, you'll also be doing an upper-body workout one day and a lower-body workout another day. This way, you can really challenge and target those trouble spots. You will need an elastic resistance band (available wherever exercise equipment is sold); a soccer ball, a basketball, or a toy ball; and a low bench or step to stand on.

The next week, you'll be doing toning walks (see page 113). This routine alternates muscle-building moves that target the entire body with brisk bouts of walking, so you get both cardio and strength bene-

fits in one workout. Like other strength workouts, don't do Toning Walks on consecutive days.

In addition, you'll be doing two longer walks a week to maximize fat-burning, and two shorter, faster walks to kick up your calorie burn. Higher-intensity cardio workouts like these may also help to build a little extra muscle. Plus, cardio is key to burning off the fat that's hiding your muscles.

Choose some hilly routes for additional lower-body toning, but avoid doing hill walks and lower-body strength training on the same day or back-to-back days. Here's your workout plan.

YOUR FIRM-UP TRAINING PLAN

WEEK 4

- *2 or 3 days a week:* Moderate Walk—3-minute warmup, 55-minute moderate pace, 2-minute cooldown (60 minutes total)

- *2 or 3 days a week:* Fast Walk—3-minute warmup, 30-minute fast pace, 2-minute cooldown (35 minutes total)

- *2 days a week:* Upper-body strength training

- *2 days a week:* Lower-body strength training

WEEK 5

- *1 or 2 days a week:* Moderate Walk—3-minute warmup, 55-minute moderate pace, 2-minute cooldown (60 minutes total)

- *1 day a week:* Fast Walk—3-minute warmup, 30-minute fast pace, 2-minute cooldown (35 minutes total)

- *3 days a week:* Toning Walk (page 113)— 3-minute warmup, 25-minute toning walk, 2-minute cooldown (30 minutes total)

WEEK 6

- *2 or 3 days a week:* Moderate Walk—3-minute warmup, 55-minute moderate pace, 2-minute cooldown (60 minutes total)

- *2 or 3 days a week:* Fast Walk—3-minute warmup, 30-minute fast pace, 2-minute cooldown (35 minutes total)

- *2 days a week:* Upper-body strength training

- *2 days a week:* Lower-body strength training

Moderate walk

TIME	DURATION	ACTIVITY	INTENSITY
0:00	3 minutes	Warmup	3
3:00	55 minutes	Moderate	5–6
58:00	2 minutes	Cooldown	3
60:00	TOTAL: 60 minutes		

Fast walk

TIME	DURATION	ACTIVITY	INTENSITY
0:00	3 minutes	Warmup	3
3:00	30 minutes	Fast	7–8
33:00	2 minutes	Cooldown	3
35:00	TOTAL: 35 minutes		

Sample Schedules

Below you'll find are several options for how to organize your workouts. Feel free to arrange them as you wish to fit within your schedule using the following guidelines.

1. Don't do two complete walks on the same day. For example, don't do a full-length Moderate Walk and a full-length Fast Walk on the same day. It is however, fine to break up one of those walks to do over the course of a day instead of all at one time.

2. Don't do strength workouts or Toning Walks on consecutive days.

3. If you walk and do strength training on the same day, you can do them at different times (make sure you warm up and stretch before and after each) or consecutively. When doing them consecutively, do the workout that offers you the benefits you most desire first. So, if burning fat is what you want, walk first. If you're more interested in firming up, then do the strength workout first. You get more benefits from a workout when you are fresh.

Weeks 4 and 6

	Sunday	Monday	Tuesday	Wednesday	Thursday	Friday	Saturday
Option 1: No rest days	Moderate walk and upper-body strength	Fast walk	Moderate walk (optional) and lower-body strength	Fast walk	Upper-body strength	Fast walk (optional) and lower-body strength	Moderate walk
Option 2: Rest days	Moderate walk and upper-body strength	Fast walk	Moderate walk (optional) and lower-body strength	Fast walk	Rest day	Fast walk (optional) and upper-body strength	Moderate walk and lower-body strength

Week 5

	Sunday	Monday	Tuesday	Wednesday	Thursday	Friday	Saturday
	Moderate walk	Toning walk	Rest day	Fast walk	Toning walk	Moderate walk (optional)	Toning walk

HOW TO GET EVEN FIRMER

For more toning benefits, try these subtle moves during your Moderate Walks or during your warmup or cooldown for your Fast Walks.

Drive your elbows back. You should feel your shoulder blades contracting as you swing your arms back, but let your arm swing forward naturally. Don't punch forward. This works and tones your back muscles. It also powers up your arm swing to help you walk faster. When your arms swing faster, your feet want to keep up. Remember to keep your arms bent the entire time—as if you were wearing a cast.

Squeeze your buttocks. You should be landing on your heel when you walk. As you land, pay attention to squeezing your butt to help firm up your backside. This technique also prevents you from reaching your foot too far out in front of you. You'll take a shorter step, which is the secret to going faster. It helps to power up your stride, too.

Imagine your legs extend up to your ribs. There are muscles that you use for walking that run all the way up there. If you pay attention to them, you should notice them working more, which will give you an abdominal workout along with your walk.

For more on techniques that can help you firm up and go faster, see page 118.

Walk Your Way to Confidence

Test panelist Eileen Gradwell admitted that she was uncomfortable with PDE—public displays of exercise—like doing squats and lunges while outside where others could see her. Though she would sometimes do them in less-public areas, she also challenged herself to deal with her fear and do them in more visible areas. When she did, the following mantras helped: "You can do this," "At least you are out moving," and "Keep up the good work." Laughing at herself as she described her attempts at pushups on the park bench to her adult children also helped to make her less stressed and less self-conscious the next time she went out.

YOUR FIRM-UP UPPER-BODY STRENGTH ROUTINE

This workout will tone up your chest, shoulders, back, and arms. Do 1 set of each exercise in Week 4, 2 sets of each in Week 5, and 3 sets of each in Week 6.

- Upright row
- Chest press
- Reverse fly
- Biceps curl
- Triceps kickback

UPRIGHT ROW

(A) Stand with your feet about shoulder-width apart and hold a dumbbell in each hand with your arms extended down in front of you, palms facing your thighs. (B) Pull the dumbbells up, bending your elbows out to the sides, as you raise them to chest height. Hold for a second, and then slowly lower.

A   B

Back it off: Use lighter weights.

Pump it up: Use heavier weights.

CHEST PRESS

(A) Lie on your back on the floor with your legs bent and your feet flat on the floor. Hold a dumbbell in each hand and bend your arms so your elbows are resting on the floor and pointing out to the sides and the dumbbells are by your chest. (B) Slowly extend your arms, pressing the dumbbells straight up over your chest. Hold for a second, and then slowly lower. Do 8 to 12 reps.

Back it off: Use lighter weights.

Pump it up: Use heavier weights.

REVERSE FLY

(A) Sit on the edge of a chair, holding a dumbbell in each hand. Lean forward from your hips so the dumbbells are hanging down toward your feet, palms facing in. (B) Keeping your elbows straight, but not locked, contract your shoulder blades and raise the dumbbells out to the sides and up to shoulder height. Hold for a second, then slowly lower. Do 8 to 12 reps.

A   B

Back it off: Use lighter weights.

Pump it up: Use heavier weights.

BICEPS CURL

(A) Stand with your feet about shoulder-width apart, and hold a dumbbell in each hand with your arms extended down at your sides, palms facing forward. (B) Keeping your upper arms still, bend your elbows and raise the dumbbells toward your shoulders. Hold for a second, then slowly lower. Do 8 to 12 reps.

A   B

Back it off: Use lighter weights.

Pump it up: Use heavier weights.

TRICEPS KICKBACK

(A) Stand behind a chair with your legs split, left foot in front, and hold a dumbbell in your right hand. Place your left hand on the back of the chair and lean forward, bending at your hips. Bend your right elbow at a 90-degree angle and hold it close to your side. (B) Without moving your shoulder, extend your right arm back, pressing the dumbbell behind you. Hold for a second, then slowly bend your elbow again, lowering the weight back to the starting position. Do 8 to 12 reps, then switch sides and repeat with your left arm.

Back it off: Use lighter weights.

Pump it up: Use heavier weights.

YOUR FIRM-UP LOWER-BODY STRENGTH ROUTINE

This workout will help you to tone up your hips, thighs, and buttocks. Do 1 set of each exercise in Week 4, 2 sets of each in Week 5, and 3 sets of each in Week 6.

- ■ Stepup
- ■ Squat with band
- ■ Hip extension
- ■ Ball squeeze
- ■ Clamshell

STEPUP

(A) Hold a dumbbell in each hand with your arms hanging naturally at your sides. Stand in front of a step or bench. Place your left foot on the bench and press into the bench to lift your body up onto the bench. (B) Lift your right leg up, tap your right toes on the bench, and then slowly lower. Do 8 to 12 reps, and repeat with your other leg.

Back it off: Use lighter weights, no weights at all, or a lower step.

Pump it up: Use heavier weights and/or a higher step. As you step up with one foot, extend your other leg behind you, squeezing your buttocks.

SQUAT WITH BAND

(A) Stand with your feet about shoulder-width apart and tie an exercise band around your calves. Make sure it is securely fastened before starting the exercise. (B) Step your right foot out to the side, pulling against the resistance band, and then lower into a squat (bend at your hips and knees, stick your butt out, and keep your back straight and your chest lifted). As you stand up, bring your left foot in toward your right. Step to the right and squat one more time. Then, repeat, doing two squats to the left. Do 8 to 12 reps on each side.

> **Back it off:** Do the move without using an exercise band.
>
> **Pump it up:** Take wider steps or use a stronger band for more resistance.

HIP EXTENSION

Securely fasten an exercise band to a railing, pole, or sturdy piece of furniture at floor level. (A) Loop the band around your right leg. (B) Place your hand on a chair or wall for balance. Standing tall, with shoulders straight and back, shift your weight onto your left foot. Raise your right leg straight out behind you, squeezing your buttocks. Keep your toes, knees, and hips pointing forward. Hold for a second, then slowly lower. Do 8 to 12 reps, then switch legs and repeat.

> **Back it off:** Do the move without using an exercise band.
>
> **Pump it up:** Use a stronger band.

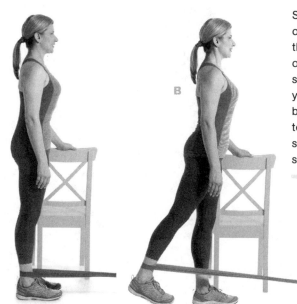

BALL SQUEEZE

Stand tall with a soft (slightly deflated) ball between your thighs. With your hands on your hips, squeeze and release the ball without letting it fall. Do 8 to 12 reps.

Back it off: Do the exercise while lying on the floor with your knees bent and hands at your sides. Squeeze the ball between your thighs.

Pump it up: Do the exercise while holding a squat position (bend at your hips and knees, stick your butt out, and keep your back straight and your chest lifted).

CLAMSHELL

(A) Lie on your left side with your legs stacked and bent. Place your left arm under your head, with your right arm in front of your body for support. **(B)** Slowly rotate your right knee upward, while keeping your feet together. Don't roll your hips forward or back as you lift. Hold for a second, then slowly lower. Do 8 to 12 reps on each side.

Back it off: Don't lift your knee as high.

Pump it up: Hold a weight against your top thigh for more resistance.

TONING WALK

You'll be interspersing bouts of brisk walking with strength exercises. You'll find descriptions of the strength moves beginning on page 114.

Don't rush through the moves. Keep them controlled and maintain good form.

Week 5

TIME	DURATION	ACTIVITY	INTENSITY
0:00	3 minutes	Warmup	3–5
3:00	4 minutes	Moderate to brisk walk	5–7
7:00	1 minute	Walking lunges (20 reps)	5–7
8:00	4 minutes	Brisk walk	6–7
12:00	1 minute	Bench pushups (10–12 reps)	5–7
13:00	4 minutes	Brisk walk	6–7
17:00	1 minute	Traveling squats (20 reps)	5–7
18:00	4 minutes	Brisk walk	6–7
22:00	2 minutes	Plank walks (10–12 reps)	5–7
24:00	4 minutes	Brisk walk	6–7
28:00	2 minutes	Cooldown	3–5
30:00	TOTAL: 30 minutes		

YOUR FIRM-UP TONING WALK ROUTINE

Combine these moves with walking intervals for a cardio strength workout that will shape you up from head to toe.

- Walking lunge
- Bench pushup
- Traveling squat
- Plank walk

WALKING LUNGE

(A) Stand tall with your feet together and your arms at your sides. Take a giant step forward with your right foot. Bend your knees and lower your body straight down toward the ground. Your right thigh should be parallel or almost parallel to the ground. Keep your right knee over your right ankle. Your back (left) knee should be pointing toward the ground. Your left heel will come off of the ground. Press into both feet to stand back up, bringing your left foot forward to meet your right foot. (B) Repeat, stepping forward with your left foot. Do 20 lunges, alternating legs. You'll be moving forward as you do these so make sure that you have enough space.

Back it off: Do forward lunges in place. When you stand back up, bring your front foot back to meet your back foot, so you don't move forward as you continue.

Pump it up: Don't stop in between lunges. Instead swing your back foot forward and immediately lower into the next lunge. No stopping with your feet together.

BENCH PUSHUP

(A) Place your hands shoulder-width apart on a chair, bench, wall, railing, picnic table, piece of playground equipment, or anything else sturdy you can find. Walk your feet back so your body forms a plank. (B) Bend your elbows out to the sides and lower your chest toward the chair. Keep your back straight and your head in line with your spine. Don't bend at the hips. Hold for a second, then straighten your arms, pressing back to the starting position. Do 10 to 12 reps.

Back it off: Place your hands on an object that is higher, such as the back of a chair instead of the seat. The more upright your body position is, the easier the pushup will be.

Pump it up: Place your hands on an object that is lower to the ground, such as the seat of a bench instead of the back. Or, find a low wall or log to use. Of course, you can put your hands on the ground to do standard pushups.

TRAVELING SQUAT

(A) Stand tall with your feet together. Step your left foot out to the side so your feet are just wider than shoulder-width apart. (B) Bend your hips and knees, stick your butt out behind you, and lower as if you were sitting in a chair. Keep your knees behind your toes, so that if you look down, you can see your toes. Keep your head up and chest lifted. Lower until your butt is just above knee height. Hold for a second, then press into your feet to stand up, bringing your right foot in to meet your left. Repeat stepping to the left. Do 10 reps moving to the left, and then do 10 reps stepping to the right.

A   B

Back it off: Don't lower as far into the squat.

Pump it up: As you stand up, add a little hop as you bring your feet together. It doesn't have to be high.

PLANK WALK

(A) Stand with your feet together. Bend your knees and squat all the way down, leaning forward and placing your hands on the floor. (B) Keep your feet stationary and walk your hands forward until your body forms a plank. (Your body should be in a straight line, (C) balancing on the palms of your hands and your toes and balls of your feet—like a pushup position.) (D) (E) (F) Then, keeping your hands stationary, walk your feet toward your hands. Repeat walking your hands out, and then your feet to meet them. Do 10 to 12 reps.

Back it off: Do pikes instead of planks. Walk your hands out only a few feet so that your body forms an upside-down V, a pike position. As you become stronger, you can walk your hands farther out, getting closer to a full plank.

Pump it up: Hold each plank position for a count of 5 before you start to move again. You can also work up to keeping your legs straight when your hands and feet are walked together in between the planks. (This requires greater flexibility in your hamstrings.)

Chapter 11

Get Faster

Before I tell you how you'll get faster, I want to be blunt about a common excuse for not even trying. Many "height-challenged" people tell me that they can't get faster without long legs.

That's when I tell them about the Chinese athlete who won the gold medal at the 2016 Olympics in the women's 20K (12.4-mile) race walk. She stands at only 5'3". She finished in 1 hour 28 minutes. That's about a 7-minute-per-mile pace—and she did it while *walking*! The American who had 2 extra inches of height on her came in 5 minutes later, finishing in 22nd place. That's still an impressive 7½ minutes per mile (8 mph)!

I hope I've just convinced you that the key to walking faster isn't longer legs. Rather, it's this: taking shorter, quicker steps. This plan will help to train your legs to do just that. Also, review the technique suggestions in Chapter 6 (see page 67). It really makes a difference. After just one session, one of my clients reported back that she was finally able to break past 3.8 mph on her treadmill, and was now comfortably striding at 4.0 mph. And if you experience any shin pain, a common complaint when you speed up, see Excuse Buster #1: Survive Shin Pain, page 333.

HOW YOU'LL WALK YOUR WAY FASTER

This plan includes three different types of walks.

Tempo walks—Once a week, you'll be doing a slightly longer tempo walk, which helps train your body to go faster for longer, while minimizing negative body effects, like burning muscles that can make you want to slow down. You should be walking at a brisk-to-fast pace for most of your workout. Each week, the duration will increase.

30-20-10 intervals—Most interval routines have two intervals, but this one really cranks it up by adding a third interval to really challenge yourself. After warming up by walking at an easy-to-moderate pace for 3 minutes, you speed up to a brisk pace for 30 seconds, then a fast pace for 20 seconds, and finally your speediest pace possible for 10 seconds. You'll repeat the 30-, 20-, and 10-second set of intervals for 4 minutes, followed by a 1-minute recovery at a moderate pace. Repeat the series for the recommended workout time.

Recovery walks—These are moderate-to-brisk paced walks that help you to maintain the gains you are making, while giving your body some rejuvenation time by going at a lower intensity. Doing too many high-intensity workouts can lead to burnout or injuries. Do at least two recovery walks a week, three if you want to walk every day. Just don't overdo it.

YOUR GET-FASTER TRAINING PLAN

WEEK 4

- *1 day a week:* Tempo Walk—3-minute warmup, 30-minute brisk-fast pace, 2-minute cooldown (35 minutes total)

- *2 days a week:* Interval Walk—3-minute warmup, 15-minute 30-20-10 intervals, 2-minute cooldown (20 minutes total)

- *2 or 3 days a week:* Recovery Walk—3-minute warmup, 30-minute moderate-brisk pace, 2-minute cooldown (35 minutes total)

- *2 or 3 days a week:* Strength training

WEEK 5

- *1 day a week:* Tempo Walk—3-minute warmup, 35-minute brisk-fast pace, 2-minute cooldown (40 minutes total)

- *2 days a week:* Interval Walk—3-minute warmup, 20-minute 30-20-10 intervals, 2-minute cooldown (25 minutes total)

- *2 or 3 days a week:* Recovery Walk—3-minute warmup, 30-minute moderate-brisk pace, 2-minute cooldown (35 minutes total)

- *2 or 3 days a week:* Strength training

WEEK 6

- *1 day a week:* Tempo Walk—3-minute warmup, 40-minute brisk-fast pace, 2-minute cooldown (45 minutes total)

- *2 days a week:* Interval Walk—3-minute warmup, 25-minute 30-20-10 intervals, 2-minute cooldown (30 minutes total)

- *2 or 3 days a week:* Recovery Walk—3-minute warmup, 30-minute moderate-brisk pace, 2-minute cooldown (35 minutes total)

- *2 or 3 days a week (nonconsecutive days):* Strength training

Tempo walk

TIME	DURATION	ACTIVITY	INTENSITY
0:00	3 minutes	Warmup	3
3:00	30 minutes*	Brisk-to-fast	6–8
33:00	2 minutes	Cooldown	3
35:00	**TOTAL:** 35 minutes		

* For week 5, increase to 35 minutes. For week 6, to 40 minutes.

Recovery walk

TIME	DURATION	ACTIVITY	INTENSITY
0:00	3 minutes	Warmup	3
3:00	30 minutes	Moderate-to-brisk	5–7
33:00	2 minutes	Cooldown	3
35:00	**TOTAL:** 35 minutes		

30-20-10 Interval walk

TIME	DURATION	ACTIVITY	INTENSITY
0:00	3 minutes	Warmup	3
3:00	30 seconds	Brisk	6
3:30	20 seconds	Fast	8
3:50	10 seconds	Speed	9
4:00	Repeat 30-20-10 intervals (minutes 3:00–4:00) 4 more times for a total of 5 circuits		
8:00	1 minute	Recovery	4
9:00	Repeat 30-20-10 intervals (minutes 3:00–4:00) 5 times total		
14:00	1 minute	Recovery	4
	Week 5: Stop at 15:00 minutes and cool down		
15:00	Repeat 30-20-10 intervals (minutes 3:00–4:00) 5 times total		
20:00	1 minute	Recovery	4
	Week 6: Stop at 21:00 minutes and cool down		
21:00	Repeat 30-20-10 intervals (minutes 3:00–4:00) 5 times		
26:00	1 minute	Recovery	4
27:00	3 minutes	Cooldown	3
30:00	**TOTAL:** 30 minutes		

Count how many steps you take during several of the 30-, 20-, and 10-second intervals to gauge an estimated baseline. Please note this on your exercise log. The goal is to see these numbers increase as you progress through the program. You don't have to count every interval. Aim to count for one or two cycles within each 5-minute circuit.

Cycle is the 1 minute that begins with a 30-second interval, is followed by a 20-second interval, and ends with a 10-second interval.

Circuit is made up of five cycles and is followed by a 1-minute recovery interval.

Sample Schedules

Here are just two options for how to organize your workouts. Feel free to arrange them as you wish to fit within your schedule with the following guidelines.

1. Don't do two complete walks on the same day. For example, don't do a full-length Tempo Walk and a full-length Interval Walk on the same day. It is however, fine to break up one of those walks to do over the course of a day instead of all at one time.

2. Don't do strength workouts on consecutive days.

3. If you walk and do strength training on the same day, you can do them at different times (make sure you warm up and stretch before and after each) or consecutively. When doing them consecutively, do the workout that offers you the benefits that you most desire first. So, if burning fat is what you want, walk first. But if you're more interested in firming up, then do the strength workout first. You get more benefits from a workout when you are fresh.

	Sunday	Monday	Tuesday	Wednesday	Thursday	Friday	Saturday
Option 1: No rest days	30-20-10 interval walk	Recovery walk and strength train (optional)	Tempo walk	Recovery walk (optional) and strength train	30-20-10 interval walk	Strength train	Recovery walk
Option 2: Rest days	30-20-10 interval walk	Recovery walk (optional) and strength train (optional)	Tempo walk	Recovery walk and strength train	30-20-10 interval walk	Rest day	Recovery walk and strength train

YOUR GET-FASTER STRENGTH ROUTINE

Strong muscles give you more power to go faster, so it's important that you not only continue to strength train 1 but challenge yourself. You'll continue to do two moves (Bent-Over Row and Bridge) from the Basic Strength Workout. To keep the results coming, lift heavier weights or try the "Pump It Up" modifications. In addition, you'll be doing two new moves that add another level of difficulty. Do 3 sets of 8 to 12 reps of each exercise, 2 or 3 nonconsecutive days a week.

- Squat with overhead press
- Bent-over row
- Bridge
- Side plank

SQUAT WITH OVERHEAD PRESS

(A) Stand with your feet about shoulder-width apart, toes pointing forward or slightly out to the sides. Hold a dumbbell in each hand, with your arms bent so the dumbbells are by your shoulders, palms facing forward. (B) Sit back into a squat, hinging forward at your hips and bending your knees. Keep your knees behind your toes as you lower. (C) Hold for a second, and then stand back up, pressing the dumbbells straight up overhead. Hold for a second. Then, lower the dumbbells to shoulder height as you sit back into a squat. Do 8 to 12 reps.

A   B   C

Back it off: Use lighter weights. Don't lower as far into the squat.

Pump it up: Use heavier weights. Add a heel lift when you press the dumbbells overhead.

BENT-OVER ROW

Place your left hand and left knee on a chair or bench. (A) Hold a dumbbell in your right hand with your arm hanging straight beneath your shoulder. (B) Bend your elbow and pull the dumbbell up toward your chest, keeping your arm in toward your body and your elbow pointing toward the ceiling. Hold for a second. Slowly lower the dumbbell. Do 8 to 12 reps with each arm for a set.

Back it off: Holding a dumbbell in your right hand, stand behind a chair with your left foot in front of your right. Lean forward slightly from your hips and place your left hand on the back of a chair. Perform the move in this position and/or use a lighter weight.

Pump it up: Hold dumbbells in both hands and hinge forward from your hips so your arms are hanging beneath your shoulders. Keeping your abs tight, do rows with both arms at the same time in this position. (Do not do this if you have back problems.) Or do one-arm rows with heavier weights.

BRIDGE

(A) Lie on the floor on your back with your legs bent and your feet flat on the floor. Place your arms at your sides with your palms facing down. (B) Contract your abdominals and buttocks, and lift your hips and back off the floor so your body is in line from your shoulders to your knees. Hold for a second. Slowly lower. Do 8 to 12 reps for a set.

Back it off: Instead of doing reps, hold the bridge position for as long as possible, up to 1 minute.

Pump it up: Raise one leg off the floor, and perform one-leg bridges, repeating with the opposite leg.

SIDE PLANK

Lie on your left side with your feet stacked. Press yourself up onto your left elbow and forearm to balance. Extend your right arm toward the ceiling. Don't roll forward or back. Imagine your body is between two panes of glass. Hold for up to 1 minute. If you're not able to hold that long, hold as long as possible, then lower and repeat. Continue until you've held the side plank for a total of 1 minute. Then, repeat on the opposite side.

Back it off: Bend your knees so you are balancing on your lower leg.

Pump it up: Hold your top leg in the air as you balance.

Chapter 12

Train for a 5K

In the following pages, you'll find a training plan that will take you from your current level of fitness to 5K ready in just 3 weeks. Amazing, right? Here's the great thing about signing up for a race: It can both boost your motivation *and* refresh your walking. A 5K is just 3.1 miles, so it's doable for even novice walkers.

As you follow the training plans, use this advice.

- **Find an event that welcomes both runners and walkers (or walkers only).** Make sure the race has a long enough time limit for you to complete the 3.1 miles. If you walk a 15-minute mile, then you'd want an event that's open for at least 45 minutes. Or, if you can't find an event that's just 3 weeks away, you can do a 5K on your own. Just map out 3.1 miles, and go!

- **Be flexible.** The training plan is organized to maximize results but flexible to help you fit everything into your individual schedule. Feel free to adjust the days on which you do most of your workouts. For example, you could make Friday a rest day and do your easy walk on Sunday. Just don't schedule fast walks on back-to-

back days, and do the shorter fast walk before you do the longer one each week, except during Week 6. I've also designed the weeks to show examples of how to allow for rest days (walk and do strength training on the same day) or to skip rest days in favor of shorter workouts each day (spread your workouts over 7 days).

- **Rest before race day.** You'll notice that the week leading up to the race is when you'll taper or cut back in preparation for the race, so your body is well rested. That's why you'll see the longer fast walk earlier in the week this time. Also, make sure you have at least 2 days of easy walks or rest days before the event.

- **Strength train.** You'll be doing two or three strength workouts a week. You can do these any day of the week, including on rest days. Just don't do a strength workout on the 2 days leading up to the event.

- **Speed walk.** If a speedy finish is your goal, check out the fast walking techniques in Chapter 19 (see page 201).

YOUR TRAIN-FOR-A-5K TRAINING PLAN

WEEK 4

- *1 day a week:* Easy Walk—3-minute warmup, 20–30-minute easy pace, 2-minute cooldown (25–35 minutes total)

- *1 day a week:* Moderate Walk—3-minute warmup, 60-minute moderate pace, 2-minute cooldown (65 minutes total)

- *1 day a week:* Brisk Walk—3-minute warmup, 30-minute brisk pace, 2-minute cooldown (35 minutes total)

- *2 days a week:* Fast Walk—3-minute warmup, 1- or 1.5-mile fast pace, 2-minute cooldown (17–35 minutes total, depending on the distance and your pace; estimates based on a 12- to 20-minute-per-mile pace, or 3 to 5 mph)

- *2 or 3 days a week:* Strength training

WEEK 5

- *1 day a week:* Easy Walk—3-minute warmup, 20–30-minute easy pace, 2-minute cooldown (25–35 minutes total)

- *1 day a week:* Moderate Walk—3-minute warmup, 60-minute moderate pace, 2-minute cooldown (65 minutes total)

- *1 day a week:* Brisk Walk—3-minute warmup, 35-minute brisk pace, 2-minute cooldown (40 minutes total)

- *2 days a week:* Fast Walk—3-minute warmup, 2- or 2.5-mile fast pace, 2-minute cooldown (29–55 minutes total, depending on the distance and your pace; estimates based on a 12- to 20-minute-per-mile pace, or 3 to 5 mph)

- *2 or 3 days a week:* Strength training

WEEK 6*

- *2 days a week:* Easy Walk—3-minute warmup, 15–30-minute easy pace, 2-minute cooldown (20–35 minutes total)

- *1 day a week:* Moderate Walk—3-minute warmup, 45-minute moderate pace, 2-minute cooldown (50 minutes total)

- *2 days a week:* Fast Walk—3-minute warmup, 2- or 3-mile fast pace, 2-minute cooldown (29–65 minutes total, depending on the distance and your pace; estimates based on a 12- to 20-minute-per-mile pace, or 3 to 5 mph)

- *2 days a week:* Strength training

* This is a taper week to prepare for the race.

Sample Schedules

Here is just one option for how to organize your workouts. Feel free to organize them as you wish to fit within your schedule using the guidelines on page 126.

	Monday	Tuesday	Wednesday	Thursday	Friday	Saturday	Sunday
Week 4: Rest days (example)	1 mile fast walk and strength train	Rest	30-min. brisk walk and strength train (optional)	1.5 miles fast walk	20–30-min. easy walk and strength train	60-min. moderate walk	Rest
Week 5: No rest days (example)	2 miles fast walk	Strength train	35-min. brisk walk	2.5 miles fast walk	20–30-min. easy walk	60-min. moderate walk	Strength train
Week 6: Rest day (example)	3 miles fast walk and strength train	Rest	2 miles fast walk	45-min. moderate walk and strength train	20–30-min. easy walk	15-min. easy walk	Race day

Easy walk

TIME	DURATION	ACTIVITY	INTENSITY
0:00	3 minutes	Warmup	3
3:00	15–30 minutes	Easy	3–5
18:00–33:00	2 minutes	Cooldown	3
20:00–35:00	**TOTAL: 20–35 minutes**		

Moderate walk

TIME	DURATION	ACTIVITY	INTENSITY
0:00	3 minutes	Warmup	3
3:00	45–60 minutes	Moderate	5–6
48:00–63:00	2 minutes	Cooldown	3
50:00–65:00	**TOTAL: 50–65 minutes**		

Brisk walk

TIME	DURATION	ACTIVITY	INTENSITY
0:00	3 minutes	Warmup	3
3:00	30–35 minutes	Brisk	6–7
33:00–38:00	2 minutes	Cooldown	3
35:00–40:00	**TOTAL: 35–40 minutes**		

Fast walk

TIME	DURATION	ACTIVITY	INTENSITY
0:00	3 minutes	Warmup	3
3:00	12–60 minutes*	Fast (1–3 miles)	8–9
15:00–63:00	2 minutes	Cooldown	3
17:00–65:00	**TOTAL: 17–65 minutes**		

Estimates based on a 12- to 20-minute-per-mile pace, or 3 to 5 mph

YOUR TRAIN-FOR-A-5K STRENGTH ROUTINE

You'll continue to do the Strength Workout from the Basic Walking Plan. Try to challenge yourself with more reps or sets, or try the more-challenging version of an exercise. In addition, you will be adding another lower-body exercise, Stepups, to give your stride even more power. Do 1 to 3 sets of 8 to 12 reps of each exercise, 2 or 3 days a week.

- Squat and Lift
- Bent-over row
- Bridge
- Plank
- Stepup

SQUAT AND LIFT

(A) Stand with your feet about shoulder-width apart, toes pointing straight ahead or slightly out, and arms relaxed at your sides. (B) Bend your knees and hinge forward from your hips, lowering yourself as if you are sitting back into a chair. Stick your butt out, shift your weight into your heels, and raise your arms out in front of you as you bend your knees and lower as far as possible, while maintaining good form. Stop before your hips are in line with your knees. Hold for a second. (C) Press into your heels, squeeze your buttocks, and stand back up. As you come up, rise up onto your toes, lifting your heels as high as possible. Hold for a second. Lower back to the starting position. Do 8 to 12 reps for a set.

Back it off: Do the squat only (without raising up onto your toes).

Pump it up: Hold dumbbells at your sides as you do the move.

BENT-OVER ROW

Place your left hand and left knee on a chair or bench. (A) Hold a dumbbell in your right hand with your arm hanging straight beneath your shoulder. (B) Bend your elbow and pull the dumbbell up toward your chest, keeping your arm in toward your body and your elbow pointing toward the ceiling. Hold for a second. Slowly lower the dumbbell. Do 8 to 12 reps with each arm for a set.

Back it off: Holding a dumbbell in your right hand, stand behind a chair with your left foot in front of your right. Lean forward slightly from your hips and place your left hand on the back of a chair. Perform the move in this position and/or use a lighter weight.

Pump it up: Hold dumbbells in both hands and hinge forward from your hips so your arms are hanging beneath your shoulders. Keeping your abs tight, do rows with both arms at the same time in this position. (Do not do this if you have back problems.) Or do one-arm rows with heavier weights.

BRIDGE

(A) Lie on the floor on your back with your legs bent and your feet flat on the floor. Place your arms at your sides with your palms facing down. (B) Contract your abdominals and buttocks, and lift your hips and back off the floor so your body is in line from your shoulders to your knees. Hold for a second. Slowly lower. Do 8 to 12 reps for a set.

Back it off: Instead of doing reps, hold the bridge position for as long as possible, up to 1 minute.

Pump it up: Raise one leg off the floor, and perform one-leg bridges, repeating with the opposite leg.

PLANK

Lie facedown on the floor with your arms bent and your elbows under your shoulders. Tuck your toes under and lift your body off the floor so you are balancing on your forearms, elbows, balls of your feet, and toes. Hold for up to 1 minute. If you're not able to hold for that long, hold for as long as possible, then lower and repeat. Keep your body in line from your head to your heels. Continue until you've held the plank for a total of 1 minute.

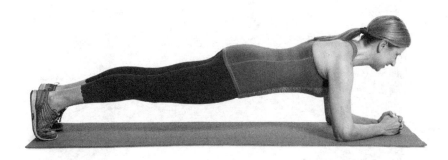

Back it off: Keep your knees on the floor.

Pump it up: After you push up into the plank, lift one foot off the floor and hold. Work up to holding for 1 minute on each leg, resting in between.

STEPUP

(A) Hold a dumbbell in each hand with your arms hanging naturally at your sides. Stand in front of a step or bench. Place your left foot on the bench and press into the bench to lift your body up onto the bench. (B) Lift your right leg up, tap your right toes on the bench, and then slowly lower. Do 8 to 12 reps, and repeat with your other leg.

A   B

Back it off: Use lighter weights, no weights at all, or a lower step.

Pump it up: Use heavier weights. As you step up with one foot, extend your other leg behind you, squeezing your buttocks.

RACE-DAY PREP

For first-timers, here's what you can expect from the start of your 5K, all the way to the finish line—and advice on how to react. Even if you've done races in the past, you might find some new tips to make this experience better than previous ones.

- Pin your bib number onto the front of your shirt, using a safety pin on each corner. A number that flaps around as you're walking gets annoying very quickly.

- Don't line up too close to the starting line. Walkers should be at the back of the pack. Some races have corrals based on your estimated finish time—don't overestimate when deciding what corral to be in. Besides, the closer to the front you are, the more people will pass you, and that can feel discouraging.

- Hold back at the beginning. You'll feel better if you start out slow. A common mistake is going out faster than you normally walk because of all the people and excitement. You can burn out well before the finish line.

- Don't walk more than two abreast.

- Cheer runners and other walkers on as you see them.

- Thank the volunteers for helping and the spectators for cheering.

- Don't stop in the middle of the road. If you need to stretch or tie your shoe, move to the side or completely off the road to avoid a collision with other walkers and runners.

- Alert others by saying something like "on your left" when you are about to pass them.

- Look for other runners before you throw your cup or wrappers, and, whenever possible, try to throw them in a trash receptacle.

- Pinch your cup for easier drinking while walking.

- You're not racing to win. You're racing to achieve a personal goal. Don't worry about being passed. Just focus on you!

- Push any negative thoughts out of your head. Instead focus on something positive like the beautiful scenery.

- Get out of the finish area as quickly as possible, so you don't interfere with other participants as they come in.

- Smile! Especially when you see photographers.

Chapter 13

Train for a 10K

So, you may wonder why to choose a 10K when you could do a 5K instead? Here's why: It could seriously fire up your motivation.

Are you the kind of person who needs a more challenging goal in order to stay on track? Then, this goal might be for you. After all, the Basic Walking Plan has already built your fitness up to the point that you could go out and do a 5K tomorrow, right? You might not be able to do it as quickly as you'd like or if you push yourself to, you probably won't feel so great afterward or the next day—but you could do it without training. So, a tougher goal, like a 10K (6.2 miles), may keep you more focused on sticking with the schedule. A 10K is also a great intermediate step, if you have a desire to walk a half- or full marathon one day.

If you choose this goal, you'll be training for 6 weeks rather than for just 3 weeks. That means you won't be switching things up in Stage 3.

You'll find a training plan for the first 3 weeks and sample schedules in the pages that follow. Here's some advice for getting the best results.

- **Find the right event for you.** You'll want an event that welcomes both runners and walkers (or walkers only) and has a long enough time limit for you to complete the 6.2 miles. If you

walk a 15-minute mile, then you'd want an event that's open for at least 90 minutes, preferably longer in case you fatigue more quickly or run into other obstacles and need more time to finish.

- **Make the schedule work for you.** When you're training for an event like a 10K, the order of some of the walks is important, so your plan is laid out as you should execute it; however, there is some flexibility to make it best fit your schedule. You can adjust the days you do most workouts. Move the Rest days, too. For example, you could do your Long Walk on Sunday instead of Saturday. Just make sure that you do an Easy Walk the day after your Long Walk. Also, don't do your Fast Walk and Long Walk on consecutive days. I've also designed the weeks to show examples of how to allow for rest days (walk and do strength training on the same day) or to skip rest days in favor of shorter workouts each day (spread your workouts over 7 days).

- **Strength train.** You'll be doing two or three strength workouts a week. You can do these any day of the week, including on rest days. Just don't do them on consecutive days. In the schedule below, there are examples of how to slot your strength workouts, in order to allow rest days or to have no rest days, but keep exercise time shorter each day.

- **Speed walk.** If a speedy finish is your goal, check out the fast walking techniques in Chapter 19 (see page 201) and Excuse Buster #1: Survive Shin Pain (see page 333) if you start to have problems.

YOUR TRAIN-FOR-A-10K TRAINING PLAN

WEEK 4

- *1 day a week:* Easy Walk—3-minute warmup, 20–30-minute easy pace, 2-minute cooldown (25–35 minutes total)

- *1 day a week:* Moderate Walk—3-minute warmup, 30-minute moderate pace, 2-minute cooldown (35 minutes total)

- *1 day a week:* Brisk Walk—3-minute warmup, 30-minute brisk pace, 2-minute cooldown (35 minutes total)

- *1 day a week:* Fast Walk—3-minute warmup, 1-mile fast pace, 2-minute cooldown (17–25 minutes total, depending on your pace; estimates based on a 12- to 20-minute-per-mile pace, or 3 to 5 mph)

- *1 day a week:* Long Walk—3-minute warmup, 4-mile long walk, 2-minute cooldown (65–85 minutes total, depending on your pace; estimates based on a 15- to 20-minute-per-mile pace, or 3 to 5 mph)

- *2 or 3 days a week:* Strength training

WEEK 5

- *1 day a week:* Easy Walk—3-minute warmup, 20–30-minute easy pace, 2-minute cooldown (25–35 minutes total)

- *1 day a week:* Moderate Walk—3-minute warmup, 30-minute moderate pace, 2-minute cooldown (35 minutes total)

- *1 day a week:* Brisk Walk—3-minute warmup, 30-minute brisk pace, 2-minute cooldown (35 minutes total)

- *1 day a week:* Fast Walk—3-minute warmup, 2-mile fast pace, 2-minute cooldown (29–45 minutes total, depending on your pace; estimates based on a 12- to 20-minute-per-mile pace, or 3 to 5 mph)

- *1 day a week:* Long Walk—3-minute warmup, 4.5-mile long walk, 2-minute cooldown (63–95 minutes total, depending on your pace; estimates based on a 15- to 20-minute-per-mile pace, or 3 to 5 mph)

- *2 or 3 days a week:* Strength training

WEEK 6

- *1 day a week:* Easy Walk—3-minute warmup, 20–30-minute easy pace, 2-minute cooldown (25–35 minutes total)

- *1 day a week:* Moderate Walk—3-minute warmup, 30-minute moderate pace, 2-minute cooldown (35 minutes total)

- *1 day a week:* Brisk Walk—3-minute warmup, 45-minute brisk pace, 2-minute cooldown (50 minutes total)

- *1 day a week:* Fast Walk—3-minute warmup, 3-mile fast pace, 2-minute cooldown (41–65 minutes total, depending on your pace; estimates based on a 12- to 20-minute-per-mile pace, or 3 to 5 mph)

- *1 day a week:* Long Walk—3-minute warmup, 5-mile long walk, 2-minute cooldown (80–105

minutes total, depending on your pace; estimates based on a 15- to 20-minute-per-mile pace, or 3 to 5 mph)

- *2 or 3 days a week:* Strength training

Sample Schedule

Follow this schedule to get yourself ready for a 10K. You'll find the final 3 weeks of training in Stage 3 on page 212.

	Monday	Tuesday	Wednesday	Thursday	Friday	Saturday	Sunday
Week 4: Rest days (example)	20–30-min. easy walk and strength train	30-min. brisk walk	Rest day	1 mile fast walk and strength train	Rest day	30-min. moderate walk and strength train (optional)	4-mile long walk
Week 5: Rest days (example)	20–30-min. easy walk and strength train	30-min. brisk walk	Strength train	2 miles fast walk	Rest day	30-min. moderate walk and strength train (optional)	4.5-mile long walk
Week 6: No rest days (example)	20–30-min. easy walk and strength train (optional)	45-min. brisk walk	Strength train	3 miles fast walk	Strength train	30-min. moderate walk	5-mile long walk

Easy walk

TIME	DURATION	ACTIVITY	INTENSITY
0:00	3 minutes	Warmup	3–5
3:00	20–30 minutes	Easy	3–5
23:00–33:00	2 minutes	Cooldown	3–5
25:00–35:00	**TOTAL: 25–35 minutes**		

Moderate walk

TIME	DURATION	ACTIVITY	INTENSITY
0:00	3 minutes	Warmup	3–5
3:00	30 minutes	Moderate	5–6
33:00	2 minutes	Cooldown	3–5
35:00	**TOTAL: 35 minutes**		

Brisk walk

TIME	DURATION	ACTIVITY	INTENSITY
0:00	3 minutes	Warmup	3–5
3:00	30–45 minutes	Brisk	6–7
33:00–48:00	2 minutes	Cooldown	3–5
35:00–50:00	**TOTAL: 35–50 minutes**		

Long walk

TIME	DURATION	ACTIVITY	INTENSITY
0:00	3 minutes	Warmup	3–5
3:00	60–100 minutes*	Moderate to brisk (4–5 miles)	5–7
63:00–103:00	2 minutes	Cooldown	3–5
65:00–105:00	**TOTAL: 65–105 minutes**		

Estimates based on a 15- to 20-minute-per-mile pace, or 4 to 5 mph

Fast walk

TIME	DURATION	ACTIVITY	INTENSITY
0:00	3 minutes	Warmup	3–5
3:00	12–60 minutes*	Fast (1–3 miles)	7–8
15:00–63:00	2 minutes	Cooldown	3–5
17:00–65:00	**TOTAL: 17–65 minutes**		

Estimates based on a 12- to 20-minute-per-mile pace or 3 to 5 mph

YOUR TRAIN-FOR-A-10K STRENGTH ROUTINE

The longer your walking distance, the stronger you're going to want to be. Muscle strength is what holds you up and helps you stand tall. You don't want to be slouching when you cross the finish line. It doesn't look good in photos, but more important, it will slow you down, and you'll feel less like celebrating. This is a total-body strength routine, but focuses more on your lower body and core, to keep you walking tall and strong as you go the distance. Do 1 to 3 sets of 8 to 12 reps of each exercise, 2 or 3 nonconsecutive days a week.

- Row with deadlift
- Squat and lift
- Hip extension
- Pushup
- Clamshell
- Lunge with a twist
- Ball squeeze

ROW WITH DEADLIFT

(A) Stand with your feet about shoulder-width apart and hold a dumbbell in each hand with your arms extended down in front of your thighs, your knees slightly bent, and your palms facing your thighs. (B) Slowly lean forward, bending at the hips, and lower your torso until almost parallel with the floor. Keep the weights close to your body, your back straight, and your abdominals tight, to protect your back as you lower. (C) Then, bend your elbows up and out to the sides and pull the dumbbells toward your chest. Hold for a second. Slowly lower the dumbbells and stand back up, pressing your feet into the floor and squeezing your buttocks. Do 8 to 12 reps. (If you have back problems, replace this move with the Bent-Over Row in the workout on page 131.)

A   B   C

Back it off: Use lighter weights. Just do rows without doing the deadlift in between.

Pump it up: Use heavier weights.

SQUAT AND LIFT

(A) Stand with your feet about shoulder-width apart, toes pointing straight ahead or slightly out, and arms relaxed at your sides. **(B)** Bend your knees and hinge forward from your hips, lowering yourself as if you are sitting back into a chair. Stick your butt out, shift your weight into your heels, and raise your arms out in front of you as you bend your knees and lower as far as possible, while maintaining good form. Stop before your hips are in line with your knees. Hold for a second. **(C)** Press into your heels, squeeze your buttocks, and stand back up. As you come up, rise up onto your toes, lifting your heels as high as possible. Hold for a second. Lower back to the starting position. Do 8 to 12 reps for a set.

Back it off: Do the squat only (without raising up onto your toes).

Pump it up: Hold dumbbells at your sides as you do the move.

HIP EXTENSION

Securely fasten an exercise band to a railing, pole, or sturdy piece of furniture at floor level. (A) Loop the band around your right leg. Place your hand on a chair or wall for balance. Standing tall, with shoulders straight and back, shift your weight onto your left foot. (B) Raise your right leg straight out behind you, squeezing your buttocks. Keep your toes, knees, and hips pointing forward. Hold for a second, then slowly lower. Do 8 to 12 reps, then switch legs and repeat.

Back it off: Do the move without using an exercise band.

Pump it up: Use a stronger band.

PUSHUP

(A) Kneel on the floor and walk your hands out so you are balancing on your hands with your fingers forward, and on your knees with your feet in the air. (B) Bend your elbows out to the sides and lower your chest toward the floor. Your body should be in line from your head to your knees; don't bend at your hips or round your upper back. Hold for a second, then push back up. Do 8 to 12 reps.

Back it off: Do pushups while you are standing with your hands placed on a desk, table, or counter.

Pump it up: Lift your knees off the floor and do pushups, balancing on your hands and toes.

CLAMSHELL

(A) Lie on your left side with your legs stacked and bent. Place your left arm under your head, with your right arm in front of your body for support. (B) Slowly rotate your right knee upward, while keeping your feet together. Don't roll your hips forward or back as you lift. Hold for a second, then slowly lower. Do 8 to 12 reps on each side.

Back it off: Don't lift your knee as high.

Pump it up: Hold a weight against your top thigh for more resistance.

LUNGE WITH A TWIST

(A) Stand with your feet together and hold a dumbbell with both hands in front of you at waist height.

(B) Step your right leg forward and lower into a lunge, keeping your right knee directly over your ankle and your left knee pointing down toward the floor. As you lunge, rotate your torso to the right. Hold for a second, and then press into your right foot to stand back up, rotating to the center as you do. Repeat to the opposite side. Do 8 to 12 reps to each side.

Back it off: Do the move without holding any weight.

Pump it up: Press into your right foot to stand back up, bringing your left knee up in front of you. Balance on your right leg for a second before lowering your left foot to the starting position.

BALL SQUEEZE

Stand tall with a soft (slightly deflated) ball between your thighs. With your hands on your hips, squeeze and release the ball without letting it fall. Do 8 to 12 reps.

Back it off: Do the exercise while lying on the floor with your knees bent and hands at your sides. Squeeze the ball between your thighs.

Pump it up: Do the exercise while holding a squat position (bend at your hips and knees, stick your butt out, and keep your back straight and your chest lifted).

WEEKS 7 THROUGH 9

Chapter 14

Boost Your Results

You've completed 6 weeks of walking. Way to go! You're really on the path to making walking a lifelong habit and to achieving your goals. Keep up the great work!

It's time to mix things up again. You don't want all the good results that you've been getting to plateau or your mind to get bored. With that in mind, you have a choice. You can stick to your original goal and add new challenges, or you can pick a new goal.

STICK TO YOUR ORIGINAL GOAL

The Stage 3 plan builds on the Stage 2 plans with new challenges, like longer distances and higher intensity, as well as new walking routines or walking drills like skipping. (If you're doing the Train for a 10K plan, you should go to page 212 to continue your training and prepare for race day.) You'll also get new strength-training moves to build and shape your muscles, so you look better and walk faster. So, if you want to stick to your original goal and build on those results, just flip to the Stage 3 chapter focusing on your goal, and get moving. However, if you did the 5K plan or want to change your goal, keep reading.

SELECT A NEW GOAL

If you'd like to select a new goal, you, again, have several options. The first, which I highly recommend, is to choose your new goal for Stage 3, but start with the Stage 2 version of that plan. The workouts in Stage 2 and Stage 3 are progressive, so you'll build up your endurance, stamina, and muscles before tackling faster speeds, longer distances, and more challenging exercises. This will maximize your chances of success and minimize your risk of an injury from doing too much too soon. This really isn't a step backward. Moving forward, I'm going to encourage you to use all of the routines in the program.

The second option is to choose a new goal and jump right into the Stage 3 plan. As I've mentioned, everyone is different, and this is all about you! You may be fine with stepping it up more quickly. (One exception is if you were following the Maximize Your Health plan for Weeks 4 through 6, which wasn't focused on building intensity that will be required in Stage 3. You would do best to take on another Stage 2 plan for Weeks 7 through 9, unless you're confident that your fitness level will support a bit of a leap forward at this stage.) So, if you want to give it a try, I'd encourage you to look at the plans in Stages 2 and 3 for the goals that you are interested in. Then, decide on which one feels right for you.

Here are the workout goals you can choose from for Stage 3.

- **Lose Weight**—interval walks for overall weight loss (page 152)

- **Flatten Your Belly**—longer, faster walks and interval walks for weight loss, with a focus on shrinking your midsection (page 164)

- **Maximize Your Health**—build a walking habit with flexible walking goals to feel good and prevent diseases (page 177)

- **Firm Up**—walking workouts with extra strength training to tone your body from head to toe, along with losing weight (page 183)

- **Get Faster**—interval and fast walks, along with fun drills, to pick up your speed and maximize benefits in less time (page 201)

- **Train for a 5K**—signing up for an event can boost your motivation; if you opt for this strategy, you'll follow the plan as laid out in Stage 2 (page 126)

- **Train for a 10K (6-week plan)**—this is the plan (page 212) for you if you've already completed Weeks 4 through 6 of the Train for a 10K on page 136; if you were pursuing another goal in Stage 2 but would now like to train for a 10K, you'll want to start with the Stage 2 training plan for best results (page 136).

Got your plan for the next 3 weeks? Then, let's rock and roll!

PROFILE: Janet Starner, 66

Lost 3.4 pounds & 2.5 inches

Janet may have been the oldest member of the Walk Your Way to Better Health test group, but she was one of the speediest. She outpaced more than half of the group during the initial 1-mile walk test, finishing at 15:03. But, Janet was a disgruntled walker.

At age 60, Janet took up running and loved it, completing her first half-marathon in 2011. Unfortunately, she developed severe knee pain during her training and had surgery later that year. But the thrill and sense of accomplishment of crossing the finish line drove her to do another half-marathon in 2013, and in 2014, she had to walk segments of it in between running. Despite her knee pain, she desperately wanted to remain a part of the amazing experience and community that surrounds races.

But, she hung up her running shoes.

Janet went from what she described as "the best shape of her life" to "feeling old and rickety" over the next 2 years.

"It took a long while for me to come to terms with the fact that I could NOT run—I was very depressed," Janet said. But, finally, at the beginning of 2016, she was ready to get back in shape.

Right before starting the Walk Your Way to Better Health program, Janet walked a half-marathon, but she was disappointed in her performance. "Walking seemed a pale second-best option," she said. She wasn't losing weight or feeling as fit as she did when she had trained in the past.

During the program, Janet stopped pushing herself hard like she had when she ran or when she was training for her first walking marathon. Instead, she shifted her focus to improving her walking technique—landing on her heel, rolling through her foot, and pushing off with her toes; taking shorter steps; and driving her elbows back, instead of punching forward as she swung her arms.

"I gave myself permission to let go of any pressure to compete with myself," she said. Her husband joined her for most of the walks, and they strolled in a variety of locations. Janet started to enjoy the scenery instead of just focusing on how fast she was going. "The walks felt less like 'training' and more like fun outings. I reframed the experience in my own mind, and after I did that, I fell in love with walking. Getting out in the fresh air was restorative, refreshing, and rejuvenating."

When she walked her next half-marathon in November 2016, she did so "simply for the joy of it." And she beat her previous half-marathon time! Not surprising since she got significantly faster over the 9-week program. At the final 1-mile walk test, Janet was speedier than three-quarters of the test panelists, some 20-plus years younger than her. She covered the distance in an impressive 13:17—nearly 2 minutes faster than her original time.

BEFORE

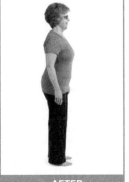

AFTER

Chapter 15

Lose Weight

For this Stage 3 weight-loss plan, you'll step up your results by increasing your Interval Walks to 35 minutes. That could rev your calorie burn by up to 75 percent during your workout.

Even better, you'll continue to burn more calories after your workout, too. This is called the excess post-exercise oxygen consumption (EPOC), which is technospeak for the afterburn that you learned in Chapter 2. As I mentioned in that chapter, your calorie burn doesn't instantly revert back to normal as soon as you stop exercising. It takes time for all of the systems in your body to return to normal and, while that happens, your calorie burn remains elevated.

Interval walking seems to really crank up your afterburn, unlike other types of walks. In one study, the afterburn following interval walking was more than double compared to steady-paced walking.[1] The longer you work out and the higher your intensity, the longer you maintain that bonus burn.

YOUR LOSE-WEIGHT TRAINING PLAN

WEEK 7

- *2 days a week:* Moderate Walk—3-minute warmup, 55-minute moderate pace, 2-minute cooldown (60 minutes total)

- *3 days a week:* Interval Walk—3-minute warmup, 25-minute intervals (1 minute fast, 1 minute brisk), 2-minute cooldown (30 minutes total)

- *2 or 3 days a week:* Strength training

WEEK 8

- *2 days a week:* Moderate Walk—3-minute warmup, 55-minute moderate pace, 2-minute cooldown (60 minutes total)

- *3 days a week:* Interval Walk—3-minute warmup, 30-minute intervals (1 minute fast,

Walk Your Way to a Firmer Rear End

Every time your heel lands on the ground, squeeze your glutes. Not only will it firm up your butt but it also helps you shorten your steps for a speedier pace. Feel a need for speed? Get more technique advice on page 201.

1 minute brisk), 2-minute cooldown (35 minutes total)

- *2 or 3 days a week:* Strength training

WEEK 9

- *2 days a week:* Moderate Walk—3-minute

warmup, 55-minute moderate pace, 2-minute cooldown (60 minutes total)

- *3 days a week:* Interval Walk—3-minute warmup, 35-minute intervals (1 minute fast, 1 minute brisk), 2-minute cooldown (40 minutes total)

- *2 or 3 days a week:* Strength training

Moderate walk

TIME	DURATION	ACTIVITY	INTENSITY
0:00	3 minutes	Warmup	3
3:00	55 minutes	Moderate	5–6
58:00	2 minutes	Cooldown	3
60:00	**TOTAL:** 60 minutes		

Sample Schedules

Below you'll find two options for how to organize your workouts. Arrange them as you wish to fit within your schedule using the following guidelines.

1. Don't do two complete walks on the same day. For example, don't do a full-length Moderate Walk and a full-length Interval Walk on the same day. It is, however, fine to break up one of those walks to do over the course of a day instead of all at one time.

2. Don't do strength workouts on consecutive days.

3. If you walk and do strength training on the same day, you can do them at different times (make sure you warm up and stretch before and after each) or consecutively. When doing them consecutively, do the workout that offers you the benefits you most desire first. So if burning fat is what you want, walk first. If you're more interested in firming up, then do the strength workout first. You get more benefits from a workout when you are fresh.

	Sunday	Monday	Tuesday	Wednesday	Thursday	Friday	Saturday
Option 1: No rest days	Interval walk	Strength train	Interval walk	Strength train	Moderate walk	Interval walk (optional)	Moderate walk and strength train (optional)
Option 2: Rest days	Interval walk and strength train	Rest day	Interval walk and strength train	Rest day	Moderate walk and strength train	Interval walk (optional)	Moderate walk

Fat-Burning Interval

Walk #1 (Week 7)

TIME	DURATION	ACTIVITY	INTENSITY
0:00	3 minutes	Warmup	3
3:00	1 minute	Moderate	5
4:00	1 minute	Brisk	6
5:00	1 minute	Fast	8
6:00	1 minute	Brisk	6
7:00	1 minute	Fast	8
8:00	1 minute	Brisk	6
9:00	1 minute	Fast	8
10:00	1 minute	Brisk	6
11:00	1 minute	Fast	8
12:00	1 minute	Brisk	6
13:00	1 minute	Fast	8
14:00	1 minute	Brisk	6
15:00	1 minute	Fast	8
16:00	1 minute	Brisk	6
17:00	1 minute	Fast	8
18:00	1 minute	Brisk	6
19:00	1 minute	Fast	8
20:00	1 minute	Brisk	6
21:00	1 minute	Fast	8
22:00	1 minute	Brisk	6
23:00	1 minute	Fast	8
24:00	1 minute	Brisk	6
25:00	1 minute	Fast	8
26:00	1 minute	Brisk	6
27:00	1 minute	Fast	8
28:00	1 minute	Brisk	6
29:00	2 minute	Cooldown	3
31:00	**TOTAL: 31 minutes**		

Fat-Burning Interval

Walk #2 (Week 8)

TIME	DURATION	ACTIVITY	INTENSITY
0:00	3 minutes	Warmup	3
3:00	1 minute	Moderate	5
4:00	1 minute	Brisk	6
5:00	1 minute	Fast	8
6:00	1 minute	Brisk	6
7:00	1 minute	Fast	8
8:00	1 minute	Brisk	6
9:00	1 minute	Fast	8
10:00	1 minute	Brisk	6
11:00	1 minute	Fast	8
12:00	1 minute	Brisk	6
13:00	1 minute	Fast	8
14:00	1 minute	Brisk	6
15:00	1 minute	Fast	8
16:00	1 minute	Brisk	6
17:00	1 minute	Fast	8
18:00	1 minute	Brisk	6
19:00	1 minute	Fast	8
20:00	1 minute	Brisk	6
21:00	1 minute	Fast	8
22:00	1 minute	Brisk	6
23:00	1 minute	Fast	8
24:00	1 minute	Brisk	6
25:00	1 minute	Fast	8
26:00	1 minute	Brisk	6
27:00	1 minute	Fast	8
28:00	1 minute	Brisk	6
29:00	1 minute	Fast	8
30:00	1 minute	Brisk	6
31:00	1 minute	Fast	8
32:00	1 minute	Brisk	6
33:00	2 minutes	Cooldown	3
35:00	**TOTAL:** 35 minutes		

Fat-Burning Interval

Walk #3 (Week 9)

TIME	DURATION	ACTIVITY	INTENSITY
0:00	3 minutes	Warmup	3
3:00	1 minute	Moderate	5
4:00	1 minute	Brisk	6
5:00	1 minute	Fast	8
6:00	1 minute	Brisk	6
7:00	1 minute	Fast	8
8:00	1 minute	Brisk	6
9:00	1 minute	Fast	8
10:00	1 minute	Brisk	6
11:00	1 minute	Fast	8
12:00	1 minute	Brisk	6
13:00	1 minute	Fast	8
14:00	1 minute	Brisk	6
15:00	1 minute	Fast	8
16:00	1 minute	Brisk	6
17:00	1 minute	Fast	8
18:00	1 minute	Brisk	6
19:00	1 minute	Fast	8
20:00	1 minute	Brisk	6
21:00	1 minute	Fast	8
22:00	1 minute	Brisk	6
23:00	1 minute	Fast	8
24:00	1 minute	Brisk	6
25:00	1 minute	Fast	8
26:00	1 minute	Brisk	6
27:00	1 minute	Fast	8
28:00	1 minute	Brisk	6
29:00	1 minute	Fast	8
30:00	1 minute	Brisk	6
31:00	1 minute	Fast	8
32:00	1 minute	Brisk	6
33:00	1 minute	Fast	8
34:00	1 minute	Brisk	6
35:00	1 minute	Fast	8
36:00	1 minute	Brisk	6
37:00	2 minutes	Cooldown	3
39:00	**TOTAL: 39 minutes**		

YOUR LOSE-WEIGHT STRENGTH ROUTINE

If you're just starting out on the Lose-Weight plan, start with 1 set for all of the exercises, then add another set each week until you are doing 3 sets.

If you followed the Stage 2 Lose-Weight plan, you'll notice that the strength routine is similar except for two new moves: the Stepup and the Twisting Side Plank. You may walk to start with 1 set of each and progress up to 3 sets. Continue to do 3 sets of the exercises you are already familiar with from weeks 4 through 6.

- Squat with overhead press
- Bridge with pullover
- Row with deadlift
- Pushup
- Stepup
- Twisting side plank

SQUAT WITH OVERHEAD PRESS

(A) Stand with your feet about shoulder-width apart, toes pointing forward or slightly out to the sides. Hold a dumbbell in each hand, with your arms bent so the dumbbells are by your shoulders, palms facing forward. (B) Sit back into a squat, hinging forward at your hips and bending your knees. Keep your knees behind your toes as you lower. (C) Hold for a second, and then stand back up, pressing the dumbbells straight up overhead. Hold for a second. Then, lower the dumbbells to shoulder height as you sit back into a squat. Do 8 to 12 reps.

A   B   C

Back it off: Use lighter weights. Don't lower as far into the squat.

Pump it up: Use heavier weights. Add a heel lift when you press the dumbbells overhead.

BRIDGE WITH PULLOVER

(A) Lie on your back, with your legs bent and your feet flat on the floor. Hold a dumbbell with both hands and extend your arms over your head, resting the dumbbell on the floor. (B) Contract your abdominals and buttocks, and press your feet into the floor to lift your butt and back off of the floor. Your body should be in line from your knees to your shoulders. As you do that, also raise the dumbbell up over your chest and toward your knees, without lifting your head off the floor. Hold for a second, then slowly return to the starting position. Do 8 to 12 reps.

Back it off: Use a lighter weight. Hold the bridge position and do reps for the pullover only.

Pump it up: Use heavier weights. Lift one foot off the floor to perform one-legged bridges.

ROW WITH DEADLIFT

(A) Stand with your feet about shoulder-width apart and hold a dumbbell in each hand with your arms extended down in front of your thighs, your knees slightly bent, and your palms facing your thighs. (B) Slowly lean forward, bending at the hips, and lower your torso until almost parallel with the floor. Keep the weights close to your body, your back straight, and your abdominals tight, to protect your back as you lower. (C) Then, bend your elbows up and out to the sides and pull the dumbbells toward your chest. Hold for a second. Slowly lower the dumbbells and stand back up, pressing your feet into the floor and squeezing your buttocks. Do 8 to 12 reps. (If you have back problems, replace this move with the Bent-Over Row in the workout on page 131.)

Back it off: Use lighter weights. Just do rows without doing the deadlift in between.

Pump it up: Use heavier weights.

PUSHUP

(A) Kneel on the floor and walk your hands out so you are balancing on your hands with your fingers forward, and on your knees with your feet in the air. (B) Bend your elbows out to the sides and lower your chest toward the floor. Your body should be in line from your head to your knees; don't bend at your hips or round your upper back. Hold for a second, then push back up. Do 8 to 12 reps.

Back it off: Do pushups while you are standing with your hands placed on a desk, table, or counter.

Pump it up: Lift your knees off the floor and do pushups, balancing on your hands and toes.

STEPUP

(A) Hold a dumbbell in each hand with your arms hanging naturally at your sides. Stand in front of a step or bench. Place your left foot on the bench and press into the bench to lift your body up onto the bench. (B) Lift your right leg up, tap your right toes on the bench, and then slowly lower. Do 8 to 12 reps, and repeat with your other leg.

Back it off: Use lighter weights, no weights at all, or a lower step.

Pump it up: Use heavier weights and/or a higher step. As you step up with one foot, extend your other leg behind you, squeezing your buttocks.

TWISTING SIDE PLANK

(A) Lie on your left side with your feet stacked. Press yourself up onto your left hand to balance with your right arm extended toward the ceiling. Don't roll forward or back. Imagine your body is between two panes of glass. (B) Slowly swoop your right arm down, across, and under your body. Hold for a second, and then return to the starting position. Do 8 to 12 reps, then repeat on the opposite side.

Back it off: Bend your knees and rest your bottom knee on the floor.

Pump it up: Before twisting, raise your top leg toward the ceiling and lower it as you balance. Then twist. That's one rep.

Chapter 16

Flatten Your Belly

This 3-week walking plan takes the belly-flattening moves from Weeks 4 through 6 and adds intervals to help crank up your results even more.

Didn't know that intervals could flatten your belly? Well, they can! In addition to revving up your calorie-burning during and after your workouts, intervals also seem to home in on that dangerous belly fat. In a

Sample Schedules

Here are just two options for how to organize your workouts. Feel free to arrange them as you wish to fit within your schedule with the following guidelines.

1. Don't do two complete walks on the same day. For example, don't do a full-length moderate and a full-length Fast Walk on the same day. It is, however, fine to break up one of those walks to do over the course of a day instead of all at one time.

2. Don't do strength workouts on consecutive days.

3. If you walk and do strength training on the same day, you can do them at different times (make sure that you warm up and stretch before and after each) or consecutively. When doing them consecutively, do the workout that offers you the benefits you most desire first. So, if burning fat is what you want, walk first. If you're more interested in firming up, do the strength workout first. You get more benefits from a workout when you are fresh.

	Sunday	Monday	Tuesday	Wednesday	Thursday	Friday	Saturday
Option 1: No rest days	Fast walk	Strength train	Interval walk	Strength train	Moderate walk	Fast walk	Moderate walk and strength train (optional)
Option 2: Rest days	Fast walk and strength train	Rest day	Interval walk	Rest day	Moderate walk and strength train	Fast walk	Moderate walk and strength train (optional)

Danish study, interval walkers lost nine times more weight than steady-paced walkers—and almost twice as much belly fat. They shrunk their waistlines more than double the amount of the non–interval walkers![1]

So, what are you waiting for? Let's get moving. (If you get shin pain as you quicken your pace, see Excuse Buster #1: Survive Shin Pain, page 333.)

YOUR FLATTEN-YOUR-BELLY TRAINING PLAN

WEEK 7

- *2 days a week:* Moderate Walk—3-minute warmup, 55-minute moderate pace, 2-minute cooldown (60 minutes total)

- *2 days a week:* Fast Walk—3-minute warmup, 40-minute fast pace, 2-minute cooldown (45 minutes total)

- *1 day a week:* Interval Walk—3-minute warmup, 20-minute intervals (1 minute fast, 1 minute brisk), 2-minute cooldown (25 minutes total)

- *2 or 3 days a week:* Strength training

WEEK 8

- *2 days a week:* Moderate Walk—3-minute warmup, 55-minute moderate pace, 2-minute cooldown (60 minutes total)

- *2 days a week:* Fast Walk—3-minute warmup, 40-minute fast pace, 2-minute cooldown (45 minutes total)

- *1 day a week:* Interval Walk—3-minute warmup, 25-minute intervals (1 minute fast, 1 minute brisk), 2-minute cooldown (30 minutes total)

- *2 or 3 days a week:* Strength training

WEEK 9

- *2 days a week:* Moderate Walk—3-minute warmup, 55-minute moderate pace, 2-minute cooldown (60 minutes total)

- *2 days a week:* Fast Walk—3-minute warmup, 40-minute fast pace, 2-minute cooldown (45 minutes total)

- *1 day a week:* Interval Walk—3-minute warmup, 30-minute intervals (1 minute fast, 1 minute brisk), 2-minute cooldown (35 minutes total)

- *2 or 3 days a week:* Strength training

Walk Your Way to a Firmer Back

For a knockout figure, don't forget to tone your back along with your belly. You can work this area while you walk by squeezing your shoulder blades and driving your elbows back as you swing your arms. The power you get from this can also help propel you forward at a faster pace. For more speed and toning techniques, see page 201.

Moderate walk

TIME	DURATION	ACTIVITY	INTENSITY
0:00	3 minutes	Warmup	3
3:00	55 minutes	Moderate	5–6
58:00	2 minutes	Cooldown	3
60:00	**TOTAL:** 60 minutes		

Fast walk

TIME	DURATION	ACTIVITY	INTENSITY
0:00	3 minutes	Warmup	3
3:00	40 minutes	Fast	7–10
43:00	2 minutes	Cooldown	3
45:00	TOTAL: 45 minutes		

Belly-Blasting Interval

Walk #1 (Week 7)

TIME	DURATION	ACTIVITY	INTENSITY
0:00	3 minutes	Warmup	3
3:00	1 minute	Moderate	5
4:00	1 minute	Brisk	6
5:00	1 minute	Fast	8
6:00	1 minute	Brisk	6
7:00	1 minute	Fast	8
8:00	1 minute	Brisk	6
9:00	1 minute	Fast	8
10:00	1 minute	Brisk	6
11:00	1 minute	Fast	8
12:00	1 minute	Brisk	6
13:00	1 minute	Fast	8
14:00	1 minute	Brisk	6
15:00	1 minute	Fast	8
16:00	1 minute	Brisk	6
17:00	1 minute	Fast	8
18:00	1 minute	Brisk	6
19:00	1 minute	Fast	8
20:00	1 minute	Brisk	6
21:00	1 minute	Fast	8
22:00	1 minute	Brisk	6
23:00	2 minutes	Cooldown	3
25:00	TOTAL: 25 minutes		

Belly-Blasting Interval

Walk #2 (Week 8)

TIME	DURATION	ACTIVITY	INTENSITY
0:00	3 minutes	Warmup	3
3:00	1 minute	Moderate	5
4:00	1 minute	Brisk	6
5:00	1 minute	Fast	8
6:00	1 minute	Brisk	6
7:00	1 minute	Fast	8
8:00	1 minute	Brisk	6
9:00	1 minute	Fast	8
10:00	1 minute	Brisk	6
11:00	1 minute	Fast	8
12:00	1 minute	Brisk	6
13:00	1 minute	Fast	8
14:00	1 minute	Brisk	6
15:00	1 minute	Fast	8
16:00	1 minute	Brisk	6
17:00	1 minute	Fast	8
18:00	1 minute	Brisk	6
19:00	1 minute	Fast	8
20:00	1 minute	Brisk	6
21:00	1 minute	Fast	8
22:00	1 minute	Brisk	6
23:00	1 minute	Fast	8
24:00	1 minute	Brisk	6
25:00	1 minute	Fast	8
26:00	1 minute	Brisk	6
27:00	1 minute	Fast	8
28:00	1 minute	Brisk	6
29:00	2 minutes	Cooldown	3
31:00	**TOTAL:** 31 minutes		

Belly-Blasting Interval

Walk #3 (Week 9)

TIME	DURATION	ACTIVITY	INTENSITY
0:00	3 minutes	Warmup	3
3:00	1 minute	Moderate	5
4:00	1 minute	Brisk	6
5:00	1 minute	Fast	8
6:00	1 minute	Brisk	6
7:00	1 minute	Fast	8
8:00	1 minute	Brisk	6
9:00	1 minute	Fast	8
10:00	1 minute	Brisk	6
11:00	1 minute	Fast	8
12:00	1 minute	Brisk	6
13:00	1 minute	Fast	8
14:00	1 minute	Brisk	6
15:00	1 minute	Fast	8
16:00	1 minute	Brisk	6
17:00	1 minute	Fast	8
18:00	1 minute	Brisk	6
19:00	1 minute	Fast	8
20:00	1 minute	Brisk	6
21:00	1 minute	Fast	8
22:00	1 minute	Brisk	6
23:00	1 minute	Fast	8
24:00	1 minute	Brisk	6
25:00	1 minute	Fast	8
26:00	1 minute	Brisk	6
27:00	1 minute	Fast	8
28:00	1 minute	Brisk	6
29:00	1 minute	Fast	8
30:00	1 minute	Brisk	6
31:00	1 minute	Fast	8
32:00	1 minute	Brisk	6
33:00	2 minutes	Cooldown	3
35:00	**TOTAL: 35 minutes**		

YOUR FLATTEN-YOUR-BELLY STRENGTH ROUTINE

You don't want to neglect other muscle groups just because your goal is to have flat abdominals. If you do, it can cause imbalances that may make you more susceptible to injury. Besides, who wants flabby arms or a saggy butt when your abdominals are looking nice and firm? So, this phase combines targeted core moves with some leg and arm toners that also work your core muscles for additional belly tightening. They are also multimuscle exercises, which means you'll increase your calorie burn, compared to doing isolated ab moves, to burn off any of the fat that may be hiding your six-pack. Do 1 to 3 sets of each exercise, 2 or 3 nonconsecutive days a week.

- Squat with overhead press
- Balance twist
- Bridge with pullover
- Plank curl
- Lunge with a twist
- Crunch
- Row with deadlift
- Twisting side plank

SQUAT WITH OVERHEAD PRESS

(A) Stand with your feet about shoulder-width apart, toes pointing forward or slightly out to the sides. Hold a dumbbell in each hand, with your arms bent so the dumbbells are by your shoulders, palms facing forward. (B) Sit back into a squat, hinging forward at your hips and bending your knees. Keep your knees behind your toes as you lower. (C) Hold for a second, and then stand back up, pressing the dumbbells straight up overhead. Hold for a second. Then, lower the dumbbells to shoulder height as you sit back into a squat. Do 8 to 12 reps.

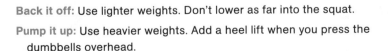

Back it off: Use lighter weights. Don't lower as far into the squat.

Pump it up: Use heavier weights. Add a heel lift when you press the dumbbells overhead.

BALANCE TWIST

(A) Sit on the floor with your legs bent and your feet flat on the floor. Shift your weight back and raise your feet into the air with your knees bent, so you are balancing on your sits bones. Bend your arms, and hold your hands in front of your chest. (B) With your abdominals contracted, slowly twist to the right as far as possible. Hold for a second. Rotate back to center, and then twist to the left. That's 1 rep. Hold for a second, and then repeat twisting to alternate sides. Do 8 to 12 reps.

Back it off: Rest your heels on the floor as you twist.

Pump it up: Hold a weight as you twist.

BRIDGE WITH PULLOVER

(A) Lie on your back, with your legs bent and your feet flat on the floor. Hold a dumbbell with both hands and extend your arms over your head, resting the dumbbell on the floor. (B) Contract your abdominals and buttocks, and press your feet into the floor to lift your butt and back off of the floor. Your body should be in line from your knees to your shoulders. As you do that, also raise the dumbbell up over your chest and toward your knees, without lifting your head off the floor. Hold for a second, then slowly return to the starting position. Do 8 to 12 reps.

Back it off: Use a lighter weight. Hold the bridge position and do reps for the pullover only.

Pump it up: Use heavier weights. Lift one foot off the floor to perform one-legged bridges.

PLANK CURL

(A) Balance on your hands and toes, like for a pushup. (B) Contract your abdominals and pull your right knee in toward your chest. Hold for a second, and then extend your leg back down to the floor. Repeat with your left leg. Do 8 to 12 reps with each leg.

Back it off: Skip pulling your knees into your chest. Instead lift one foot off the floor at a time. Hold for a second, then lower. Alternate legs.

Pump it up: Pull each knee in toward the opposite elbow for a twist.

LUNGE WITH A TWIST

(A) Stand with your feet together and hold a dumbbell with both hands in front of you at waist height.

(B) Step your right leg forward and lower into a lunge, keeping your right knee directly over your ankle and your left knee pointing down toward the floor. As you lunge, rotate your torso to the right. Hold for a second, and then press into your right foot to stand back up, rotating to the center as you do. Repeat to the opposite side. Do 8 to 12 reps to each side.

Back it off: Do the move without holding any weight.

Pump it up: Press into your right foot to stand back up, bringing your left knee up in front of you. Balance on your right leg for a second before lowering your left foot to the starting position.

CRUNCH

(A) Lie on your back with your legs bent and your feet flat on the floor. Place your hands gently behind your head. (B) Contract your abdominals, and slowly raise your head, shoulders, and upper back off the floor. Don't pull on your neck. Hold for a second, and then slowly lower. Do 8 to 12 reps.

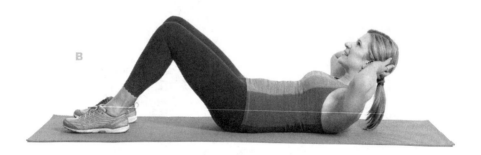

Back it off: Extend your arms in front of you on either side of your knees.

Pump it up: Extend your arms above your head.

ROW WITH DEADLIFT

(A) Stand with your feet about shoulder-width apart and hold a dumbbell in each hand with your arms extended down in front of your thighs, your knees slightly bent, and your palms facing your thighs. (B) Slowly lean forward, bending at the hips, and lower your torso until almost parallel with the floor. Keep the weights close to your body, your back straight, and your abdominals tight, to protect your back as you lower. (C) Then, bend your elbows up and out to the sides and pull the dumbbells toward your chest. Hold for a second. Slowly lower the dumbbells and stand back up, pressing your feet into the floor and squeezing your buttocks. Do 8 to 12 reps. (If you have back problems, replace this move with the Bent-Over Row in the workout on page 131.)

A　　　　B　　　　C

Back it off: Use lighter weights. Just do rows without doing the deadlift in between.

Pump it up: Use heavier weights.

TWISTING SIDE PLANK

(A) Lie on your left side with your feet stacked. Press yourself up onto your left hand to balance with your right arm extended toward the ceiling. Don't roll forward or back. Imagine your body is between two panes of glass. (B) Slowly swoop your right arm down, across, and under your body. Hold for a second, and then return to the starting position. Do 8 to 12 reps, then repeat on the opposite side.

Back it off: Bend your knees and rest your bottom knee on the floor.

Pump it up: Before twisting, raise your top leg toward the ceiling and lower it as you balance. Then twist. That's 1 rep.

Chapter 17

Maximize Your Health

During Stage 2, the focus for this goal was to make walking a daily habit. Additional goals were to get 10,000 steps a day and to avoid sitting for more than 2 hours at a time. In a Dutch study, sitting less and walking more allowed for better improvements in insulin and cholesterol levels than 1 hour of vigorous exercise.[1]

This Stage-3 workout will build on the habit you've started to create (no matter which goal you were following in Stage 2) by combining some shorter bouts of walking into longer ones, at least a few times a week. While any walking you do provides benefits, there are additional ones to be had by adding some continuous longer walks into your routine. In a study out of the United Kingdom, increasing from the standard 150 minutes of physical activity a week recommendation to about an hour daily or 420 minutes a week significantly reduced the risk of developing diabetes from 26 to 40 percent. (See also "Walk Your Way to Less Inflammation," right.) In addition, by walking more every day, even in short bouts, you'll further reduce sitting time and get more steps in.

Your goal is to walk longer a few times a week, starting with staying on your feet for at least 30 minutes once a week and gradually building to three times a week. On alternate days, aim to increase the total minutes of walking you get throughout the day, working up to 60 minutes at least once or twice a week. Increase your walking time according to your level of fitness. Even an extra 5 minutes can be beneficial. Or, walk a little faster. There are benefits of both increasing duration and intensity.

Walk Your Way to Less Inflammation

Inflammation can help you heal after an injury, but chronic inflammation has been associated with diabetes, heart disease, arthritis, and obesity. New research, published in the journal *Brain, Behavior, and Immunity,* shows that just 20 minutes of moderate intensity treadmill walking can act like an anti-inflammatory and bring down levels of inflammation.[2]

YOUR MAXIMIZE-YOUR-HEALTH TRAINING PLAN

WEEK 7

- *6 days a week:* Walk a total of 30–60 minutes at a comfortable pace.* You can split it up or do it all at one time.

- *1 day a week:* Walk 30 continuous minutes at a comfortable pace.

- *2 or 3 days a week:* Strength training

WEEK 8

- *5 days a week:* Walk a total of 30–60 minutes at a comfortable pace.* You can split it up or do it all at one time.

- *2 days a week:* Walk 30 continuous minutes at a comfortable pace.

- *2 or 3 days a week:* Strength training

WEEK 9

- *4 days a week:* Walk a total of 30–60 minutes at a comfortable pace.* You can split it up or do it all at one time.

- *3 days a week:* Walk 30 continuous minutes at a comfortable pace.

- *2 or 3 days a week:* Strength training

Sample Schedule

TIME	ACTIVITY
7 a.m.	20-min. walk around the block
Noon	15-min. walk during lunch break
3 p.m.	10-min.walk during work break
6 p.m.	10-min. walk around the shopping center before grocery shopping for dinner

*A comfortable pace is whatever you feel like doing that day. Some days, you might be up for a challenge or just want to have a good sweat, so you go faster. Other days, a leisurely stroll feels good to you. Research shows that self-selecting your pace helps you to walk more consistently—and that's the key to long-term, health-maximizing results. Once you've established your walking habit, aim to add some intensity, such as doing moderate or brisk walks, for even more benefits.

YOUR MAXIMIZE-YOUR-HEALTH STRENGTH ROUTINE

For Stage 3, you're going to do total-body strength moves that have you on your feet more and working multiple body parts at the same time—like upper and lower body. All of this creates more resistance to build strong bones and better balance to make you steadier on your feet and avoid falls.

Do 1 to 3 sets of 8 to 12 reps of each exercise. For Week 7, do 1 set of each exercise. For Week 8, do 2 sets. For Week 9, do 3 sets.

- Squat with overhead press
- Bridge with pullover
- Row with deadlift
- Pushup

SQUAT WITH OVERHEAD PRESS

(A) Stand with your feet about shoulder-width apart, toes pointing forward or slightly out to the sides. Hold a dumbbell in each hand, with your arms bent so the dumbbells are by your shoul-

ders, palms facing forward.

(B) Sit back into a squat, hinging forward at your hips and bending your knees. Keep your knees behind your toes as you lower.

(C) Hold for a second, and then stand back up, pressing the dumbbells straight up overhead. Hold for a second. Then, lower the dumbbells to shoulder height as you sit back into a squat. Do 8 to 12 reps.

A   B   C

Back it off: Use lighter weights. Don't lower as far into the squat.

Pump it up: Use heavier weights. Add a heel lift when you press the dumbbells overhead.

BRIDGE WITH PULLOVER

(A) Lie on your back, with your legs bent and your feet flat on the floor. Hold a dumbbell with both hands and extend your arms over your head, resting the dumbbell on the floor. (B) Contract your abdominals and buttocks, and press your feet into the floor to lift your butt and back off of the floor. Your body should be in line from your knees to your shoulders. As you do that, also raise the dumbbell up over your chest and toward your knees, without lifting your head off the floor. Hold for a second, then slowly return to the starting position. Do 8 to 12 reps.

Back it off: Use a lighter weight. Hold the bridge position and do reps for the pullover only.

Pump it up: Use heavier weights. Lift one foot off the floor to perform one-legged bridges.

ROW WITH DEADLIFT

(A) Stand with your feet about shoulder-width apart and hold a dumbbell in each hand with your arms extended down in front of your thighs, your knees slightly bent, and your palms facing your thighs. (B) Slowly lean forward, bending at the hips, and lower your torso until almost parallel with the floor. Keep the weights close to your body, your back straight, and your abdominals tight, to protect your back as you lower. (C) Then, bend your elbows up and out to the sides and pull the dumbbells toward your chest. Hold for a second. Slowly lower the dumbbells and stand back up, pressing your feet into the floor and squeezing your buttocks. Do 8 to 12 reps. (If you have back problems, replace this move with the Bent-Over Row in the workout on page 131.)

Back it off: Use lighter weights. Just do rows without doing the lift at the end.

Pump it up: Use heavier weights.

PUSHUP

(A) Kneel on the floor and walk your hands out so you are balancing on your hands with your fingers forward, and on your knees with your feet in the air. (B) Bend your elbows out to the sides and lower your chest toward the floor. Your body should be in line from your head to your knees; don't bend at your hips or round your upper back. Hold for a second, then push back up. Do 8 to 12 reps.

Back it off: Do pushups while you are standing with your hands placed on a desk, table, or counter.

Pump it up: Lift your knees off the floor and do pushups, balancing on your hands and toes.

Chapter 18

Firm Up

To help you to get stronger and firmer faster, this routine doubles the bang for your exercise buck by combining cardio and strength into one workout. If you followed the Stage 2 Firm Up plan, challenge yourself by using heavier weights and/or stronger resistance bands and/or by trying some of the "Pump it up" modifications. You'll also increase the duration of your Toning Walks by doing more sets of the toning moves. Also, choose a hilly route for some of your walks for an added leg- and booty-shaping workout. (Avoid doing hill walks and lower body strength workouts on consecutive days.)

If this is a new goal for you, you'll spend about half of your exercise time on cardio and the other half on strength training. Along with moderate- and fast-pace walking, you'll also be doing a Toning Walk (page 113) during 2 of the 3 weeks. On the alternate week, you'll be doing two strength routines, one that targets your upper body and the other that targets your lower body for some super shaping. You will need an elastic resistance band, a ball, and a low bench or step to stand on.

YOUR FIRM-UP TRAINING PLAN

WEEK 7

- *1 or 2 days a week:* Moderate Walk—3-minute warmup, 55-minute moderate pace, 2-minute cooldown (60 minutes total)

- *1 day a week:* Fast Walk—3-minute warmup, 30-minute fast pace, 2-minute cooldown (35 minutes total)

- *3 days a week:* Toning Walk—3-minute warmup, 30-minute toning walk, 2-minute cooldown (35 minutes total)

WEEK 8

- *2 or 3 days a week:* Moderate Walk—3-minute warmup, 55-minute moderate pace, 2-minute cooldown (60 minutes total)

- *2 or 3 days a week:* Fast Walk—3-minute warmup, 30-minute fast pace, 2-minute cooldown (35 minutes total)

- *2 days a week:* Upper-body strength training

- *2 days a week:* Lower-body strength training

WEEK 9

- *1 or 2 days a week:* Moderate Walk—3-minute warmup, 55-minute moderate pace, 2-minute cooldown (60 minutes total)

- *1 day a week:* Fast Walk—3-minute warmup, 30-minute fast pace, 2-minute cooldown (35 minutes total)

- *3 days a week:* Toning Walk—3-minute warmup, 35-minute toning walk, 2-minute cooldown (40 minutes total)

Moderate walk

TIME	DURATION	ACTIVITY	INTENSITY
0:00	3 minutes	Warmup	3
3:00	55 minutes	Moderate	5–6
58:00	2 minutes	Cooldown	3
60:00	**TOTAL:** 60 minutes		

Fast walk

TIME	DURATION	ACTIVITY	INTENSITY
0:00	3 minutes	Warmup	3
3:00	30 minutes	Fast	7–8
33:00	2 minutes	Cooldown	3
35:00	**TOTAL:** 35 minutes		

Sample Schedules

Here are some options for how to organize your workouts. Feel free to arrange them as you wish to fit within your schedule using the following guidelines.

1. Don't do two complete walks on the same day. For example, don't do a full-length Moderate Walk and a full-length Fast Walk on the same day. It is, however, fine to break up one of those walks to do over the course of a day instead of all at one time.

2. Don't do strength workouts or Toning Walks on consecutive days.

3. If you walk and do strength training on the same day, you can do them at different times (make sure you warm up and stretch before and after each), or consecutively. When doing them consecutively, do the workout that offers you the benefits you most desire first. So, if burning fat is what you want, walk first. If you're more interested in firming up, then do the strength workout first. You get more benefits from a workout when you are fresh.

Weeks 7 and 9

	Sunday	Monday	Tuesday	Wednesday	Thursday	Friday	Saturday
	Moderate walk	Toning walk	Rest day	Fast walk	Toning walk	Moderate walk (optional)	Toning walk

Week 8

	Sunday	Monday	Tuesday	Wednesday	Thursday	Friday	Saturday
Option 1: No rest days	Moderate walk and upper-body strength train	Fast walk	Moderate walk (optional) and lower-body strength train	Fast walk	Upper-body strength train	Fast walk (optional) and lower-body strength train	Moderate walk
Option 2: Rest days	Moderate walk and upper-body strength train	Fast walk	Moderate walk (optional) and lower-body strength train	Fast walk	Rest day	Fast walk (optional) and upper-body strength train	Moderate walk and lower-body strength train

TONING WALK

This routine builds on the Stage 2 Toning Walk by adding more sets of each exercise to the workout. If Firm Up is a new goal for you, jump right in if your fitness allows. Or, you may want to start with the Stage 2 Toning Walk routine on page 113 for week 7 and then do the first routine below for week 9. Descriptions of the exercises follow.

Week 7

TIME	DURATION	ACTIVITY	INTENSITY
0:00	3 minutes	Easy warmup	3
3:00	4 minutes	Moderate to brisk walk	5–7
7:00	1 minute	Walking lunges (20 reps)	5–7
8:00	1 minute	Bench pushups (10–12 reps)	5–7
9:00	4 minutes	Brisk walk	6–7
13:00	1 minute	Traveling squats (20 reps)	5–7
14:00	2 minutes	Plank walks (10–12 reps)	5–7
16:00	4 minutes	Brisk walk	6–7
20:00	1 minute	Walking lunges (20 reps)	5–7
21:00	1 minute	Bench pushups (10–12 reps)	5–7
22:00	4 minutes	Brisk walk	6–7
26:00	1 minute	Traveling squats (20 reps)	5–7
27:00	2 minutes	Plank walks (10–12 reps)	5–7
29:00	4 minutes	Brisk walk	6–7
33:00	2 minutes	Easy cooldown	3
35:00	**TOTAL:** 35 minutes		

Week 9

TIME	DURATION	ACTIVITY	INTENSITY
0:00	3 minutes	Easy warmup	3
3:00	5 minutes	Moderate to brisk walk	5–7
8:00	1 minute	Walking lunges (20 reps)	5–7
9:00	1 minute	Bench pushups (10–12 reps)	5–7
10:00	1 minute	Traveling squats (20 reps)	5–7
11:00	2 minutes	Plank walks (10–12 reps)	5–7
13:00	5 minutes	Brisk walk	6–7
18:00	1 minute	Walking lunges (20 reps)	5–7
19:00	1 minute	Bench pushups (10–12 reps)	5–7
20:00	1 minute	Traveling squats (20 reps)	5–7
21:00	2 minutes	Plank walks (10–12 reps)	5–7
23:00	5 minutes	Brisk walk	6–7
28:00	1 minute	Walking lunges (20 reps)	5–7
29:00	1 minute	Bench pushups (10–12 reps)	5–7
30:00	1 minute	Traveling squats (20 reps)	5–7
31:00	2 minutes	Plank walks (10–12 reps)	5–7
33:00	5 minutes	Brisk walk	6–7
38:00	2 minutes	Easy cooldown	3
40:00	**TOTAL: 40 minutes**		

YOUR FIRM-UP TONING WALK ROUTINE

Combine these moves with walking intervals for a cardio strength workout that will shape you up from head to toe.

- ■ Walking lunge
- ■ Bench pushup
- ■ Traveling squat
- ■ Plank walk

WALKING LUNGE

(A) Stand tall with your feet together and your arms at your sides. Take a giant step forward with your right foot. Bend your knees and lower your body straight down toward the ground. Your right thigh should be parallel or almost parallel to the ground. Keep your right knee over your right ankle. Your back (left) knee should be pointing toward the ground. Your left heel will come off of the ground. Press into both feet to stand back up, bringing your left foot forward to meet your right foot. (B) Repeat, stepping forward with your left foot. Do 20 lunges, alternating legs. You'll be moving forward as you do these, so make sure that you have enough space.

Back it off: Do forward lunges in place. When you stand back up, bring your front foot back to meet your back foot, so you don't move forward as you continue.

Pump it up: Don't stop in between lunges. Instead, swing your back foot forward and immediately lower into the next lunge. No stopping with your feet together.

BENCH PUSHUP

(A) Place your hands shoulder-width apart on a chair, bench, wall, railing, picnic table, piece of play-ground equipment, or anything else sturdy you can find. Walk your feet back so your body forms a plank. Keep your back straight and your head in line with your spine. Don't bend at the hips. (B) Bend your elbows out to the sides and lower your chest toward the chair. Hold for a second, then straighten your arms, pressing back to the starting position. Do 10 to 12 reps.

Back it off: Place your hands on an object that is higher, such as the back of a chair instead of the seat. The more upright your body position is, the easier the pushup will be.

Pump it up: Place your hands on an object that is lower to the ground, such as the seat of a bench instead of the back. Or, find a low wall or log to use. Of course, you can put your hands on the ground to do standard pushups.

TRAVELING SQUAT

(A) Stand tall with your feet together. Step your left foot out to the side so your feet are just wider than shoulder-width apart. (B) Bend your hips and knees, stick your butt out behind you, and lower as if you were sitting in a chair. Keep your knees behind your toes, so that if you look down, you can see your toes. Keep your head up and chest lifted. Lower until your butt is just above knee height. Hold for a second, then press into your feet to stand up, bringing your right foot in to meet your left. Repeat stepping to the left. Do 10 reps moving to the left, and then do 10 reps stepping to the right.

A   B

Back it off: Don't lower as far into the squat.

Pump it up: As you stand up, add a little hop as you
bring your feet together. It doesn't have to be high.

PLANK WALK

(A) Stand with your feet together. Bend your knees and squat all the way down, leaning forward and placing your hands on the floor. (B)(C) Keep your feet stationary and walk your hands forward until your body forms a plank. (Your body should be in a straight line, balancing on the palms of your hands and your toes and balls of your feet—like a pushup position.) (D)(E)(F) Then, keeping your hands stationary, walk your feet toward your hands. Repeat walking your hands out, and then your feet to meet them. Do 10 to 12 reps.

Back it off: Do pikes instead of planks. Walk your hands out only a few feet so that your body forms an upside-down V, a pike position. As you become stronger, you can walk your hands farther out, getting closer to a full plank.

Pump it up: Hold each plank position for a count of 5 before you start to move again. You can also work up to keeping your legs straight when your hands and feet are walked together in between the planks. (This requires greater flexibility in your hamstrings.)

YOUR FIRM-UP UPPER-BODY STRENGTH ROUTINE

If you were following Firm Up in Stage 2 (see page 100), you should do 3 sets of each exercise to start. You may wish to start with 1 set of each exercise in Week 7, 2 sets in Week 8, and 3 sets in Week 9. This routine will tone up your chest, shoulders, back, and arms.

- Upright row
- Chest press
- Reverse fly
- Biceps curl
- Triceps kickback

UPRIGHT ROW

(A) Stand with your feet about shoulder-width apart and hold a dumbbell in each hand with your arms extended down in front of you, palms facing your thighs. (B) Pull the dumbbells up, bending your elbows out to the sides, as you raise them to chest height. Hold for a second, and then slowly lower.

A   B

Back it off: Use lighter weights.

Pump it up: Use heavier weights.

CHEST PRESS

(A) Lie on your back on the floor with your legs bent and your feet flat on the floor. Hold a dumbbell in each hand and bend your arms so your elbows are resting on the floor and pointing out to the sides and the dumbbells are by your chest. (B) Slowly extend your arms, pressing the dumbbells straight up over your chest. Hold for a second, and then slowly lower. Do 8 to 12 reps.

Back it off: Use lighter weights.

Pump it up: Use heavier weights.

REVERSE FLY

(A) Sit on the edge of a chair, holding a dumbbell in each hand. Lean forward from your hips so the dumbbells are hanging down toward your feet, palms facing in. (B) Keeping your elbows straight but not locked, contract your shoulder blades and raise the dumbbells out to the sides and up to shoulder height. Hold for a second, then slowly lower. Do 8 to 12 reps.

A   B

Back it off: Use lighter weights.

Pump it up: Use heavier weights.

BICEPS CURL

(A) Stand with your feet about shoulder-width apart and hold a dumbbell in each hand with your arms extended down at your sides, palms facing forward. (B) Keeping your upper arms still, bend your elbows and raise the dumbbells toward your shoulders. Hold for a second, then slowly lower. Do 8 to 12 reps.

A

B

Back it off: Use lighter weights.

Pump it up: Use heavier weights.

TRICEPS KICKBACK

(A) Stand behind a chair with your legs split, left foot in front, and hold a dumbbell in your right hand. Place your left hand on the back of the chair and lean forward, bending at your hips. Bend your right elbow at a 90-degree angle and hold it close to your side. (B) Without moving your shoulder, extend your right arm back, pressing the dumbbell behind you. Hold for a second, then slowly bend your elbow again, lowering the weight back to the starting position. Do 8 to 12 reps, then switch sides and repeat with your left arm.

Back it off: Use lighter weights.

Pump it up: Use heavier weights.

YOUR FIRM-UP LOWER-BODY STRENGTH ROUTINE

If you were following Firm Up in Stage 2 (see page 100), you should do 3 sets of each exercise to start. If you're new to Firm Up, then you may wish to start with 1 set of each exercise in Week 7, progress to 2 sets in Week 8, and do 3 sets in Week 9. This routine will tone up your butt and legs, while also working your abdominals.

- Stepup
- Squat with band
- Hip extension
- Ball squeeze
- Clamshell

STEPUP

(A) Hold a dumbbell in each hand with your arms hanging naturally at your sides. Stand in front of a step or bench. Place your left foot on the bench and press into the bench to lift your body up onto the bench.
(B) Lift your right leg up, tap your right toes on the bench, and then slowly lower. Do 8 to 12 reps, and repeat with your other leg.

Back it off: Use lighter weights, no weights at all, or a lower bench.

Pump it up: Use heavier weights and/or a higher step. As you step up with one foot, extend your other leg behind you, squeezing your buttocks.

SQUAT WITH BAND

(A) Stand with your feet about shoulder-width apart and tie an exercise band around your calves. (B) Step your right foot out to the side, pulling against the resistance band, and then lower into a squat (bend at your hips and knees, stick your butt out, and keep your back straight and your chest lifted). As you stand up, bring your left foot in toward your right. Step to the right and squat one more time. Then, repeat, doing two squats to the left. Do 8 to 12 reps on each side.

Back it off: Do the move without using an exercise band.

Pump it up: Take wider steps or use a stronger band for more resistance.

HIP EXTENSION

(A) Loop an exercise band around your ankle. Make sure it is securely fastened before performing the exercise. Place your hand on a chair or wall for balance. (B) Standing tall, with shoulders straight and back, shift your weight onto your left foot. Raise your right leg straight out behind you, squeezing your buttocks. Keep your toes, knees, and hips pointing forward. Hold for a second, then slowly lower. Do 8 to 12 reps, then switch legs and repeat.

Back it off: Do the move without using an exercise band.

Pump it up: Use a stronger band.

BALL SQUEEZE

Stand tall with a soft (slightly deflated) ball between your thighs. With your hands on your hips, squeeze and release the ball without letting it fall. Do 8 to 12 reps.

Back it off: Do the exercise while lying on the floor with your knees bent and hands at your sides. Squeeze the ball between your thighs.

Pump it up: Do the exercise while holding a squat position (bend at your hips and knees, stick your butt out, and keep your back straight and your chest lifted).

CLAMSHELL

(A) Lie on your left side with your legs stacked and bent. Place your left arm under your head, with your right arm in front of your body for support. (B) Slowly rotate your right knee upward, while keeping your feet together. Don't roll your hips forward or back as you lift. Hold for a second, then slowly lower. Do 8 to 12 reps on each side.

Back it off: Don't lift your knee as high.

Pump it up: Hold a weight against your top thigh for more resistance.

Chapter 19

Get Faster

During this Stage 3 option, you'll add techniques and fun drills to help increase your foot speed. Speed intervals like the 30-20-10 Walks that you did if you were following the Stage 2 Get Faster Plan will continue to help and the addition of drills will get them moving even more quickly. If Get Faster is a new goal for you, feel free to modify the walks by doing fewer intervals during a session or shortening your entire session and gradually build up.

The strength routine also has an increased focus in your lower body. Stronger leg, butt, and core muscles give you more power and stamina with every step. You will need an elastic resistance band (available wherever exercise equipment is sold); a soccer ball, a basketball, or a toy ball; and a low bench or step to stand on.

THE GET-FASTER DRILLS

Include these drills as a part of your tempo walks. Either mix and match them or simply pick one and do it for the recommended amount of time.

Hill climbs—Find a hill and walk up it. Focus on keeping your front leg straight as you land, which will force you to take shorter steps. On the downhill, focus on a quick foot turnover (fast steps). When going up or down a hill, stand tall; don't lean into the hill and don't lock your knees.

Chalk walks—Mark your starting point with chalk. Walk as quickly as you can for a set period of time, like 10 to 60 seconds, depending upon how much space you have. Mark your finish spot with chalk, too. Slowly walk back to your starting point. Repeat the walking fast for the same amount of time, and try to get a little farther. Mark it again, and repeat.

Skip it—Practice skipping for a set distance or period of time that is comfortable for you. Alternate bouts of skipping in which you focus on bounding as high as possible (choose a soft surface like some level grass or smooth gravel) with bouts in which you bound forward as far as possible with each skip. Walk at an easy pace in between bouts of skipping to recover. Count only the time that you are skipping for your recommended drill time.

Retro walks—Turn around and walk backward. Make sure that you do this only in safe areas such as on a smooth track or paved path when there are not a lot of people around. Even better, do it with a friend so you can spot each other.

Fast feet—Mark a starting and ending point at least 50 feet apart (roughly measure it by taking

50 short steps). Walk as fast as you can, and count each step until you complete the distance. Recover by walking at an easy pace. Repeat, trying to take more steps in that same distance. During this drill, you're exaggerating the small quick steps. Think about what kids do when they are running at the pool and the lifeguard blows the whistle and yells, "No running!" They keep both feet on the ground, and they take quick, tiny steps with stiff legs. Give it a try, but don't lock your knees.

YOUR GET-FASTER TRAINING PLAN

WEEK 7

- *1 day a week:* Tempo Walk—3-minute warmup, 30-minute Tempo (brisk-fast) pace, 5-minute drills, 2-minute cooldown (50 minutes total)

- *2 days a week:* 30-20-10 Walk—3-minute warmup, 25-minute 30-20-10 intervals, 2-minute cooldown (30 minutes total)

- *2 or 3 days a week:* Recovery Walk—3-minute warmup, 30-minute Recovery (moderate-brisk) pace, 2-minute cooldown (35 minutes total)

- *2 or 3 days a week:* Strength training

WEEK 8

- *1 day a week:* Tempo Walk—3-minute warmup, 35-minute tempo (brisk-fast) pace, 10-minute drill, 2-minute cooldown (50 minutes total)

- *2 days a week:* 30-20-10 Walk—3-minute warmup, 25-minute 30-20-10 intervals, 2-minute cooldown (30 minutes total)

- *2 or 3 days a week:* Recovery Walk—3-minute warmup, 30-minute recovery (moderate-brisk) pace, 2-minute cooldown (35 minutes total)

- *2 or 3 days a week:* Strength training

WEEK 9

- *1 day a week:* Tempo Walk—3-minute warmup, 30-minute tempo (brisk-fast) pace, 15-minute drills, 2-minute cooldown (50 minutes total)

- *2 days a week:* 30-20-10 Walk—3-minute warmup, 25-minute 30-20-10 intervals, 2-minute cooldown (30 minutes total)

- *2 or 3 days a week:* Recovery Walk—3-minute warmup, 30-minute Recovery (moderate-brisk) pace, 2-minute cooldown (35 minutes total)

- *2 or 3 days a week:* Strength training

Tempo walk

TIME	DURATION	ACTIVITY	INTENSITY
0:00	3 minutes	Warmup	3
3:00	30 minutes*	Brisk to fast	6–8
43:00	5 minutes**	Drills	6–8
48:00	2 minutes	Cooldown	3
50:00	**TOTAL:** 50 minutes		

*For week 8, increase to 35 minutes. For week 9, to 40 minutes.
**Increase by 5 minutes each week.

Recovery walk

TIME	DURATION	ACTIVITY	INTENSITY
0:00	3 minutes	Warmup	3
3:00	30 minutes	Moderate to brisk	5–7
33:00	2 minutes	Cooldown	3
35:00	**TOTAL: 35 minutes**		

30-20-10 Interval walk

TIME	DURATION	ACTIVITY	INTENSITY
0:00	3 minutes	Warmup	5
3:00	30 seconds	Brisk	6
3:30	20 seconds	Fast	8
3:50	10 seconds	Speed	9
4:00	Repeat 30-20-10 intervals (minutes 3:00–4:00) 4 more times for a total of 5 circuits		
8:00	1 minute	Recovery	4
9:00	Repeat 30-20-10 intervals (minutes 3:00–4:00) 5 times total		
14:00	1 minute	Recovery	4
Week 5: Stop at 15:00 minutes and cool down			
15:00	Repeat 30-20-10 intervals (minutes 3:00–4:00) 5 times total		
20:00	1 minute	Recovery	4
Week 6: Stop at 21:00 minutes and cool down			
21:00	Repeat 30-20-10 intervals (minutes 3:00–4:00) 5 times		
26:00	1 minute	Recovery	4
27:00	3 minutes	Cooldown	3
30:00	**TOTAL: 30 minutes**		

Count how many steps you take during several of the 30-, 20-, and 10-second intervals to gauge an estimated baseline. Please note this on your exercise log. The goal is to see these numbers increase as you progress through the program. You don't have to count every interval. Aim to count for one or two intervals within each 5-minute circuit.

Cycle is the 1 minute that begins with a 30-second interval, is followed by a 20-second interval, and ends with a 10-second interval.

Circuit is made up of five cycles and is followed by a 1-minute recovery interval.

Sample Schedules

Here are just two options for how to arrange your workouts. Feel free to arrange them as you wish to fit within your schedule using the following guidelines.

1. Don't do two complete walks on the same day. For example, don't do a full-length Tempo and a full-length 30-20-10 Walk on the same day. It is, however, fine to break up one of those walks to do over the course of a day instead of all at one time.

2. Don't do strength workouts on consecutive days.

3. If you walk and do strength training on the same day, you can do them at different times (make sure you warm up and stretch before and after each) or consecutively. When doing them consecutively, do the workout that offers you the benefits you most desire first. So, if burning fat is what you want, walk first. But if you're more interested in firming up, then do the strength workout first. You get more benefits from a workout when you are fresh.

	Sunday	Monday	Tuesday	Wednesday	Thursday	Friday	Saturday
Option 1: No rest days	30-20-10 walk	Recovery walk and strength train (optional)	Tempo walk	Recovery walk (optional) and strength train	30-20-10 walk	Strength train	Recovery walk
Option 2: Rest days	30-20-10 walk	Recovery walk (optional) and strength train (optional)	Tempo walk	Recovery walk and strength train	30-20-10 walk	Rest day	Recovery walk and strength train

GET-FASTER TECHNIQUE

You've already learned how to walk with your arms bent, by rolling from heel to toe, and by taking shorter, quicker steps. Now, it's time to sharpen your technique even more to further crank up your speedometer.

A word of caution: Don't try to do all of these techniques at once. Otherwise, you'll start walking like a robot. Instead, pick one and practice it sporadically during your warmup, cooldown, or recovery walks. Then, try it out during your speedier sessions for a few minutes. Also, as you're learning a technique, you may slow down a bit until it feels natural.

If shin pain strikes as you're getting up to speed, see Excuse Buster #1: Survive Shin Pain, page 333.

Straighten your leg. When your foot lands in front of you, your leg should be straight, without locking your knee. Keep it straight until it is underneath you. If you bend your knee upon landing, it puts more pressure on your joints and creates a bouncy, runninglike motion that is harder on your joints and interferes with the forward momentum you want for a speedy pace.

Squeeze your buttocks. Stand tall and place your right hand on your right butt cheek. Raise your right leg a bit in front of you, and then slowly swing it behind you. (You can hold on to something with your left hand for balance, if needed.) Feel your muscles working? They're responsible for hip extension, or pulling your leg behind you. Now that you know where they are, and what they are supposed to be doing, start using them. Each time your heel lands on the ground, squeeze your glutes as if they are helping to pull your body over your front legs. By activating them with every step, you'll make them stronger, firm up your butt, and put more power in your pace.

Drive your elbows back. Now we're going to add some power and speed to your arm swing, which will encourage your legs to move faster. I see a lot of people who punch forward as they swing their arms. The real power to propel you forward is behind you, in your back muscles. To activate them, drive your elbows back and squeeze your shoulder blades. Then, let your arm swing forward naturally. In addition to speeding up your legs by quickening your arm swing, this also tones your back. Remember to keep your arms bent the entire time—as if you were wearing a cast.

Bare your sole. The foot motion of walking is landing on your heel, rolling through your foot, and pushing off with the ball of your foot and toes. I want you to focus on that push-off. Think about keeping your toes on the ground as long as possible as your heel and midfoot come off of the ground. If you do this, someone who is walking behind you would see more of the sole of your shoe. Think of pushing off forward, not up, for a smooth stride. This will really kick in your calf muscles for shapelier legs and a quicker gait.

Move your hips. You'll want to add this technique once you've gotten everything out of the others, and feel like the only way to go faster is to start running. Slow down! There's still room for you to walk faster. You just need to get your hips in on the action. The movement is forward and back, not the side-to-side kind you do on the dance floor. You want to keep your body streamlined, with all motions going forward and back, not side to side or up and down. To help you use your hips effectively, imagine that your legs extend all the way up to your rib cage. So as your right foot comes forward, your right hip follows forward, and then it follows your leg backward. The movement is small, though. Here are two strategies, from my colleague Lee Scott, creator of the DVD *Simple Secrets for a Great Walking Workout*, to help you get more comfortable with the hip swivel, which is probably the toughest technique to implement.

1. Stand with your feet a few inches apart and place your hands on your hips. Now pull your right hip back, allowing the left one to go forward. Your right leg will straighten and your left one will bend. Just make sure your hips, not your legs, are driving the action. Your hips will be moving only an inch or so back and forth.

2. Imagine that you are walking on a plank or balance beam. Bring each foot to the midline of the plank or beam you are imagining as you step forward. You can also practice this in a parking lot or road where there is a line to walk on; just stay alert to traffic. As you do this, feel how your abdominal muscles are activated.

YOUR GET-FASTER STRENGTH ROUTINE

This routine puts extra emphasis on your lower body, to build your leg muscles and give you more power. Do 1 set of each exercise in Week 7, 2 sets in Week 8, and 3 sets in Week 9.

- Lunge with a twist
- Stepup
- Pushup
- Hip extension
- Ball squeeze
- Clamshell

LUNGE WITH A TWIST

(A) Stand with your feet together and hold a dumbbell with both hands in front of you at waist height. Step your right leg forward and lower into a lunge, keeping your right knee directly over your ankle and your left knee pointing down toward the floor. (B) As you lunge, rotate your torso to the right. Hold for a second, and then press into your right foot to stand back up, rotating to the center as you do. Repeat to the opposite side. Do 8 to 12 reps to each side.

Back it off: Do the move without holding any weight.

Pump it up: Press into your right foot to stand back up, bringing your left knee up in front of you. Balance on your right leg for a second before lowering your left foot to the starting position.

STEPUP

(A) Hold a dumbbell in each hand with your arms hanging naturally at your sides. Stand in front of a step or bench. Place your left foot on the bench and press into the bench to lift your body up onto the bench. (B) Lift your right leg up, tap your right toes on the bench, and then slowly lower. Do 8 to 12 reps, and repeat with your other leg.

Back it off: Use lighter weights or none at all.

Pump it up: Use heavier weights and/or a higher step. As you step up with one foot, extend your other leg behind you, squeezing your buttocks.

PUSHUP

(A) Kneel on the floor and walk your hands out so you are balancing on your hands with your fingers forward, and on your knees with your feet in the air. **(B)** Bend your elbows out to the sides and lower your chest toward the floor. Your body should be in line from your head to your knees; don't bend at your hips or round your upper back. Hold for a second, then push back up. Do 8 to 12 reps.

Back it off: Do pushups while you are standing with your hands placed on a desk, table, or counter.

Pump it up: Lift your knees off the floor and do pushups, balancing on your hands and toes.

HIP EXTENSION

Securely fasten an exercise band to a railing, pole, or sturdy piece of furniture at floor level. Loop the band around your right ankle. (A) Place your hand on a chair or wall for balance. Standing tall, with shoulders straight and back, shift your weight onto your left foot. (B) Raise your right leg straight out behind you, squeezing your buttocks. Keep your toes, knees, and hips pointing forward. Hold for a second, then slowly lower. Do 8 to 12 reps, then switch legs and repeat.

Back it off: Do the move without using an exercise band.

Pump it up: Use a stronger band.

BALL SQUEEZE

Stand tall with a soft (slightly deflated) ball between your thighs. With your hands on your hips, squeeze and release the ball without letting it fall. Do 8 to 12 reps.

Back it off: Do the exercise while lying on the floor with your knees bent and hands at your sides. Squeeze the ball between your thighs.

Pump it up: Do the exercise while holding a squat position (bend at your hips and knees, stick your butt out, and keep your back straight and your chest lifted).

CLAMSHELL

(A) Lie on your left side with your legs stacked and bent. Place your left arm under your head, with your right arm in front of your body for support. (B) Slowly rotate your right knee upward, while keeping your feet together. Don't roll your hips forward or back as you lift. Hold for a second, then slowly lower. Do 8 to 12 reps on each side.

Back it off: Don't lift your knee as high.

Pump it up: Hold a weight against your top thigh for more resistance.

Chapter 20

Train for a 10K

In this section, you'll find the second half of the training plan to help you get ready to walk a full 10K (6.2 miles). (The first half of it was in Chapter 13 and detailed what to do for Weeks 4 through 6 on page 137.)

By the end of Week 9, you'll be able to line up at the starting line with the confidence of knowing that you can reach the finish.

This is your final preparation. Feel welcome to adjust the days you do most workouts and move the rest days to best fit your schedule.

Remember, this plan is the one exception for customization in this program—don't jump in here for Stage 3 if you haven't already completed the Train for a 10K plan in Stage 2 on page 136.

The week leading up to the race is when you taper or cut back in preparation for the race, so your body is well rested. Make sure you have at least 2 days of easy walks or rest days before the event. And, no strength training on those days, either.

Most important, stick to the training schedule, and you'll have a fun, successful race.

YOUR TRAIN-FOR-A-10K TRAINING PLAN

WEEK 7

- *1 day a week:* Easy Walk—3-minute warmup, 20–30-minute easy pace, 2-minute cooldown (25–35 minutes total)

- *1 day a week:* Moderate Walk—3-minute warmup, 30-minute moderate pace, 2-minute cooldown (35 minutes total)

Walk Your Way to the Finish Line

To get to the finish, really push it. Push off harder with your toes and ball of your foot. Lift your heel and midfoot off of the ground as high as possible before pushing off. It's as if you are trying to show the sole of your shoe to someone behind you. Make sure you are propelling yourself forward, not up. For more ways to get to the finish line faster, see page 204.

- *1 day a week:* Brisk Walk—3-minute warmup, 45-minute brisk pace, 2-minute cooldown (50 minutes total)

- *1 day a week:* Fast Walk—3-minute warmup, 4-mile fast pace, 2-minute cooldown

- *1 day a week:* Long Walk—3-minute warmup, 5.5-mile long walk, 2-minute cooldown (88–115 minutes total, depending upon your pace; estimates based on a 15- to 20-minute-per-mile pace, or 3 to 5 mph)

- *2 or 3 days a week:* Strength training

WEEK 8

- *1 day a week:* Easy Walk—3-minute warmup, 20–30-minute easy pace, 2-minute cooldown (25–35 minutes total)

- *1 day a week:* Moderate Walk—3-minute warmup, 30-minute moderate pace, 2-minute cooldown (35 minutes total)

- *1 day a week:* Brisk Walk—3-minute warmup, 45-minute brisk pace, 2-minute cooldown (50 minutes total)

- *1 day a week:* Fast Walk—3-minute warmup, 4-mile fast pace, 2-minute cooldown (53–85 minutes total, depending upon your pace; estimates based on a 12- to 20-minute-per-mile pace, or 3 to 5 mph)

- *1 day a week:* Long Walk—3-minute warmup, 6-mile long walk, 2-minute cooldown (95–125 minutes total, depending upon your pace; estimates based on a 15- to 20-minute-per-mile pace, or 3 to 5 mph)

- *2 or 3 days a week:* Strength training

WEEK 9*

- *2 days a week:* Easy Walk—3-minute warmup, 15–30-minute easy pace, 2-minute cooldown (20–35 minutes total)

- *1 day a week:* Moderate Walk—3-minute warmup, 30-minute moderate pace, 2-minute cooldown (35 minutes total)

- *1 day a week:* Brisk Walk—3-minute warmup, 30-minute brisk pace, 2-minute cooldown (35 minutes total)

- *1 day a week:* Fast Walk—3-minute warmup, 3-mile fast pace, 2-minute cooldown (41–105 minutes total, depending upon your pace; estimates based on a 12- to 20-minute-per-mile pace, or 3 to 5 mph)

- *2 days a week:* Strength training

*This is a taper week to prepare for the race.

Easy walk

TIME	DURATION	ACTIVITY	INTENSITY
0:00	3 minutes	Warmup	3
3:00	15–30 minutes	Easy	3–5
18:00–33:00	2 minutes	Cooldown	3
20:00–35:00	**TOTAL: 20–35 minutes**		

Moderate walk

TIME	DURATION	ACTIVITY	INTENSITY
0:00	3 minutes	Warmup	3–5
3:00	30 minutes	Moderate	5–6
33:00	2 minutes	Cooldown	3–5
35:00	**TOTAL: 35 minutes**		

Brisk walk

TIME	DURATION	ACTIVITY	INTENSITY
0:00	3 minutes	Warmup	3–5
3:00	30–45 minutes	Brisk	6–7
33:00–48:00	2 minutes	Cooldown	3–5
35:00–50:00	**TOTAL: 35–50 minutes**		

Long walk

TIME	DURATION	ACTIVITY	INTENSITY
0:00	3 minutes	Warmup	3–5
3:00	83–120 minutes*	5.5 to 6-mile moderate to brisk	5–7
86:00–123:00	2 minutes	Cooldown	3–5
88:00–125:00	**TOTAL: 88–125 minutes**		

Estimates based on a 15- to 20-minute-per-mile pace, or 4 to 5 mph

Fast walk

TIME	DURATION	ACTIVITY	INTENSITY
0:00	3 minutes	Warmup	3–5
3:00	36–80 minutes*	3- to 4-mile fast	7–8
39:00–83:00	2 minutes	Cooldown	3–5
41:00–85:00	**TOTAL: 41–85 minutes**		

Estimates based on a 12- to 20-minute-per-mile pace, or 3 to 5 mph

Sample Schedule

Here are some options for how to organize your workouts. Feel free to arrange them as you wish to fit within your schedule using the following guidelines.

1. Don't do two complete walks on the same day. For example, don't do a full-length Moderate Walk and a full-length Fast Walk on the same day. It is, however, fine to break up one of those walks to do over the course of a day instead of all at one time.

2. Don't do strength workouts on consecutive days.

3. If you walk and do strength training on the same day, you can do them at different times (make sure you warm up and stretch before and after each), or consecutively. When doing them consecutively, do the workout that offers you the benefits you most desire first. So, if burning fat is what you want, walk first. If you're more interested in firming up, then do the strength workout first. You get more benefits from a workout when you are fresh.

	Monday	Tuesday	Wednesday	Thursday	Friday	Saturday	Sunday
Week 7 Rest day	20–30-min. easy walk and strength train	45-min. brisk walk	Strength train	4 miles fast walk	Rest day	30-min. moderate walk and strength train (optional)	5.5-mile moderate-pace long walk
Week 8 No rest day	20–30 min. easy walk and strength train (optional)	45-min. brisk walk	Strength train	4 miles fast walk	Strength train	30-min. moderate walk	6-mile moderate-pace long walk
Week 9	20–30 min. easy walk	30-min. brisk walk and strength train	30-minute moderate walk	3 miles fast walk and strength train	Rest day	15-min. easy walk	Race day

YOUR TRAIN-FOR-A-10K STRENGTH ROUTINE

This routine is a total-body, multimuscle move routine. That means you're using a variety of muscles during each move, as well as challenging your balance. Your body is working in a coordinated effort—just what you want it to do on race day. Do 1 to 3 sets of 8 to 12 reps of each exercise, 2 or 3 nonconsecutive days a week.

- Row with deadlift
- Squat and lift
- Bridge
- Pushup
- Lunge with a twist

ROW WITH DEADLIFT

(A) Stand with your feet about shoulder-width apart and hold a dumbbell in each hand with your arms extended down in front of your thighs, your knees slightly bent, and your palms facing your thighs. (B) Slowly lean forward, bending at the hips, and lower your torso until almost parallel with the floor. Keep the weights close to your body, your back straight, and your abdominals tight, to protect your back as you lower. (C) Then, bend your elbows up and out to the sides and pull the dumbbells toward your chest. Hold for a second. Slowly lower the dumbbells and stand back up, pressing your feet into the floor and squeezing your buttocks. Do 8 to 12 reps. (If you have back problems, replace this move with the Bent-Over Row in the workout on page 131.)

A   B   C

Back it off: Use lighter weights. Just do rows without doing the lift at the end.

Pump it up: Use heavier weights.

SQUAT AND LIFT

(A) Stand with your feet about shoulder-width apart, toes pointing straight ahead or slightly out, and arms relaxed at your sides. (B) Bend your knees and hinge forward from your hips, lowering yourself as if you are sitting back into a chair. Stick your butt out, shift your weight into your heels, and raise your arms out in front of you as you bend your knees and lower as far as possible, while maintaining good form. Stop before your hips are in line with your knees. Hold for a second. (C) Press into your heels, squeeze your buttocks, and stand back up. As you come up, rise up onto your toes, lifting your heels as high as possible. Hold for a second. Lower back to the starting position. Do 8 to 12 reps for a set.

Back it off: Do the squat only (without raising up onto your toes).

Pump it up: Hold dumbbells at your sides as you do the move.

BRIDGE

(A) Lie on the floor on your back with your legs bent and your feet flat on the floor. Place your arms at your sides with your palms facing down. (B) Contract your abdominals and buttocks, and lift your hips and back off the floor so your body is in line from your shoulders to your knees. Hold for a second. Slowly lower. Do 8 to 12 reps for a set.

Back it off: Instead of doing reps, hold the bridge position for as long as possible, up to 1 minute.

Pump it up: Raise one leg off the floor, and perform one-leg bridges, repeating with the opposite leg.

PUSHUP

(A) Kneel on the floor and walk your hands out so you are balancing on your hands with your fingers forward, and on your knees with your feet in the air. (B) Bend your elbows out to the sides and lower your chest toward the floor. Your body should be in line from your head to your knees; don't bend at your hips or round your upper back. Hold for a second, then push back up. Do 8 to 12 reps.

Back it off: Do pushups while you are standing with your hands placed on a desk, table, or counter.

Pump it up: Lift your knees off the floor and do pushups, balancing on your hands and toes.

LUNGE WITH A TWIST

(A) Stand with your feet together and hold a dumbbell with both hands in front of you at waist height.

(B) Step your right leg forward and lower into a lunge, keeping your right knee directly over your ankle and your left knee pointing down toward the floor. As you lunge, rotate your torso to the right. Hold for a second, and then press into your right foot to stand back up, rotating to the center as you do. Repeat to the opposite side. Do 8 to 12 reps to each side.

A   B

Back it off: Do the move without holding any weight.

Pump it up: Press into your right foot to stand back up, bringing your left knee up in front of you. Balance on your right leg for a second before lowering your left foot to the starting position.

MEALS, RECIPES, AND MORE

Chapter 21

Eat Your Way to Better Health

The his book promises that you can walk your way to better health. So why is there an eating plan in this program? Exercise goes hand in hand with a healthy diet if you want to achieve the best results possible, especially if you want to lose weight. I wouldn't be doing my job if I didn't tell you that walking alone probably won't be enough to achieve your goals. What you eat has a big impact on your health!

That's why I worked with the experts at *Prevention* magazine and Rodale Test Kitchen to come up with sensible advice, menus, and recipes that deliver results. In this chapter, you'll find the advice. In Chapter 22, you'll find a 21-day meal plan that you can follow to the letter, or, as with nearly everything in this program, customize to better suit your lifestyle. In Chapter 23, you'll find delicious, quick-and-easy recipes that you can mix and match to, quite literally, cook your way to optimal results.

This trio of chapters marries my nearly 20 years

of coordinating test panels with scientific research to give you a winning combination that will offer you the best chance of success.

This eating plan is all about eating the types of foods that will fuel your workouts so you can go hard, fill you up so you will eat less, keep you satiated between meals so you won't feel hungry, and provide the nutrients you need for all-day energy. I've seen firsthand the effects of different diet and fitness programs on people just like you, and I promise that when you find the right combination, you'll feel amazing and get great results.

GUIDELINES ON FOLLOWING THE GUIDELINES

Before we get started, I want you to remember two things:

1. These are *only* guidelines.

2. The 80-20 rule. (See the next page.)

Let's start with "guidelines." I chose to call them this instead of rules because this is not a rigid eating plan. I don't want you to feel like you're breaking any rules if you have a piece of birthday cake at your best friend's party. Or, if you eat a whole bag of almonds when you were stressing over a work project. (In my book, that's better than if you ate your way through a bag of potato chips or a carton of ice cream. Even if you consumed more calories, you got a lot of other good stuff. Just don't make it a habit!) Back to my point about guidelines: They are suggestions—goals to aim for. They are not meant to rule your life, and if you don't follow them, you're not a bad person. This is a guilt-free zone.

That brings us to the 80-20 rule. I don't expect anyone to eat 100 percent healthy 100 percent of the time. It's just not realistic. If you eat healthy and make healthful choices 80 percent of the time, you are rockin' it! Let the other 20 percent go. So, you ate dessert at your neighbor's potluck. Or, maybe you had a second helping at dinner. Or, maybe it was the leftover bacon on your kid's plate that you couldn't resist. Skip the guilt, and make your next meal or snack a healthy one.

Now, I'm not talking about allowing all-out pig-outs. In fact, hopefully by letting small slips go—even if it lasts an entire day—and getting back on track right away, you'll avoid the downward shame spiral that ends with you completely throwing in the towel and going back to your old habits. That's exactly what we *don't* want! You've worked too hard to undo it all because of a setback here and there.

Speaking of which, let's not forget all-or-nothing thinking (see page 24). You don't have to implement *all* of these guidelines at once. You can pick one or two of them to start—that's way better than doing *nothing*. After a week or two, you can add another one or two changes. Or, maybe you'll need

a month or more to make a particular guideline a part of your life. That's okay! There might even be one or two guidelines that you never incorporate into your life. Again, it's okay! You decide what *you* want to achieve and which steps you're going to take to make it happen.

For example, you may be willing to switch to different brands of peanut butter, pasta sauce, and salad dressing to cut added sugar, but perhaps you draw the line at your favorite, slightly sugary yogurt. That's okay. Again, you decide how into the program you want to be.

When Sue, one of our test panelists, told me that she wasn't going to drink coffee during the program, because she couldn't give up her half-and-half, I said, "Stop right there!" This is not an eating plan that you do for 9 weeks and then abandon with relief. I want it to be a plan you can stick to for life. And if you can't do that as it's laid out, then I want you to adjust it, customize it, personalize it until it is "your way." I'll help by offering suggestions.

So, instead of being miserable drinking her coffee with nonfat milk or skipping her daily Joe entirely, Sue made an adjustment: She felt confident that she could cut back on the amount of half-and-half she used in her cup of coffee each day, and that's just what she did. She also identified some other things that she could do more easily to get on track with healthier eating. Looking at the big picture, that one compromise didn't sabotage her results (check them out on page 238). In fact, it may have helped her stick with the rest of the program, since she didn't feel deprived or miserable every morning. As a coffee person myself, I can imagine how much her loved ones appreciated this little tweak, as well. It can be dangerous to get between a gal and her morning cuppa!

The meal plans in Chapter 22 are designed

according to the guidelines below, but you can still eat *your* way, keeping the guidelines in mind, of course, as you customize your plan. Besides the meal recipes, I'll offer you some guidance on how to make healthy choices when you're eating out (let's face it, sometimes takeout is the only way dinner is getting on the table!) and when you're putting together your own meals (see page 231).

All of that said, it's important to understand that depending on how much you customize away from the meal plans, it may affect your results. For example, you may lose 5 pounds instead of 8, because you're not following all the guidelines or because you're deviating from the plan's recommended meals more often than not. But, in my experience, it's better to lose 5 and keep them off than to struggle to lose 10 pounds and regain them because you can't stick to the changes you made.

THE ACTUAL GUIDELINES

Here are the key principles to think about when you're grocery shopping, preparing meals, and eating.

Eat naturally. Simply put, choose whole foods over processed ones; that is, eat foods as close to their natural form as possible—like a baked sweet potato instead of sweet potato fries. When you do that, you avoid all of the chemicals (such as aspartame) and artificial ingredients (such as food coloring) that get added as a food is processed more. Of course, the more foods are processed, the more their good-for-you nutrients are lost.

Eating naturally is relatively easy to do with fruits, vegetables, meats, fish, and poultry. For other foods, like dairy products, breads, cereals, and other grain products that require some processing, the ingredient list on their labels will come in handy as you make your choices.

The key with semiprocessed foods is to choose items that have ingredient lists that you can read and understand. Avoid the ones with ingredients that you need a PhD in chemistry to pronounce, like butylated hydroxyanisole. And stay away from fast food! You probably don't need another reason to do so, but here it is: A new study[1] from George Washington University showed that the more fast food you eat, the more potentially dangerous chemicals like phthalates and bisphenol A (BPA) show up in your body. (And by the way, the study defined fast food as food obtained from restaurants, regardless of waiter/waitress service. All carryout and delivery food was also considered fast food.)

Load up on veggies and fruits. This may sound a little awkward, because most of us say "fruits and veggies." It just rolls off the tongue more easily and, for some reason, it sounds better (maybe just because we're used to it). But I flipped it, because veggies have a bit of an edge over fruit in providing more of the good stuff. But, that doesn't mean you shouldn't eat fruit. Please do! Both are so good for you.

In fact, if you're going to make only one dietary change, this is the one I'd encourage you to choose. Why? For one thing, vegetables and fruits fill you up for a lot fewer calories than foods like cereal, bread, or cheese. If losing or maintaining your weight is one of your goals, load up your plate with produce because the side effect may be eating less of other high-calorie foods.

The best reason, though, is that veggies and fruits are chock-full of benefits with very little downside. They are loaded with vitamins and minerals, fiber, and other phytochemicals, such as lycopene in tomatoes and sulforaphane in broccoli. If you're eating them naturally (without sauces or syrups), they don't have any added sugars, added sodium, or any artificial chemicals, preservatives, or coloring.

All of this good stuff contributes to their having a big impact on your health. Studies show that the more produce you eat, the lower your risk is for developing a host of problems, like heart disease, stroke, diabetes, high blood pressure, and cancer. They may even help you live longer. Analysis of multiple studies[2] that followed participants for an average of 13 years showed that eating five servings of vegetables and fruits a day reduced people's risk of dying by about 25 percent during the follow-up period. Other studies suggest that eating more may provide additional benefits.

The goal for the program is to have at least one serving with every meal and snack. That will get you to the minimum recommendation of five a day. Since there's no harm in having more, and there could be a big upside, you could also aim for two servings with some or all your meals.

One possible downside may be pesticides and chemicals that veggies and fruits are exposed to. More research is being done in this area, but we still don't know the long-term effects. On the flip side, the evidence supporting the consumption of veggies and fruit is pretty solid. The most important thing is that you're eating enough of them. Next is to minimize your exposure to harmful chemicals by choosing organic whenever possible. But that doesn't mean you have to buy everything organic. Each year since 2004, the Environmental Working Group has been analyzing pesticide residue testing data from the US Department of Agriculture and Food and Drug Administration for 48 popular produce items. From that data, they develop yearly lists of the Dirty Dozen (see page 232)—foods with the most pesticide residue—and Clean 15 (see page 232)—those with the least—to help you determine which foods you should buy organic and which ones you don't have to.

But remember, it's more important to eat veggies and fruit than to worry about organic versus nonorganic. "The health benefits of a diet rich in fruits and vegetables outweigh the risks of pesticide exposure," according to the Environmental Working Group. "Eating conventionally grown produce is far better than skipping fruits and vegetables."

And fresh isn't the only way to get your produce. Frozen is another great way to always have veggies and fruits on hand. Just make sure you choose products without any added sugar, sauces, or syrups. Canned can be an option, too. Avoid products with added sugar, added salt, or syrup (look for those canned in 100 percent juice or water) and look for brands that use BPH-free cans or glass jars.

Eat more omega-3s. These fatty acids play a key role in brain function and are essential to a well-functioning body. Unlike other essential fats, however, your body can't make them, so you need to get them from foods. Research shows that they can protect against heart disease by reducing inflammation and lowering cholesterol and blood pressure levels. They may also lower your risk for cancer and help with conditions such as arthritis, depression, and even Alzheimer's disease.

Omega-3s are found in abundance in fish, especially fatty varieties like salmon, anchovies, trout, and certain canned light tunas, which also tend to be low in mercury. Avoid or limit your intake of the highest-mercury fish: shark, swordfish, king mackerel, and tilefish. If you love canned tuna, look for brands like Wild Planet that source younger fish (which tend to have lower mercury content) and use cooking methods to preserve the omega-3s.

Aim for eating fish two to four times a week. If you don't like fish, here are some nonfishy sources of omega-3s: flaxseeds, flaxseed oil, chia seeds, walnuts, edamame, enriched eggs, pumpkin seeds, and canola (rapeseed) oil.

Cut back on added sugar. Just because you don't eat candy or don't put sugar in your coffee doesn't mean you can skip this guideline. More than two-thirds of Americans are eating more added sugar than they should be. The reason: It's hiding in plain sight in bread, yogurt, salad dressing, pasta sauce, and peanut butter, to name just a few.

Sugar had traditionally been blamed for cavities, diabetes, and weight gain. But recently, the case against it has grown with studies showing that too much sugar can increase your risk of dying from heart disease,[3] make you more likely to have a stroke, raise your blood pressure and cholesterol levels, and jack up your chances of developing rheumatoid arthritis. Remember those telomeres back in Chapter 2 (page 19), the end caps on DNA that are markers of aging? While walking may help you keep them longer or even lengthen them, sugar appears to have exactly the opposite effect. Not to mention, it can contribute to an expanding waistline.

Based on the evidence, the *Dietary Guidelines for Americans* that were updated in 2015 included (for the first time) a recommendation on sugar: Limit sugar to no more than 10 percent of calories. That's 12 teaspoons if you're eating 2,000 calories a day. The American Heart Association has an even stricter recommendation: no more than 6 teaspoons a day for women, and no more than 12 teaspoons a day for men. Americans eat on average 22 teaspoons of added sugar a day—up to more than three times as much as recommended.

Get some protein every time you eat. Foods with a good amount of protein—think chicken, turkey,

SUGAR'S ALIASES

Anytime you see the word *sugar* in an ingredient list, even if it's combined with something healthy like beet, coconut, or date, steer clear. It's added sugar, and you don't want it. Here are some other common names you should know about, so you can spot the added sugary ingredients in your food.

Agave nectar	Crystalline fructose	Malt syrup
Barley malt	Dextrose	Molasses
Brown rice syrup	Fructose	Rice brand syrup
Cane crystals	Fruit juice concentrates	Rice syrup
Cane juice	Glucose	Sorghum
Caramel	High-fructose corn syrup	Sucrose
Carob syrup	Honey	Syrup
Corn sweetener	Lactose	
Corn syrup	Maltose	

fish (another reason to eat more of this superfood), lean meat, eggs, dairy, soybeans, and nuts—help you to feel fuller for longer than carbs and fats. Protein is also important for muscle repair and maintaining muscle as you get older.

If you eat meat regularly, you're probably getting an adequate amount of protein, but depending upon the source, you could be getting too much saturated fat, which can wreak havoc on your heart and blood vessels. If this is you, you'll want to choose lean protein options . . . another reason this program recommends more fish. It's a great source of protein and, instead of nasty saturated fat, many varieties contain heart-healthy omega-3s.

If you don't eat a lot of meat, fish, or poultry, you might not be getting enough protein. A good guideline for how much protein you need is 0.75 gram per pound of body weight. So, if you weigh 150 pounds, you should aim for about 112 grams of protein per day. See the list of high-protein foods below for foods to choose from.

By having just one serving of protein every time you eat, you'll spread your protein intake throughout the day, so you'll feel more satisfied all day long—and maybe eat less. And, this includes snacks! Instead of having just a banana, add peanut butter.

HIGH-PROTEIN FOODS

Eat a variety of these foods to ensure that you're getting enough protein, which will help you to feel more satisfied and less hungry. Protein grams correspond to cooked servings, where appropriate. Check labels, because amounts may vary among brands.

Food	Serving Size	Protein (g)
Turkey or chicken breast	3 ounces	25
Lean beef and veal	3 ounces	23
Lean pork	3 ounces	22
Fish (tuna, salmon, halibut)	3 ounces	19–23
0% Greek yogurt	6 ounces	15
Cottage cheese	½ cup	12
Fat-free or soy milk	1 cup	8
Quinoa	1 cup	8
Soybeans (edamame)	½ cup	8
Tofu	3 ounces	8
Nuts and seeds	¼ cup	6–10
Beans, lentils, split peas, and chickpeas	½ cup	6–9
Egg	1 large	6
Low-fat cheeses	1 ounce	4–7

Having a salad? Add chicken or nuts.

Watch portion sizes. Calories count, even if you're eating only healthy foods. While vegetables and fruit tend to be low-calorie, if eaten in their natural form, other healthy foods like nuts, seeds, quinoa, and avocados can pack a calorie wallop, if you're eating oversize portions. The best way to rein in calories is to get familiar with appropriate portion sizes. That means measuring foods like these and salad dressing, oil, pasta, grains, and spreads like hummus. After measuring them a few times, you should be able to eyeball it moving forward. Using smaller plates and dishes can also help to keep portion sizes under control. If you get stuck on a plateau, start measuring again. You may be surprised at how portion sizes can grow over time. Be particularly careful about portions when dining out. Restaurant portions are notoriously supersized. In most cases, you can immediately cut your portion in half and take one-half home for another entire meal.

Eat more beans. Beans are already a part of the guidelines because they are a good source of protein and fiber. I'm calling them out with their own entry because making a point of eating beans every day offers a heap of help if you're trying to lose weight.

A recent study[4] found that simply eating ¾ cup serving of beans daily—without changing anything else—led to an average ½-pound weight loss over 6 weeks. Okay, that's not much weight loss, but the people in the study didn't have to do anything else. No giving up chocolate, cutting portions, exercising . . . *nada*!

That's pretty amazing for one simple change!

All the fiber you get in beans may be one of the reasons it's an effective weight-loss aid. A recent study[5] from Denmark found that meatless meals consisting of beans and peas fill you up more and curb your appetite better than similar meals made with meat. The meals were similar in calories and amount, but testers reported feeling more satisfied after the bean meals and ate 13 percent fewer calories at their next meal than they did when they ate the meat dish.

I know, you don't like beans, right? I didn't used to like them either! I remember having dinner at a friend's house when I was about 8 years old, and her mother served chili. That felt like the longest dinner ever, as I tried to fish out the kidney beans and hide them in my napkin. I'm still not a fan of kidney beans, but I'll add black beans, navy beans, or cannellini beans to dishes whenever possible. The dish that won me over was a black-bean-and-corn salad that was served at my bridal shower. I was trying to like beans at the time because I knew how good they were for me. Well, I loved these! So much so that the Rodale Test Kitchen re-created the recipe for me, and we published it in *Prevention* magazine (see the recipe on page 253).

To try to get my kids to eat them, I mash up white beans and mix them with tuna fish. Or, I mash black ones up into lean ground beef and roll the mixture up in a tortilla with rice and salsa. Adding them to eggs helps me feel satisfied longer.

By the way, it's okay to used canned beans. They make throwing together a quick dinner so easy: cooked quinoa or rice, black beans, chopped cooked chicken (optional), avocado, and salsa. Just rinse the beans in a colander under cold water for at least a minute. This will help to reduce the sodium content. If you have the time to soak dried beans, then go for them. They tend to be less expensive. But, again, the important thing is that you eat them.

Choose fiber-rich grains. White bread, pasta, and cereal basically act like sugar when they get into your body, causing blood sugar spikes and crashes that can leave you feeling moody and tired. They

HIGH-FIBER FOODS

Here are a variety of foods to choose from to ensure that you get 25 to 30 grams of fiber a day.

Fruits	Serving size	Total fiber (g)*
Raspberries	1 cup	8
Pear, with skin	1 medium	6
Apple, with skin	1 medium	4
Banana	1 medium	3
Orange	1 medium	3
Strawberries (halves)	1 cup	3
Grains, cereal, and pasta		
Bran flakes, high-fiber	⅓–¾ cup	9–14
Pearled barley	1 cup cooked	6
Whole-wheat spaghetti	1 cup cooked	6.
Oat bran muffin	1 medium	5
Instant oatmeal	1 cup cooked	4
Brown rice	1 cup cooked	3
Popcorn (air-popped)	3 cups	3
Rye bread	1 slice	2
Whole-wheat or multi-grain bread	1 slice	2
Legumes, Nuts, and Seeds		
Lentils	1 cup cooked	16
Split peas	1 cup cooked	16
Black beans	1 cup cooked	15
Lima beans	1 cup cooked	11
Vegetarian baked beans (canned)	1 cup	10
Almonds	1 ounce (23 nuts)	4
Sunflower seed kernels	¼ cup	4
Pecans	1 ounce (19 halves)	3
Pistachios	1 ounce (49 nuts)	3
Vegetables		
Green peas, cooked	1 cup cooked	9
Artichoke hearts	½ cup cooked	7
Broccoli	1 cup steamed	5
Turnip greens	1 cup boiled	5
Sweet corn	1 cup cooked	4
Brussels sprouts	1 cup cooked	4
Baked potato, with skin	1 small	3
Carrot	1 medium	3
Tomato paste	¼ cup	3

Fiber content can vary between brands.

Source: USDA National Nutrient Database for Standard Reference, 2012

can also have detrimental effects, such as increased inflammation and blood pressure, high risk of heart disease, and maybe even a greater chance of being depressed.

Whole grain bread, pasta, and cereal, on the other hand, have been associated with healthier cholesterol and blood pressure levels, less risk of diabetes, and less weight gain. They can even help you live longer. A study in the *Journal of the American Medical Association* (JAMA)[6] found that the consumption of whole grains lowered their risk of dying over the next 25 years.

But not all whole grain products are healthy. Some can be loaded with added sugars and sodium. So, you'll need to do some detective work to find the best ones. Thankfully, there's a simple formula that makes finding the healthiest whole grain products easier. Harvard researchers did some serious food shopping, buying 545 whole grain products and then analyzing them to come up with a reliable way to identify the healthy ones. Look for whole grain products with a 10 to 1 ratio of carbohydrates—for every 10 grams of carbohydrates that a product has, it should have 1 gram of fiber. For example, if a slice of bread has 20 grams of carbohydrates, only buy it if it also has at least 2 grams of fiber. Based on the study, whole grain products with this ratio were also likely to have less added sugar and sodium and less likely to contain trans fats—all-around a healthier choice.[7]

Don't drink your calories. Calories aren't the only problem when it comes to beverages. About half of the added sugar that Americans are consuming comes from sweetened beverages—and it's not just soda. Iced tea, coffee drinks, smoothies, and sports drinks are major contributors, too.

The problem with liquid calories is that your body doesn't register them like it does solid ones. Let's say you eat a bigger breakfast than normal, consuming an extra 300 calories' worth of pancakes. You'll feel fuller from those 300 pancake calories, so you may delay eating and/or you may even eat less later. But, let's say those 300 calories come from a sugary coffee drink instead. Unfortunately, they don't make you feel any fuller, and they don't curb your appetite later in the day, so you're more likely to end up with a net increase in calories when drinking extra calories than when you eat them.

Perhaps surprisingly, calorie-free diet beverages aren't the answer. Some research suggests that artificial sweeteners may actually increase your desire for sugary foods. In a randomized-controlled study, 81 overweight and obese women with type 2 diabetes, who regularly drank diet beverages, followed a comprehensive weight-loss program, including diet and exercise. Half of the group continued to consume diet beverages, while the other half drank water instead. While both groups lost weight and improved glucose levels and insulin sensitivity, the water-drinkers had better results after 24 weeks. They lost 22 percent more weight and had up to 37 percent greater improvements in other glucose and insulin markers.[8]

Your best bet is to stick with water, unsweetened tea and coffee, and no-calorie seltzers, whenever possible. When you do indulge, eat your treats, don't drink them.

CREATE YOUR OWN MEALS

If you're looking for an easy, throw-together meal, here's a formula to make it healthy and calorie-controlled.

- Start with 3 to 4 ounces of lean protein, such as fish, chicken or turkey breast, pork tenderloin or chops, lean beef like sirloin or eye of round, or tofu. Pair it with one of the following flavorful marinades, and then bake, grill, or broil it.

- Fill your plate with 1 to 2 cups of vegetables. Roasting is an easy healthy way to cook up tasty vegetables. For roasting instructions, see the tips and roasting chart on page 234.

- Add 1 cup of a whole grain or a medium potato. For some delicious grain combinations, see page 235.

- Round it out with 1 to 2 teaspoons of butter or oil or 2 tablespoons of nuts or seeds (unless you make a recipe that already includes them).

Bon appétit!

Flavor Your Entrée

When you want to flavor chicken breasts, pork chops, steaks, fish, or tofu, consider marinating it. You can also marinate vegetables. A basic marinade is generally composed of equal parts of:

1. Acid (citrus juice, vinegar, wine, buttermilk, yogurt)

2. Fat (oil, coconut milk, yogurt)

3. Aromatics (minced garlic, hot peppers, scallions, herbs, citrus zest, soy sauce,

DIRTY DOZEN: WHAT TO BUY ORGANIC

According to the Environmental Working Group, these are the foods that tend to have the most pesticide residue, so it's best to buy organic whenever possible.

1. Strawberries
2. Apples
3. Nectarines
4. Peaches
5. Celery
6. Grapes
7. Cherries
8. Spinach
9. Tomatoes
10. Bell peppers
11. Cherry tomatoes
12. Cucumbers

CLEAN 15

According to the Environmental Working Group, here are the vegetables and fruits that tend to have the lowest amount of pesticides. So, when you're trying to decide where to spend your money on organic, you can probably skip these.

1. Avocados
2. Sweet corn
3. Pineapples
4. Cabbage
5. Sweet peas
6. Onions
7. Asparagus
8. Mangoes
9. Papaya
10. Kiwifruit
11. Eggplant
12. Honeydew melon
13. Grapefruit
14. Cantaloupe
15. Cauliflower

Worcestershire sauce, fish sauce, sweeteners like molasses or honey)

The possibilities, however, are endless. Keep in mind that it's the acid in the marinade that tenderizes a protein, so don't keep anything delicate, such as fish, in the marinade for longer than 20 minutes. Heartier items like steak and fresh vegetables can withstand an overnight marinade in the refrigerator, either in a glass dish or a resealable plastic bag. Remember: Unless what you're marinating is strictly vegetarian, discard all marinade after use. In a pinch, you can use your favorite vinaigrette, but here are six to try for marinating 1 pound of meat:

- ¼ cup soy sauce, ¼ cup mirin, 2 tablespoons water, 1 tablespoon grated fresh ginger, and 4 chopped cloves garlic

- ½ cup olive oil, ¼ cup fresh lemon juice, 2 chopped cloves garlic, and 1 tablespoon chopped fresh parsley

- ½ cup fresh orange juice, 2 tablespoons fresh lime juice, 2 tablespoons fresh rosemary, 3 chopped cloves garlic, 1 tablespoon honey, 1 tablespoon olive oil, ¼ teaspoon salt, and ¼ teaspoon freshly ground black pepper

- 3 tablespoons rice vinegar, 2 tablespoons grated fresh ginger, 2 tablespoons canola oil, 2 tablespoons sesame oil, 2 tablespoons soy sauce, 2 tablespoons honey, 1 tablespoon chopped fresh cilantro, and 1 chopped serrano or jalapeño pepper

- 2 chopped cloves garlic, 1 teaspoon salt, ½ cup olive oil, ¼ cup fresh lemon juice, 2 tablespoons lemon zest, 3 tablespoons chopped fresh mint, 2 tablespoons chopped fresh oregano, and ½ teaspoon freshly ground black pepper

- 2 chopped scallions, ⅓ cup rice vinegar, 2 tablespoons sesame seeds, 4 teaspoons sesame oil, 1 tablespoon honey, and ¼ cup soy sauce

Easy, Tasty Veggies

Perhaps the simplest side dish you'll ever make involves roasting vegetables. All that's required is a baking sheet or roasting pan, and the rest is up to you. Heartier vegetables like potatoes, carrots, and

DIRTY DOZEN FOOD ADDITIVES

To clean up your diet, use this guide from the Environmental Working Group. Whenever possible, avoid these ingredients associated with serious health concerns, additives banned or restricted in other countries, and other substances that shouldn't be in food.

1. Nitrites and nitrates (added to cured meats)
2. Potassium bromate
3. Propyl paraben (added to tortillas, muffins, food dyes)
4. Butylated hydroxyanisole (BHA)
5. Butylated hydroxytoluene (BHT)
6. Propyl gallate
7. Theobromine
8. Secret flavor ingredients
9. Artificial colors
10. Diacetyl (butter flavoring in microwave popcorn)
11. Phosphate-based food additives
12. Aluminum-based additives

squash take longer to roast than less-hearty varieties such as Brussels sprouts, asparagus, and peppers, so if you want to mix and match, plan on adding lighter veggies midway through the roast. For the most success, follow these tips.

Roast at high heat. That's 425° to 450°F, so you can achieve a brown exterior and soft interior.

Add some fat. Olive oil lends great flavor as well as certain health benefits. Canola oil works well, too. Don't overdo it, though: 1 to 2 tablespoons is enough to coat a full baking dish of vegetables. Avoid certain oils with lower smoke points such as flax, sunflower, and walnut oils. Toss everything right on the baking sheet and mix.

HANDY ROASTING CHART

Not sure how long to roast a veggie? Use these guidelines.

Vegetable	Roasting Time (min.)
Hearty Veggies	
Beets (trimmed and cubed, if large, or quartered, if small)	30–40
Butternut and other winter squash (peeled and cubed)	40–45
Carrots (peeled and cut into bite-size pieces)	40–45
Cauliflower florets	30
Fennel (trimmed and cut into wedges)	30–40
Onions (thickly sliced or cut into large wedges)	30–40
Parsnips (peeled and cut into bite-size pieces)	40
Potatoes (baby and new potatoes unpeeled and halved; larger potatoes peeled and cut into bite-size pieces)	30–40
Sweet potatoes/yams (peeled and cut into bite-size pieces)	30–40
Tender Veggies	
Asparagus (trimmed and left whole or cut into 1-inch pieces)	10–15
Bell peppers (stemmed, seeded and cut into strips)	10–15
Broccoli florets	25–30
Brussels sprouts (trimmed and halved or quartered, if very large)	30
Eggplant (cut into rounds or bite-size pieces)	15–20
Green beans (trimmed)	20–30
Mushrooms (cleaned, trimmed, and halved or quartered)	20–30
Roma tomatoes (stemmed and halved)	20–30
Zucchini and other summer squash (cut into bite-size pieces)	15

Pay attention to the chopping details. Chop the vegetables to roughly the same size for even cooking.

Don't overcrowd the baking sheet. You want the hot air to circulate. One baking sheet can hold about 3 pounds of chopped vegetables.

Stir the veggies once during roasting—or don't! The portion of veggie touching the baking sheet will caramelize to a dark golden brown, but giving them one or two stirs during roasting will more evenly distribute the browning.

Befriend the color golden-brown because it is truly delicious. Toss the timer and roast until hard vegetables are tender and golden and soft vegetables are golden. Times in the chart (opposite) are approximate, but softer veggies can be done in 10 to 20 minutes, while harder veggies can take 30 to 45 minutes.

Make cleanup a snap. Line the baking sheet with foil—not parchment paper, which tends to hold moisture and is more likely to steam the veggies.

Keep your taste buds guessing, by continually changing it up. Here are a few tricks to try.

- Add fresh or dried herbs to the mix. Reserve more delicate herbs (basil, parsley, tarragon, chervil) for the finishing touch for serving; tougher herbs (rosemary, thyme, sage, oregano) can withstand the long roast.

- For a touch of brightness, toss in 1 tablespoon balsamic, apple-cider, or red wine vinegar during the roast, or finish the veggies with a squeeze of lemon juice before serving.

- Add a bit of sweetness by tossing in 1 to 2 tablespoons maple syrup or honey toward the end of the roast.

- Add some crunch by adding ¼ to ½ cup coarsely chopped nuts—such as hazelnuts, pecans, or cashews—midway through the roast.

- Other additions: soy sauce, nutritional yeast flakes, citrus zest and juice, bacon, or your favorite salad dressing.

MAKE GRAINS MORE INTERESTING

Mix in different combinations of ingredients into whole grains to change up the flavor profiles. Each makes one serving.

Pilaf—Combine 1 cup warm rice or quinoa with 1 tablespoon sliced almonds, 1 tablespoon golden raisins, and 1 tablespoon chopped parsley (280 calories with brown rice).

Fried rice—Combine 1 cup warm rice with ¼ cup shredded chicken, 2 tablespoons grated carrots, 2 tablespoons green peas, and 1 tablespoon reduced-sodium soy sauce. Drizzle with ½ teaspoon sesame oil and top with chopped scallions (320 calories with brown rice).

Sushi bowl—Toss 1 cup warm rice or quinoa with 1 tablespoon rice vinegar and top with 3 ounces sushi-grade salmon chunks, ¼ cup cucumber slices, and ¼ cup shredded nori. Drizzle with 1 tablespoon low-sodium tamari (372 calories with brown rice).

Cilantro lime—Toss 1 cup warm rice or quinoa with ½ cup canned black beans, 2 tablespoons finely chopped cilantro leaves, 2 tablespoons fresh lime juice, and ½ teaspoon sea salt (340 calories with brown rice).

Cajun—Combine 1 cup rice with ½ teaspoon dried thyme, ¼ teaspoon sea salt, and ⅛ teaspoon cayenne pepper. Top with ¼ cup canned red kidney beans, ¼ cup chopped green pepper, and 1 slice of crumbled cooked bacon (352 calories with brown rice).

"Pudding"—Combine 1 cup warm rice or quinoa with ½ cup warm light coconut milk and 1 tablespoon maple syrup. Top with 2 tablespoons each of diced fresh pineapple and mango and ½ teaspoon cardamom (392 calories with brown rice).

Korean bowl—Top 1 cup warm rice or quinoa with ¼ cup store-bought kimchi (a fermented Korean product, available in the international aisle of most grocery stores), 1 thinly sliced scallion, and 1 fried egg. Sprinkle with ½ teaspoon toasted sesame seeds and a squirt of hot sauce (342 calories with brown rice).

EATING ON-THE-GO

The more you can cook at home, the healthier your meals will be and the fewer calories you'll take in. But I know that that isn't always possible. Dining out and using convenience foods are a part of life, so here are some ways for you to do both, while supporting your ability to reach your exercise goals.

- Choose meals described with words such as "grilled," "steamed," "baked," "broiled," or "roasted."

- Speak up! Ask for an open-faced sandwich, half portions, or smarter sides, such as steamed vegetables or a salad instead of fries. Many restaurants will accommodate these requests.

- Start with a salad, but ask for dressing on the side, and use it sparingly. Dip your fork into the dressing and then pick up some salad—you'll be amazed at how little dressing you'll use while still enjoying the flavor. Also, order the salad without croutons or cheese.

Chinese restaurants—Order beef, chicken, or shrimp with broccoli. Order one of these same dishes with mixed vegetables instead of broccoli. Ask for more vegetables than beef, chicken, or shrimp. Get the sauce on the side, and brown rice instead of white rice. Have 1¾ cups entrée with ¾ cup steamed rice. Use 4 tablespoons sauce with your meal.

Mexican restaurants—Stick with chicken, beans, fajitas, vegetables, lettuce, tomato salsa, and half a portion of guacamole. Skip fried dishes, sour cream, and tortilla chips.

Mediterranean restaurants—Order a chicken and vegetable kebab. Have all the skewered vegetables and about 2½ ounces of the chicken (usually about a third of a serving). Take the leftover chicken home to be used in other dinners. Have a side of Greek salad (with 1½ cups greens and no feta cheese; order dressing on the side and use about 1 tablespoon) and 1 cup rice.

Steak house restaurants—Order the smallest portion possible, trim the fat, and take at least half of it home. Ask for barbecue sauce on the side. Opt for steamed or roasted veggies instead of baked potatoes or steak fries.

Salad bars—Take 1 cup mixed greens and 1½ cups chopped raw (plain, not marinated) vegetables of your choice (such as tomatoes, shredded carrots, or broccoli); toss with 1½ tablespoons dressing. Add 2 tablespoons chopped egg, tofu, or chicken and ½ cup cottage cheese. Enjoy with fresh fruit on the side.

Coffee shops—Skip the syrups and flavorings in your coffee, which are often loaded with sugar. Snack on fresh fruit or hummus and veggies instead of pastries.

Sandwich shops—Order the small size, and stick with turkey or chicken. Then, fill the sandwich with lots and lots of veggies and a little splash of vinegar or yellow mustard. Consider taking off the top bun or roll and eating it as an open-faced sandwich. Some shops will give you the option of a chopped salad using the sandwich ingredients without the bread, which will save you still more calories and carbohydrates. Have fresh fruit or a salad on the side instead of chips.

Pizza parlors—Have 1 slice of a large (14-inch) pizza or 1½ slices of a medium (12-inch) pizza, topped with two vegetables, such as mushrooms and green peppers. (Opt for thin-crust pizza and order a salad with dressing on the side to fill you up.)

Frozen pizza—Check the labels and have 265 to 280 calories' worth. Serve with a salad of 1 cup mixed greens and ½ cup chopped vegetables of your choice (such as tomatoes, peppers, and carrots) with 2 tablespoons reduced-calorie dressing.

Frozen burritos—Heat Amy's Bean and Rice Burrito; Amy's Bean, Rice; and Cheese Burrito; or Cedarlane Bean, Rice, and Cheese Burrito (check the label for 260 to 280 calories and 6 to 9 grams of fat). Enjoy with 1 cup raw vegetables of your choice dipped in 1 tablespoon light dressing.

Frozen and canned meals—Some of the best include:

- Amy's Organic Brown Rice and Vegetables Bowl

- Amy's Breakfast Tofu Scramble Breakfast Wrap

- Applegate Organic Chicken Strips

- Evol Chicken Penne Pomodoro

- Kashi Mediterranean Thin Crust Pizza

- Healthy Choice Hearty Chicken Soup

- Newman's Own Beef and Broccoli Complete Skillet Meal for Two

- Seapak Salmon Burgers

Macaroni and cheese—Heat Amy's Macaroni and Cheese according to package directions, and serve with 2 cups romaine lettuce topped with 1 teaspoon olive oil and 2 tablespoons balsamic vinegar.

Nutrition bars—Some of the best nutrition bars include:

- Luna Bar LemonZest

- Kind Fruit and Nut Delight

- Oatmega Wild Blueberry Crisp

- Annie's Gluten-Free Double Chocolate Chip Granola Bar

- ThinkThin Crunch Cranberry Apple Mixed Nuts

PROFILE: Sue Snyder, 59

Lost 6.6 pounds & 8.25 inches

Looking at Sue, you might wonder why she signed up for this program. She doesn't look like she needs to lose weight. In fact, she looks so good she could be a model. (She actually is one for QVC!)

But, before starting her walking plan, Sue was in a rut. She hadn't exercised regularly in almost a year, and she was feeling the effects. She'd collapse on the couch after work. The stress of working a full-time job and modeling on the side was getting to her. And she didn't have the energy to play with her grandchildren.

Despite looking slim, Sue was carrying around more body fat than is considered healthy. This can be a problem for women who are a healthy weight, especially as they age and lose muscle mass that is often replaced with fat. (For more on this, see page 9.)

"I was ready to make a change," she said. But "how was I going to fit in a walk when I could barely fit in a bathroom break?"

From the get-go, Sue was struggling as she tried to fit every minute of every walk into her already jam-packed schedule. She was feeling so defeated that she was ready to call it quits by Week 2.

But, following a pep talk and advice on breaking up her walks, Sue was off and walking! She'd walk in the morning, at lunch, or take a walking break from work around 4:00. "Going for walks gave me a new perspective," she said. "I never came back and said, 'Darn, I shouldn't have done that walk.'"

While Sue struggled with the walking portion of the program, she found the diet changes easier to make. She started by paying attention to what she was eating, asking herself, "Is it healthy?" and then, if it wasn't, "Is it worth the calories?" Sometimes, it was, and she enjoyed it, and sometimes, it wasn't, and she moved on. She also became aware of her oversized portions. "I'd eat the entire bowl of rice instead of just a cup." Now, she's eating more sensible portions and got rid of the chocolate in her desk drawer at work.

Despite all the healthy changes she'd made, Sue didn't think she was doing enough to see any results. "I was walking but not really pushing the limits I could have," she said. So, she was really shocked when the scale registered a 6.6-pound weight loss. And she lost 4 inches off her waist and 2½ off her thighs. Even better, she reduced her body fat by 6 percent. Now, she's getting down on the floor and playing with her grandchildren.

BEFORE   AFTER

Chapter 22

The Walk Your Way to Better Health Meal Plan

Forget about eating specific meals at precise times every day—nobody has time for a diet that rigid. Though many of us are trying to slim down or to maintain a healthy weight, I don't know too many people (okay, I don't know any!) who enjoy measuring foods and counting calories. To keep the crazy out of eating healthy, the Rodale Test Kitchen did you a favor. This chapter contains a complete, 3-week meal plan. Each meal has been portion-controlled for you. Every breakfast, lunch, and dinner on the plan clocks in around 400 calories. Each snack and dessert is about 200 calories.

So, if you're a woman, that means you can eat three squares and one or two snacks (or dessert) and end up automatically staying between 1,400 and 1,600 calories a day. Guys should add an extra 200 to 400 calories to that mark, shooting for 1,800 to 2,000 calories a day. This could mean eating an extra snack (or two!), or doubling a meal.

But that's not all we've done. I've also created three different ways to use the 3-week meal plan.

Pick one and stick to it, or mix and match the three to create one that best fits you.

Method One: Follow It to a T

If the idea of being able to enjoy the cooking process without having to think too much or fuss with last-minute decision making sounds like heaven to you, then just follow the 21-day meal plan and as provided in the following pages. When you reach the end, just start back over from Day 1, and enjoy your favorite meals all over again. You could repeat it as is, or change up the order of the days or weeks for a little variety.

Method Two: Cook It Your Way

If you're a renegade who enjoys making your own decisions, and you have the time to customize, or if you desperately need to work in some superfast meals for busier nights, then feel welcome to mix and match the meals and recipes, including the quick recipes in Chapter 23 on pages 248–255. If you just want to simplify the plan, you could alternate between only two or three breakfasts and lunches, and maybe four or five dinners, instead of changing the menus daily. (It will also pare down your shopping list.)

Method Three: Make It Your Own

Remember, the closer you adhere to the 400-/200-calorie recommendations for meals and snacks and the guidelines in Chapter 21, the better your results will be. Besides that, not much direction is needed here. Maybe you do your own thing for breakfast and lunch, and then follow the dinner recipes outlined in the 21-day meal plan. Or, follow the breakfast plan to a T and play it by ear for dinner. Flip through, and find the recipes you like the most, served when you want them. The choice is yours.

Additional Meal Plan Options

Feel free to substitute milk with the equivalent portion of soy, cashew, or almond milk, if you like. Please note that almond milk will offer less protein, so you may need to make that up elsewhere to stay satisfied longer and give your muscles enough of this building block they need as you grow stronger. Look for a brand that has about 110 calories per cup and is fortified with 30 to 40 percent of the Daily Value for calcium.

When selecting bread, muffins, and waffles, remember the guideline to select fiber-rich, whole grains. Some recommendations are:

- Nature's Own 100% Whole Wheat Bread

- Ezekiel Sprouted 100% Whole Grain Bread (all varieties)

- Ezekiel Sprouted Grain English Muffins

- Kashi 7-Grain Waffles

- Van's 8 Whole Grains Waffles

- Arnold 100% Whole Wheat Sandwich Thins

- Thomas' 100% Whole Wheat English Muffins

Week 1

	Breakfast	Snack	Lunch	Dinner	Snack
DAY 1	1 serving French Toast with Strawberry Topping (page 262) 1 slice Canadian bacon (1 ounce), pan-grilled Black coffee, black tea, or green tea	Salsa Fresca and Chips (page 323)	1 serving Mediterranean Seafood Soup (page 309) 1 medium pear	1 serving Sage-Roasted Pork Tenderloin with Stuffed Acorn Squash (page 288)	1 serving Dark Chocolate–Raspberry Patties (page 330)
	Per day: 1,543 calories, 87 g protein, 211 g carbohydrates, 62 g sugar, 45 g total fat, 11 g saturated fat, 34 g fiber, 2,323 mg sodium				
DAY 2	1 serving Blueberry-Oat Pancakes (page 257) 2 links turkey sausage 2 tablespoons low-fat cottage cheese 2 teaspoons maple syrup Black coffee, black tea, or green tea	½ serving Muesli with Dried Fruits and Walnuts (page 265) ½ cup 0% plain Greek yogurt	1 serving Pork Tender Wrap in a Corn Tortilla (page 286)	1 serving Pistachio-Crusted Wild Salmon (page 294)	1 serving Creamy Tropical Fruit Medley (page 329)
	Per day: 1,573 calories, 114 g protein, 138 g carbohydrates, 56 g sugar, 65 g total fat, 14 g saturated fat, 23 g fiber, 1,790 mg sodium				
DAY 3	1 serving Scrambled Eggs with Spinach, Tomatoes, and Canadian Bacon (page 268) Black coffee, black tea, or green tea	1 serving Spiced Sweet Potato Chips (page 325)	1 serving Greek Vegetable Sandwiches (page 273) 1 apple	1 serving Turkey Meat Loaf with Roasted Vegetables (page 283) Salad made with 1 cup prewashed mixed greens and 1 teaspoon balsamic vinegar	1 serving Warm Glazed Oranges with Walnuts (page 332)
	Per day: 1,588 calories, 78 g protein, 207 g carbohydrates, 73 g sugar, 60 g total fat, 18 g saturated fat, 44 g fiber, 3,074 mg sodium				
DAY 4	1 serving Muesli with Dried Fruits and Walnuts (page 265) 1 cup 0% plain Greek yogurt Black coffee, black tea, or green tea	1 serving Black Bean Dip with Baby Carrots (page 320) 1 ounce reduced-fat Swiss cheese	1 serving Mushroom, Beef, and Barley Soup (page 310) 2 plums	1 serving Grilled Trout with Chive and Dill Sauce (page 291) 1 cup steamed broccoli	1 serving Double Chocolate Pudding (page 330)
	Per day: 1,473 calories, 111 g protein, 178 g carbohydrates, 75 g sugar, 41 g total fat, 7 g saturated fat, 40 g fiber, 2,023 mg sodium				
DAY 5	1 serving Vegetable Quiche (page 269) Black coffee, black tea, or green tea	1 serving Seafood Antipasto (page 324)	1 serving Turkey-and-Red-Cabbage-Slaw Sandwich (page 284)	1 serving Broccoli, Mushroom, and Tofu Stir-Fry with Walnuts (page 271) 1 serving Spinach and Orange Salad with Honey-Mustard Dressing (page 304)	1 serving Blueberry-Ricotta Sundae (page 329)

Week 1 (continued)

	Breakfast	Snack	Lunch	Dinner	Snack
	Per day: 1,605 calories, 78 g protein, 169 g carbohydrates, 40 g sugar, 71 g total fat, 16 g saturated fat, 25 g fiber, 2,222 mg sodium				
DAY 6	¾ cup cooked regular or steel-cut oats mixed with 1 cup fat-free plain yogurt and topped with ¼ cup chopped fresh strawberries, 2 tablespoons chopped walnuts, and a dash of cinnamon Black coffee, black tea, or green tea	1 medium apple, sliced 1½ tablespoons natural peanut butter	1 serving Chicken Gyros with Yogurt-Cucumber Sauce (page 279) ½ cup fresh or canned-in-juice pineapple chunks topped with 1 teaspoon ground flaxseed	1 serving Pinto Beans and Pasta in Tomato-Basil Sauce (page 275) 1 serving Fast and Fresh Salad (page 303) with ¼ avocado, sliced	1 serving Strawberry Sorbet (page 331)
	Per day: 1,586 calories, 82 g protein, 206 g carbohydrates, 69 g sugar, 58 g total fat, 11 g saturated fat, 34 g fiber, 1,700 mg sodium				
DAY 7	1 serving Hummus, Tomato, and Spinach Breakfast Muffin (page 263) 1 kiwifruit Black coffee, black tea, or green tea	1 stick reduced-fat string cheese 2 pieces multigrain crispbread	1 serving Creole Cauliflower Soup (page 307) 1 navel orange	1 serving Arroz con Pollo (page 277) 1 serving Stir-Fried Curly Kale (page 317)	1 serving Baked Pears with Creamy Lemon Sauce (page 328)
	Per day: 1,497 calories, 99 g protein, 179 g carbohydrates, 69 g sugar, 52 g total fat, 10 g saturated fat, 35 g fiber, 2,256 mg sodium				

Week 2

	Breakfast	Snack	Lunch	Dinner	Snack
DAY 8	1 serving Pineapple-Strawberry Smoothie (page 267) ½ whole wheat pita (6-inch diameter), toasted, filled with 1 sliced organic hard-boiled egg and 4 sliced grape tomatoes Black coffee, black tea, or green tea	1 serving Broccoli Spears with Asian Peanut Sauce (page 321)	1 serving Curried Lentil and Spinach Soup (page 308) 1 serving Crunchy Chinese Slaw (page 314)	1 serving Oven-Fried Rosemary Chicken Breasts with Farro and Asparagus (page 282)	Sweet snack mix: 1 tablespoon bittersweet chocolate chips, 1 tablespoon chopped walnuts, and 1 tablespoon unsweetened dried cranberries
	Per day: 1,452 calories, 88 g protein, 188 g carbohydrates, 60 g sugar, 47 g total fat, 12 g saturated fat, 47 g fiber, 1,169 mg sodium				
DAY 9	1 serving Blueberry-Oat Pancakes (page 257) spread with 2 tablespoons natural almond butter Black coffee, black tea, or green tea	½ cup steamed edamame pods	1 serving Bean and Turkey Chili (page 276) mixed with ½ cup cooked mixed frozen vegetables	1 serving Orange Chicken-and-Broccoli Stir-Fry (page 281) ½ cup grapes	1 serving Strawberry Sorbet (page 331)
	Per day: 1,420 calories, 96 g protein, 170 g carbohydrates, 54 g sugar, 46 g total fat, 6 g saturated fat, 31 g fiber, 1,930 mg sodium				
DAY 10	1 100% whole wheat English muffin, toasted and spread with 1 tablespoon natural peanut butter ½ cup cherries (fresh or frozen) Black coffee, black tea, or green tea	1 medium pear ½ ounce reduced-fat Cheddar cheese	1 serving Pumpkin Bisque (page 312) 1 serving Mahi, Mango, and Avocado Quesadillas (page 293)	1 serving Roasted Arctic Char, Carrots, and Leeks with Penne (page 295)	½ cup thawed frozen blackberries topped with 2 tablespoons fat-free plain yogurt and 1 teaspoon honey
	Per day: 1,491 calories, 75 g protein, 203 g carbohydrates, 76 g sugar, 48 g total fat, 11 g saturated fat, 37 g fiber, 1,916 mg sodium				
DAY 11	1 serving French Toast with Strawberry Topping (page 262) with 2 tablespoons whipped low-fat cream cheese and 1 tablespoon chopped walnuts Black coffee, black tea, or green tea	1 medium sliced apple with 2 tablespoons almond butter	Tuna salad on crispbread: Combine ½ cup drained canned albacore tuna with 1 tablespoon prepared hummus, 1 tablespoon shredded baby carrots, and 1 teaspoon flaxseed oil. Serve on 2 pieces multi-grain crispbread 1 serving Fast and Fresh Salad (page 303)	1 serving Bean and Turkey Chili (page 276) 1 cup sparkling water with lime	1 serving Double Chocolate Pudding (page 330)
	Per day: 1,540 calories, 90 g protein, 157 g carbohydrates, 70 g sugar, 68 g total fat, 13 g saturated fat, 35 g fiber, 1,745 mg sodium				

Week 2 (continued)

	Breakfast	Snack	Lunch	Dinner	Snack
DAY 12	1 serving Scrambled Eggs with Spinach, Tomatoes, and Canadian Bacon (page 268) Black coffee, black tea, or green tea	½ serving Muesli with Dried Fruits and Walnuts (page 265) ½ cup 0% plain Greek yogurt	1 serving Chicken Gyros with Yogurt-Cucumber Sauce (page 279)	1 serving Pasta e Fagiole (page 311) 1 serving Shellfish Scampi over Cauliflower "Rice" (page 298)	½ ounce bittersweet chocolate
	Per day: 1,566 calories, 119 g protein, 152 g carbohydrates, 29 g sugar, 57 g total fat, 17 g saturated fat, 37 g fiber, 3,061 mg sodium					
DAY 13	Peanut butter–banana waffle sandwich: 2 whole grain toasted frozen waffles spread with 1 tablespoon natural peanut butter and 1 sliced banana Black coffee, black tea, or green tea	1 serving Black Bean Dip with Baby Carrots (page 320) 1 stick reduced-fat string cheese	1 serving Asparagus and Barley Salad with Dill Dressing (page 302) with ½ cup chopped cooked chicken	1 serving Wild Salmon with Swiss Chard and Couscous (page 300)	½ cup fat-free vanilla frozen yogurt
	Per day: 1,555 calories, 101 g protein, 199 g carbohydrates, 57 g sugar, 47 g total fat, 12 g saturated fat, 37 g fiber, 1,965 mg sodium					
DAY 14	1 serving Broccoli and Sausage Egg Bake (page 259) 1 medium peach Black coffee, black tea, or green tea	1 stick reduced-fat string cheese 1 piece multigrain crispbread ½ cup red grapes	1 serving Bean-and-Olive Bruschetta (page 320) with 2 ounces albacore tuna (in water, drained) 1 cup diced cantaloupe	1 serving Rosemary-Roasted Baby Potatoes and Carrots with Sirloin (page 287) 1 serving Sweet-and-Sour Red Cabbage (page 318)	½ cup fresh strawberry halves drizzled with ½ ounce melted bittersweet chocolate
	Per day: 1,531 calories, 100 g protein, 174 g carbohydrates, 78 g sugar, 53 g total fat, 17 g saturated fat, 27 g fiber, 2,340 mg sodium					

Week 3

	Breakfast	Snack	Lunch	Dinner	Snack
DAY 15	Nutty Choco-Banana Oatmeal (page 266) Black coffee, black tea, or green tea	1 serving Spicy Tomato-Parmesan Bites (page 325)	1 serving Roasted Veggie Couscous Salad with Feta Dressing (page 303)	Nachos: 1 grilled boneless, skinless chicken breast, sliced over 1 serving Salsa Fresca and Chips (page 323) topped with 2 tablespoons shredded reduced-fat Cheddar cheese 1 serving Roasted Broccoli and Cauliflower (page 315)	½ serving Pineapple-Strawberry Smoothie (page 267)
	Per day: 1,634 calories, 86 g protein, 198 g carbohydrates, 50 g sugar, 64 g total fat, 13 g saturated fat, 42 g fiber, 1,819 mg sodium				
DAY 16	¾ cup high-fiber bran flakes 1 cup fat-free milk 1 banana Black coffee, black tea, or green tea	1 serving Caramelized Onion and Lentil Spread (page 322)	1 serving Mushroom, Beef, and Barley Soup (page 310) 1 serving Warm Couscous and Bean Salad (page 305)	1 serving Sesame Scallop Skewers with Baby Bok Choy and Green Tea Rice (page 296)	1 serving Peach Smoothie (page 266)
	Per day: 1,532 calories, 80 g protein, 228 g carbohydrates, 60 g sugar, 38 g total fat, 12 g saturated fat, 40 g fiber, 2,046 mg sodium				
DAY 17	1 100% whole wheat English muffin, toasted 1 ounce shredded reduced-fat Cheddar cheese 1 slice Canadian bacon (1 ounce), pan-grilled 1 large organic egg, poached ¼ cup baby spinach leaves Black coffee, black tea, or green tea	1 serving Peach Smoothie (page 266) 1 medium apple	1 serving Crunchy Sesame Chicken and Bulgur Bowl (page 280)	1 serving Curried Black-Bean-and-Corn Burger over Quinoa Salad (page 272)	1 serving Balsamic Strawberries with Pistachios and Chocolate (page 327)
	Per day: 1,686 calories, 94 g protein, 209 g carbohydrates, 74 g sugar, 56 g total fat, 11 g saturated fat, 39 g fiber, 2,766 mg sodium				
DAY 18	1 serving Breakfast Brown Rice Fritter (page 258) Black coffee, black tea, or green tea	1 serving Caramelized Onion and Lentil Spread (page 322)	1 serving Sesame Scallop Skewers with Baby Bok Choy and Green Tea Rice (page 296)	1 serving Shellfish Scampi over Cauliflower "Rice" (page 298) 1 serving Fast and Fresh Salad (page 303)	1 serving Baked Pears with Creamy Lemon Sauce (page 327)
	Per day: 1,492 calories, 88 g protein, 178 g carbohydrates, 50 g sugar, 52 g total fat, 11 g saturated fat, 35 g fiber, 2,682 mg sodium				

Week 3 (continued)

	Breakfast	Snack	Lunch	Dinner	Snack
DAY 19	1 toasted whole grain frozen waffle spread with 2 tablespoons natural peanut butter and ¼ cup sliced fresh strawberries Black coffee, black tea, or green tea	½ cup low-fat cottage cheese 1 piece multi-grain crispbread 6 grape tomatoes	1 serving Curried Lentil and Spinach Soup (page 308) 1 serving Crunchy Chinese Slaw (page 314)	1 serving Turkey Meat Loaf with Roasted Vegetables (page 283) 1 serving Fast and Fresh Salad (page 303)	1 serving Double Chocolate Pudding (page 331)
	Per day: 1,421 calories, 81 g protein, 172 g carbohydrates, 49 g sugar, 51 g total fat, 11 g saturated fat, 48 g fiber, 1,671 mg sodium				
DAY 20	1 serving Vegetable Quiche (page 269) 1 medium clementine Black coffee, black tea, or green tea	½ ounce reduced-fat Cheddar cheese 2 tablespoons whole almonds 1 tablespoon raisins	1 serving Tangy Mediterranean Tuna Salad (page 304)	1 serving Orange Chicken-and-Broccoli Stir-Fry (page 281)	¼ cup fat-free vanilla frozen yogurt with 1 tablespoon chopped bittersweet chocolate chips
	Per day: 1,539 calories, 84 g protein, 161 g carbohydrates, 45 g sugar, 67 g total fat, 17 g saturated fat, 21 g fiber, 2,183 mg sodium				
DAY 21	Quick bread "pudding": 1 serving Irish Oats Quick Bread (page 264), halved and layered with ½ cup 0% vanilla Greek yogurt and 1 sliced banana Black coffee, black tea, or green tea	1 cup edamame pods, steamed	1 serving Mediterranean Seafood Soup (page 309)	1 Chicken and Rice Salad with Pecans (page 278)	1 serving Pineapple-Strawberry Smoothie (page 267)
	Per day: 1,552 calories, 117 g protein, 213 g carbohydrates, 78 g sugar, 30 g total fat, 5 g saturated fat, 21 g fiber, 2,147 mg sodium				

Chapter 23

The Walk Your Way to Better Health Recipes

I n Chapter 21, I offered up an 80-20 rule as a reminder that you don't need to be 100 perfect 100 percent of the time. But even so, that may seem like a pretty daunting rule for someone who isn't exactly Julia Child. Maybe you're wondering, "Who can cook fresh, healthy meals from scratch even 80 percent of the time?"

Luckily for you, all the recipes in this book are as simple to make as they are to eat. In the following pages, you'll find dozens that you can mix and match. Most of the meals (with just a few exceptions) clock in around 400 calories. Most of the snacks and desserts (again, with a few exceptions) offer about 200. So, if you eat three squares and two snacks, you'll consume about 1,600 calories a day, which is perfect for steady weight loss. In those few cases where a recipe offers a lot fewer than 400 calories, you can bulk it up by pairing it with another dish, such as a soup, salad, or snack.

But before we usher you into the kitchen, here are a few kitchen pointers that even the handiest of cooks can brush up on.

COOKING BASICS

The best culinary minds know that simple touches can lead to magical meals. Here are some kitchen tips and tricks that will ensure that every dish makes your taste buds happy.

- For deeply flavored foods, don't overcrowd the pan. Ingredient overload makes a pan's temperature plummet, and foods end up steaming rather than caramelizing. This adds cooking time and subtracts taste. All ingredients should fit comfortably in one layer, so use a pan that's big enough for the job, and cook in batches, if necessary.

- Bottled dressings are a waste of money and calories. Make your own vinaigrette by whisking together three parts oil (olive, canola, or sesame) with one part vinegar (balsamic, red wine, or rice wine), plus salt and pepper. Build extra flavor by adding, to taste, minced shallot, Dijon mustard, or fresh herbs. One of my favorites is olive oil, balsamic vinegar, spicy brown mustard, and horseradish.

- Get more pucker for the price! Zap lemons, limes, or oranges for 15 seconds in the microwave before squeezing them. The fruit will yield twice as much juice.

- Pat meat and fish dry before cooking them. Surface moisture creates steam when it hits a hot pan or grill, impeding caramelization. If the fish has skin, use a sharp knife to squeegee off the water trapped within it.

- If you want perfect al dente pasta, adapt the box directions. Drain the pasta about 1 minute before the package tells you to. Dump the noodles back into the pot and stir in the heated sauce. The pasta will finish cooking in the pot.

- Always cook fish skin side down first. The skin keeps the flesh of the fish from drying out and provides a crunchy counterpoint to the tender meat. Cook the fillet, undisturbed, for 75 percent of the time on the skin side.

- Overcooked meat? Salvage dinner by slicing the meat thinly, putting it on a plate, and topping it with chopped tomatoes, onions, and jalapeños. Add olive oil and fresh lime juice. The acid and oil will restore moisture and fat to the mistreated meat.

- Freshen up limp vegetables by dropping the aging produce into ice water before cooking. Plants wilt because of water loss. Ice water penetrates their cells to restore crispness.

- Place a damp kitchen towel underneath the cutting board, to prevent it from rocking or slipping while you're chopping or slicing foods. Avoid a visit to the ER!

SHORT ON TIME? NO PROBLEM!

Whip up one of these quick meals or snacks faster than you can lace up your walking shoes. They make good substitutions for your meal plan on busier days, when you need help sticking to the eating guidelines with less effort.

Breakfasts

Each meal serves one. Breakfasts are about 400 calories each.

ALMOND BUTTER AND APPLE SANDWICH
Open and toast ½ whole wheat pita (6½-inch diameter). Spread with 2 tablespoons almond butter, sprinkle with 1 tablespoon chia seeds, and stuff with 1 thinly sliced Granny Smith apple. (396 calories)

APPLE OATMEAL WITH NUTS
Microwave ½ cup rolled oats with 1 cup fat-free milk. Stir in ½ cup unsweetened applesauce. Top with 2 tablespoons chopped walnuts. (390 calories)

OATMEAL WITH PEANUT BUTTER OR ALMOND BUTTER AND FRUIT

Cook ½ cup rolled oats with 1 cup fat-free milk instead of water. Stir in a heaping tablespoon of peanut butter or almond butter, and top with ½ cup chopped fruit. (402 calories)

SAUSAGE AND EGG ON AN ENGLISH MUFFIN

Scramble an egg in a nonstick skillet with 1 teaspoon butter. Toast a whole wheat English muffin. Heat 1 organic chicken breakfast sausage patty according to package directions. Top one-half of the muffin with the egg and the breakfast patty and top with the other half. Take it to go with a banana. (397 calories)

SPINACH "FRITTATA"

Heat a medium nonstick skillet over medium heat and coat with olive oil spray. Beat 3 eggs with 2 tablespoons fat-free milk, ¼ teaspoon salt, and ¼ teaspoon black pepper. Add 1 packed cup fresh spinach and 1 minced clove garlic. Pour into the skillet and cook 1 minute. Tilt the skillet, lifting up the edges of the egg with a spatula so the uncooked egg can flow underneath. When the center of the egg is still wet but set (not runny), cover the skillet and cook for about 2 minutes, until the egg is puffed and fully set. Serve with a slice of whole wheat toast and a small pear or other fruit. (402 calories)

SOUTHWEST BREAKFAST WRAP

Lightly scramble 1 egg in 1 teaspoon olive oil, adding ¼ cup rinsed black beans and heat through (or skip the beans and go for 2 eggs). Transfer to a 7-inch whole grain tortilla, top with 2 tablespoons salsa, ¼ diced avocado, and a sprinkle of shredded Cheddar. Roll up like a burrito. (406 calories)

TOMATO, SPINACH, AND FETA OMELET

Quickly sauté 2 handfuls (2 cups) of baby spinach with ½ chopped tomato and a clove of minced garlic in a splash of olive oil. Add 2 tablespoons crumbled feta cheese and transfer to a bowl. Wipe out the skillet before making a 3-egg omelet, using the veggie and cheese mixture as the filling. Serve with a clementine. (403 calories)

PB&J WAFFLE

Toast a frozen whole grain waffle. Top with 2 tablespoons peanut butter and ¾ cup chopped and smashed fresh strawberries. Sprinkle with 1 teaspoon hemp seeds (available in the whole foods section of most grocery stores) and serve with ½ cup fat-free milk. (405 calories)

WESTERN OMELET

Coat a nonstick skillet with cooking spray and heat over medium heat. Cook ¾ cup finely chopped vegetables of your choice (tomatoes, peppers, mushrooms, and onions) until tender. Transfer to a plate. Wipe out the skillet, spray with cooking spray, and return to medium heat. Whisk 3 eggs with ¼ teaspoon onion powder, ¼ teaspoon salt, ¼ teaspoon ground black pepper, and 2 tablespoons fat-free milk. Pour into the skillet and cook, covered, 1 to 1½ minutes, until wet but set. Top one-half of the egg with the cooked vegetables and 1 tablespoon Monterey Jack cheese. Fold the other half over the top, and slide onto a plate. Serve with ½ cup fat-free milk and 1 slice whole wheat toast. (405 calories)

Snacks

Each snack serves one, unless otherwise noted. Snacks are about 200 calories each.

APRICOT INDULGENCE

Spread 2 graham cracker squares (2½-inch size) each with 1 teaspoon natural peanut butter, almond butter, or sunflower seed butter. Top with a sliced fresh apricot. (202 calories)

BANANA "ICE CREAM"

Blend a frozen banana with 1 tablespoon almond butter and ½ teaspoon unsweetened cocoa powder until smooth. Or, skip the almond butter and top with 1 cup of your favorite berries. (203 calories with almond butter; 181 with berries)

BEEFED-UP TRAIL MIX

Mix 1 cup air-popped popcorn, ½ ounce chopped beef jerky, 2 tablespoons salted pumpkin seeds, and 1 tablespoon dried cranberries. (197 calories)

DELI DELIGHT

Wrap a 1-ounce slice of deli ham or turkey around a piece of reduced-fat string cheese and pair it with an apple. (175 calories)

DEVILED EGGS

Hard-boil 4 eggs. Peel the eggs, slice in half, and remove the yolks and place them in a small bowl. Mash the yolks with 2 tablespoons Greek yogurt and ¼ avocado. Stuff the yolk mixture back into the eggs and enjoy. (191 calories)

FRUIT-AND-NUT BUTTER

Slice a medium pear, apple, or banana and spread with 1 tablespoon almond butter or peanut butter. (201 calories)

FRUIT SALAD

Combine 2 cups chopped fresh fruits with 1 tablespoon toasted chopped nuts and 1 teaspoon unsweetened shredded coconut. (197 calories)

FRUIT WITH CHEESE

Slice a medium pear or apple and 1 piece (1 ounce) of reduced-fat cheese. (188 calories)

FROZEN GRAPES

Put 1 cup seedless grapes in the freezer for several hours. Eat right out of the freezer; they're like candy. Serve with 1 stick reduced-fat string cheese or 1 whole grain crispbread topped with 1 tablespoon goat cheese. (184 calories)

KALE CHIPS

Rinse 3 cups (about ½ pound) torn kale pieces and pat dry with a clean kitchen towel. Toss with 2 teaspoons olive oil on a baking sheet and arrange in a single layer. Sprinkle with ¼ teaspoon salt and bake at 250°F, tossing once for 20 to 30 minutes, until crispy. Sprinkle with 1 tablespoon Parmesan cheese or nutritional yeast flakes. (209 calories)

NUTTY YOGURT

Top 8 ounces (1 cup) fat-free plain yogurt with 2 tablespoons chopped walnuts and ½ teaspoon ground cinnamon. (199 calories)

PEANUT BUTTER RICE CAKE

Spread a brown-rice cake with 1 tablespoon peanut butter (or almond butter). Sprinkle with 1 teaspoon chia seeds and top with 2 tablespoons fresh blueberries. (197 calories)

PEANUT 'N' BANANA OPEN-FACED SANDWICH

Smash ½ medium banana and spread over half a toasted whole wheat English muffin. Sprinkle with 1½ tablespoons chopped salted peanuts. (189 calories)

RAISIN-NUT CLUSTER

Melt 8 ounces chopped bittersweet chocolate in the microwave, checking every 30 seconds to avoid burning. Stir in ⅔ cup peanuts and ½ cup raisins. Drop 12 spoonfuls onto a waxed paper–lined plate. Refrigerate for about 20 minutes, until set. (1 cluster: 174 calories)

SALTY EDAMAME

Sprinkle ¼ teaspoon sea salt over 1 cup steamed shelled edamame. (200 calories)

TRAIL MIX

Mix 2 tablespoons dried sweetened cranberries, 2 tablespoons unsweetened coconut chips, and 2 tablespoons salted peanuts. (208 calories)

VEGETABLES AND HUMMUS

Serve 8 baby carrots and ½ cup sliced cucumber with ¼ cup hummus mixed with 1 tablespoon hemp seeds. (199 calories)

Lunches and Dinners

Each meal serves one, unless otherwise noted. Lunches and dinners are about 400 calories each.

VEGETARIAN

ASPARAGUS PASTA

Whisk together 2 tablespoons white wine, 2 teaspoons olive oil, 1 minced clove garlic, ¼ teaspoon salt, and ¼ teaspoon ground black pepper. Pour over 1 cup cooked whole wheat penne pasta. Steam or roast 6 large asparagus spears and slice into the pasta. Top with 2 ounces cubed firm tofu, and sprinkle with 1½ tablespoons grated Parmesan or nutritional yeast flakes. (400 calories)

BAKED POTATO WITH BROCCOLI AND CHEESE

Top 1 hot baked potato with ¼ cup shredded reduced-fat Cheddar cheese and 1 cup cooked broccoli florets (microwaved frozen broccoli is fine). Serve with ⅓ cup fresh pineapple chunks on the side. (405 calories)

BEAN BURRITO

Top 1 warmed whole wheat tortilla with ½ cup canned pinto or black beans (drained and rinsed), partly mashed; ¼ cup shredded reduced-fat Cheddar cheese; and 3 tablespoons salsa. Roll and eat with

¾ cup baby carrots and 2 tablespoons prepared guacamole. (396 calories)

PASTA WITH CHICKPEAS

Toss 1 cup cooked whole grain pasta with ½ cup canned chickpeas (drained and rinsed), 1 tablespoon Parmesan cheese, 1 teaspoon olive oil, ½ teaspoon dried basil, and ½ teaspoon minced garlic. Serve with ⅓ cup steamed snow peas. (404 calories)

VEGETABLE PITA PIZZA

Preheat an oven or toaster oven to 350°F. Slice a 6½-inch whole wheat pita lengthwise to produce 2 rounds. Spread each round with 1½ tablespoons pizza sauce or thick spaghetti sauce, ¼ cup chopped vegetables (mushrooms, zucchini, peppers), 1 tablespoon sliced black olives, and ¼ cup reduced-fat shredded mozzarella cheese. Heat for 8 minutes, or until the cheese just melts. Serve with 1 cup cooked broccoli florets. (393 calories)

POULTRY

MEXICAN CHICKEN WRAP

Preheat a toaster oven to 300°F. Combine 3 ounces (⅓ to ½ cup) shredded rotisserie chicken breast with 1 tablespoon light mayonnaise, 1 teaspoon Dijon mustard, and ½ teaspoon ground black pepper. Put the mixture onto a 6½ -inch whole grain tortilla and top with ¼ cup reduced-fat shredded Cheddar or Mexican-style cheese and 3 to 5 strips roasted red peppers from a jar (drained). Roll and heat for 5 minutes, and top with ⅓ cup salsa. Serve with ½ cup cantaloupe cubes. (411 calories)

ROASTED CHICKEN WITH BROWN RICE

Serve a 3-ounce (about the size of a deck of cards) roasted chicken breast with 1 ear fresh corn (or ½ cup cooked frozen corn), 1 cup cooked broccoli florets topped with 1 teaspoon butter, and ½ cup cooked brown rice. (393 calories)

SIZZLING STIR-FRY

Heat a nonstick skillet over medium heat and add 1 tablespoon olive oil or sesame oil. Add ⅓ cup sliced bell peppers; ⅓ cup broccoli, cauliflower, and carrots blend; and ¼ cup shelled edamame. Cook for 2 minutes. Add 3 ounces (⅓ cup) cooked, sliced chicken strips. Top with 2 teaspoons low-sodium soy sauce and continue cooking until thoroughly warmed. Serve over ½ cup cooked brown rice. (406 calories)

TURKEY, AVOCADO, AND BACON WRAP

On an 8-inch whole wheat tortilla, place 3 ounces turkey breast slices, 1 cooked crumbled bacon strip (save time by microwaving precooked bacon), ¼ of a diced avocado, 2 slices tomato or 1 tablespoon salsa, 1 tablespoon crumbled cotija or feta cheese; and a squeeze of lime juice. Roll and serve with ½ cup baby carrots and ½ cup mandarin oranges. (402 calories)

ZUCCHINI AND CHICKEN PASTA

Serve 1 cup cooked whole grain pasta with ⅓ cup spaghetti sauce and 3 ounces (about ⅓ cup) cooked chicken strips. Place ¾ cup chopped zucchini in a colander. Run hot top water over it for 1 minute (or if making the pasta fresh, drain the pasta over the zucchini in the colander). Mix all the ingredients together and serve topped with 2 tablespoons grated Parmesan. (397 calories)

MEAT

MUSHROOMS, BEEF, AND RICE

In a nonstick skillet over medium heat, cook 4 ounces crumbled raw 93% lean organic ground beef until no longer pink. Add ½ cup sliced fresh mushrooms, ⅓ cup chopped onion, ½ cup low-fat, low-sodium cream of mushroom soup, and 1 minced clove garlic. Stir thoroughly and cook for 5 to 7 minutes, until the mushrooms and onion are softened. Stir in ½ cup cooked brown rice. Serve with ½ cup cooked vegetables. (398 calories)

HAMBURGER WITH VEGETABLES

Serve a 4-ounce organic hamburger, grilled or broiled, loaded with ½ cup spinach leaves, a thick slice of tomato, and sliced onion. Smash ¼ avocado and spread on the bottom of a whole wheat hamburger bun, along with 1 tablespoon ketchup, if desired. Serve with 1 cup cooked green beans topped with 1 teaspoon slivered almonds. (402 calories)

ROAST BEEF SANDWICH

Spread 2 whole wheat bread slices with 1 tablespoon light mayonnaise each, plus ½ teaspoon horseradish mustard or Dijon mustard. Top with 3 ounces lean roast beef (about 3 slices), 2 slices tomato, and ½ cup spinach. Serve with 8 ounces V-8 vegetable juice. (406 calories)

SEAFOOD

BROCCOLI RICE WITH SHRIMP

In a medium pot, heat 1 teaspoon butter. Add 1 cup fresh broccoli, chopped into small pieces. Cook until bright green, about 2 minutes. Stir in 1 cup cooked brown rice, remove from the heat, cover, and keep warm. In a large nonstick skillet over medium heat, warm 2 teaspoons butter and 1 minced clove garlic (or ½ teaspoon garlic powder). Sauté the garlic for 30 seconds, then add about 10 large or 12 medium peeled shrimp (7 ounces). Cook for 4 to 5 minutes, stirring constantly, until the shrimp turn pink. Serve the shrimp over the broccoli rice. (396 calories)

BROILED SCALLOPS

Preheat the oven to 350°F. Rinse 6 ounces fresh scallops and place in a shallow baking pan. Sprinkle with 1 teaspoon garlic salt, 2 teaspoons melted butter, and 1 tablespoon fresh lemon juice. Broil for 8 minutes, or until the scallops turn golden brown. Serve with 1 slice French bread (about the size of your palm) and ½ cup cooked spinach seasoned with ¼ teaspoon ground black pepper and 1 teaspoon fresh lemon juice. (409 calories)

CRAB CAKES

Combine ¼ pound fresh lump crabmeat with ⅓ cup soft bread crumbs, ¼ cup chopped raw onion, ½ tablespoon fresh lemon juice, ½ tablespoon fat-free milk, ⅛ teaspoon salt, ⅛ teaspoon ground black pepper, and 1 slightly beaten egg white. Heat ½ tablespoon canola oil in a nonstick skillet over medium-high heat. Form the crab mixture into patties and cook on both sides until golden. Serve with 3 tablespoons tartar sauce and 2 cups mixed greens tossed with 1 teaspoon fresh lemon juice and 1 teaspoon olive oil. (402 calories)

GRILLED MAPLE MARINATED TUNA

Marinate 4 ounces tuna steak in 1 tablespoon maple syrup, 2 tablespoons fresh orange juice, and freshly ground black pepper to taste for 20 minutes. Remove from the marinade and grill or broil for approximately 3 minutes on each side. Serve with ½ large baked potato topped with 2 tablespoons reduced-fat sour cream and 8 large cooked asparagus spears. (404 calories)

SALMON, QUINOA, AND EDAMAME

Preheat the oven to 350°F. In a 1½-quart baking dish, pour ½ cup white wine and ½ cup water. Add 3 peppercorns, 1 bay leaf, and ½ clove garlic. Place in the oven. When it comes to a simmer, add 1 piece (3 ounces) boneless salmon fillet. Cook, skin side down, for 8 minutes, or until cooked all the way through. With a slotted spoon, remove the salmon from the liquid. Serve the salmon with 1 cup cooked quinoa and 1 cup steamed or microwaved shelled edamame with 1 teaspoon sesame seeds and a spritz of lemon. (400 calories)

SALADS

BLACK BEAN, CORN, AND PEPPER SALAD

Combine half a 15-ounce can of black beans (drained and rinsed) with ½ cup frozen, thawed corn kernels (or fresh corn from ½ cob), ½ fresh or roasted chopped red pepper, juice of ½ lime, a splash of olive oil, ½ teaspoon ground cumin, a pinch of salt, and half a palmful of chopped fresh cilantro. Serve with 4 ounces grilled or rotisserie chicken or 3 ounces grilled or baked salmon, or stir in ¾ cup cooked quinoa. (403 calories)

CHICKEN SALAD

Mix half of a 6-ounce can of chicken breast meat with 1 teaspoon horseradish spread, 2 tablespoons light mayonnaise, ¼ cup finely chopped celery, 10 sliced baby carrots, and 7 halved grapes. Spread on 1 toasted whole grain hamburger roll. (400 calories)

COBB SALAD

Combine 3 cups romaine lettuce leaves, 1 chopped plum tomato, and 1/4 cup chopped red onion and toss with 3 tablespoons light blue cheese salad dressing. Top with 1/4 cup reduced-fat shredded Cheddar cheese, 1 chopped hard-boiled egg, 1/4 sliced avocado, 2 tablespoons black olives, and 3 ounces (about 3 slices) low-sodium turkey breast cut into strips. (403 calories)

EGG SALAD WITH ROASTED RED PEPPERS

Prepare egg salad by combining 2 chopped hard-boiled eggs with 2 teaspoons horseradish spread, 2 tablespoons light mayonnaise, 1/4 cup chopped roasted red peppers from a jar (drained), and 1/4 cup finely chopped celery. Serve with 1 cup fat-free milk and 17 grapes. (394 calories)

GRILLED CHICKEN CAESAR SALAD

Begin with 3 cups chopped romaine lettuce. Warm 4 ounces (about 2/3 cup) chicken strips and add to the lettuce. Top the salad with 3 tablespoons light Caesar dressing, 1/3 cup croutons, and 2 tablespoons grated Parmesan cheese. Serve with 1 apple. (407 calories)

SPINACH-BLUE CHEESE SALAD

Toss together 2 cups spinach and 1 small tomato (cut into wedges) or 6 cherry tomatoes. Top with 2 tablespoons crumbled blue cheese, 1 sliced hard-boiled egg, 2 slices cooked and crumbled turkey bacon, and 2 tablespoons light Italian salad dressing. Serve with 2 multigrain crispbreads. (403 calories)

TACO SALAD

Begin with 2 cups romaine lettuce. Top with 1/2 cup canned (rinsed and drained) black beans, 1/4 cup reduced-fat shredded Cheddar cheese, 2 tablespoons sliced black olives, 1/2 cup salsa, and 2 tablespoons light sour cream. Top with 12 crumbled baked tortilla chips. (404 calories)

TOSSED SALAD WITH ROASTED CHICKEN AND FETA

Toss 2 cups mixed greens with 5 chopped baby carrots, 1 tablespoon sliced black olives. 1 medium sliced tomato, 1/4 avocado, 1/4 cup chopped red onion, and 2 tablespoons crumbled feta cheese. Toss with 2 teaspoons each olive oil and balsamic vinegar. Top with 2 ounces (about 1/2 cup) cold chopped roasted chicken. (399 calories)

TUNA-AVOCADO SALAD

Mash 1/2 avocado and flake in 1 can drained water-packed wild-caught tuna (5 ounces). Mix in 1/2 teaspoon white or apple-cider vinegar and 1/4 teaspoon brown mustard. Spoon onto 1 slice whole grain toast and serve with 1 cup carrot sticks. (401 calories)

TUNA, BEAN, AND CORN TOSSED SALAD

Combine half of a 6-ounce can drained water-packed tuna with 1/3 cup canned (rinsed and drained) beans (chickpeas and cannellini beans are good choices) and 1/3 cup corn kernels. Add 1/2 cup sliced cherry tomatoes, 1/2 cup chopped green or red pepper, and 1 stick reduced-fat string cheese, chopped. Toss with 2 tablespoons light salad dressing and add 1 to 2 tablespoons fresh parsley, basil, or dill, if desired. (401 calories)

SOUP

BLACK BEAN SOUP WITH SOUR CREAM

Heat 2 teaspoons olive oil in a medium saucepan over medium heat. Add 1/2 cup chopped onion, 1/4 cup chopped red bell pepper, and 1 chopped clove garlic. Cook for 5 minutes, or until tender. Add 1 cup low-sodium chicken broth, 1 cup canned black beans (drained and rinsed), 1/2 teaspoon cumin, and 1/2 teaspoon salt. Bring to a boil, then reduce the heat and simmer for 10 minutes. Gently mash the beans to thicken the soup. Serve with 1 tablespoon reduced-fat sour cream. (404 calories)

BUTTERNUT SQUASH-GINGER SOUP

In a medium saucepan over medium heat, warm 1 teaspoon olive oil. Cook ¼ cup chopped onion and 1 chopped garlic clove for about 5 minutes, until soft. Stir in 1 cup frozen thawed butternut squash, ½ cup light coconut milk, 1 teaspoon salt, and ¼ teaspoon ground ginger. Cook until warm, then blend with an immersion blender or in a regular blender until smooth. Top with ¼ cup chickpeas and 1 tablespoon pumpkin seeds. Serve with 7 thin wheat crackers. (402 calories)

CREAMY TOMATO SOUP

In a medium saucepan over medium heat, stir together 1 cup tomato puree, 1 cup fat-free milk, 1 tablespoon tomato paste, ½ teaspoon garlic powder, ½ teaspoon onion powder, and ¼ cup shredded low-fat Cheddar cheese. Heat until the cheese has melted and the soup is warmed through. Serve with a small banana and 5 small whole grain crackers. (410 calories)

LENTIL SOUP

In a medium saucepan over medium heat, warm 1 teaspoon olive oil. Add ¼ cup chopped onion, 3 chopped baby carrots, ½ teaspoon dried oregano, ½ teaspoon salt, and ½ teaspoon ground black pepper. Cook for about 5 minutes, until softened. Stir in 1½ cups low-sodium vegetable broth and 1 cup canned (rinsed and drained) lentils and heat for 10 minutes. Stir in ½ cup baby spinach and sprinkle with 1 teaspoon grated Parmesan cheese. Serve with 1 slice whole wheat toast spread with 1 teaspoon soft goat cheese. (407 calories)

MINESTRONE SOUP

In a slow cooker or large soup pot, combine 1 quart low-sodium chicken or vegetable broth, 1 can (14.5 ounces) diced tomatoes (with juice), 3 chopped carrots, 2 chopped ribs celery, 1 chopped onion, 1 or 2 minced cloves garlic, and 1 tablespoon dried oregano. Cook until the vegetables are tender, then add 1½ cups small whole grain pasta, such as ditalini, and 2 cans (15 ounces each) drained and rinsed beans—red and white kidney beans are traditional, but try swapping out 1 can for chickpeas or 1½ cups cut frozen green beans. Add 3 ounces fully cooked chopped organic chicken-apple sausage or 5 ounces baby spinach. Season to taste with salt and ground black pepper. Serve with 1 tablespoon freshly grated Parmesan cheese per serving. Makes 4 servings, so freeze 3 or refrigerate for quick lunches the rest of the week. (366 calories with just the soup; 403 calories with chicken-apple sausage; 380 calories with spinach)

RECIPES
Breakfasts

*Recipes are from the 21-day meal plan. The other recipes can be swapped into the meal plan or used to create your own meals.

BLUEBERRY-OAT PANCAKES

■ Serves 6
PREP TIME: **15 minutes**
TOTAL TIME: **35 minutes**

1¼ cups quick-cooking oats
½ cup whole wheat flour
2 tablespoons ground flaxseed
½ teaspoon baking powder
¼ teaspoon baking soda
   Pinch of salt

1 cup low-fat buttermilk or almond milk
2 large eggs
1 tablespoon canola oil
1 teaspoon freshly grated lemon zest
1½ cups blueberries
   Maple syrup (optional)

1. Combine the oats, flour, flaxseed, baking powder, baking soda, and salt in a large bowl.

2. In a medium bowl, combine the buttermilk or almond milk, eggs, oil, and lemon zest. Pour the buttermilk mixture into the oat mixture, stirring until just moistened. Gently fold in the blueberries with a rubber spatula. Set aside for 10 minutes.

3. Coat a large nonstick skillet or griddle with cooking spray and heat over medium heat. Spoon ¼ cupfuls of batter into the skillet, as many as possible without the pancakes touching. Cook 2½ to 3 minutes, until the tops begin to bubble slightly. Turn the pancakes and cook 2½ to 3 minutes longer, or until golden and cooked through. Transfer to a platter and set aside. Repeat with the remaining batter.

4. Stack 4 pancakes on each plate and drizzle with 2 teaspoons syrup, if using.

PER SERVING: 197 calories, 8 g protein, 28 g carbohydrates, 6 g sugar, 7 g total fat, 1 g saturated fat, 5 g fiber, 175 mg sodium

MAKE IT AHEAD

On the weekend, make a double or triple batch of pancakes. Cool on a rack. Pack between small pieces of waxed paper in a plastic storage container. To eat, remove the pancakes you want and heat in a toaster oven or microwave.

BREAKFAST BROWN RICE FRITTER

■ Serves 1
PREP TIME: **5 minutes**
TOTAL TIME: **15 minutes**

2 eggs
⅛ teaspoon garlic powder
⅛ teaspoon salt
⅛ teaspoon ground black pepper
¼ cup cooked brown rice
1 link fully cooked chicken sausage, chopped

2 tablespoons chopped onion
2 tablespoons coarsely chopped baby spinach
2 tablespoons chopped mushrooms
1½ teaspoons olive oil

1. In a medium bowl, whisk together the eggs, garlic powder, salt, and pepper. Stir in the rice, sausage, onion, spinach, and mushrooms. Form into a patty.

2. In a medium skillet over medium heat, heat the olive oil. Cook the patty for 6 minutes, turning once, or until browned.

PER SERVING: 380 calories, 25 g protein, 18 g carbohydrates, 3 g sugar, 23 g total fat, 6 g saturated fat, 2 g fiber, 770 mg sodium

BROCCOLI AND SAUSAGE EGG BAKE

Serves 4
PREP TIME: **15 minutes**
TOTAL TIME: **55 minutes**

1 large onion, chopped

4 cups broccoli florets, cut into small pieces

8 ounces raw turkey sausage

½ teaspoon dried sage

2½ cups 1% milk

5 eggs

¼ cup (1 ounce) cubed low-fat Cheddar cheese

4 slices 100% whole wheat bread, cubed

1. Preheat the oven to 350°F. Coat an 8 x 8-inch baking dish with cooking spray.

2. Coat a large nonstick skillet with cooking spray. Set over medium-high heat. Add the onion and broccoli. Cook for 3 to 4 minutes, or until almost soft. Add the sausage and sage. Cook, stirring often, for 5 minutes, or until the sausage is no longer pink.

3. Meanwhile, in a large bowl, combine the milk, eggs, and Cheddar. Add the bread cubes and the sausage mixture. Stir to mix, making sure that the bread cubes are moistened. Pour into the prepared baking dish. Press with the back of a spoon to pack the mixture.

4. Bake for 35 to 40 minutes, or until browned and slightly puffed. Cut into 4 pieces.

PER SERVING: 362 calories, 32 g protein, 28 g carbohydrates, 11 g sugar, 14 g total fat, 5 g saturated fat, 5 g fiber, 682 mg sodium

MAKE IT AHEAD

This dish may be assembled the night before cooking. Cover tightly with plastic wrap, and refrigerate. In the morning, remove the plastic wrap and bake according to the recipe directions.

Leftover portions also make terrific ready-made breakfasts. Store the cooled leftovers in an airtight container for up to 5 days. To reheat, remove one portion and place on a microwaveable dish. Cover with waxed paper. Microwave on medium power for 2 to 3 minutes, or until heated through.

BRUSCHETTA PANCAKES

■ Serves 1
PREP TIME: **5 minutes**
TOTAL TIME: **15 minutes**

⅓ cup rolled oats

1 tablespoon chia seeds

1 egg

3 tablespoons milk

4 tablespoons shredded part-skim mozzarella cheese

1 tablespoon + 1 teaspoon chopped fresh basil

⅛ teaspoon garlic powder

⅛ teaspoon salt

⅛ teaspoon ground black pepper

1½ teaspoons olive oil

⅓ cup chopped tomatoes

1. In a blender, combine the oats and chia seeds for about 30 seconds, until a fine crumb forms. Add the egg and milk and blend again for about 30 seconds until smooth. Stir in 2 tablespoons of the mozzarella and 1 tablespoon of the basil, then add the garlic powder, salt, and pepper.

2. Coat a medium skillet with the oil and heat over medium heat. Pour in the batter, forming 2 or 3 pancakes, and cook for 6 minutes, turning once, until golden on both sides. Top the pancakes with the remaining 2 tablespoons mozzarella, the tomatoes, and the remaining 1 teaspoon basil.

PER SERVING: 402 calories, 22 g protein, 29 g carbohydrates, 5 g sugar, 23 g total fat, 6.6 g saturated fat, 7 g fiber, 561 mg sodium

CASHEW-COCONUT MUESLI YOGURT

■ Serves 1
PREP TIME: **5 minutes**
TOTAL TIME: **10 minutes**

⅓ cup rolled oats

1½ tablespoons chopped cashews

1½ tablespoons unsweetened shredded coconut

¼ teaspoon ground cinnamon

¼ teaspoon ground ginger

½ cup plain Greek yogurt

½ banana, sliced

1. In a small bowl, combine the oats, cashews, coconut, cinnamon, and ginger. Fold in the yogurt. Set aside for 5 minutes, or until the oats soften.

2. Top with the banana.

PER SERVING: 406 calories, 18 g protein, 43 g carbohydrates, 14 g sugar, 19 g total fat, 10 g saturated fat, 6 g fiber, 38 mg sodium

CREAMY MOCHA FROST

Serves 1
PREP TIME: 5 minutes
TOTAL TIME: 5 minutes

1 small very ripe banana	1 teaspoon instant coffee granules
½ avocado, peeled and pitted	2 teaspoons chia seeds
1 cup milk	¼ cup soft (not silken) tofu, drained
2 teaspoons unsweetened cocoa powder	1 cup ice

In a blender, combine the banana, avocado, milk, cocoa, instant coffee, chia seeds, and tofu. Blend on high speed for 1 minute, or until smooth. Add the ice. Blend on high for 45 seconds, or until no ice chunks remain.

PER SERVING: 398 calories, 16 g protein, 38 g carbohydrates, 20 g sugar, 24 g total fat, 7 g saturated fat, 10 g fiber, 125 mg sodium

CRUSTLESS MINI BROCCOLI, CHEESE, AND BACON QUICHE

Serves 4
PREP TIME: 10 minutes
TOTAL TIME: 55 minutes

1 tablespoon olive oil	⅔ cup cooked quinoa
2 cups finely chopped broccoli florets	2 cups shredded reduced-fat Cheddar cheese
½ cup seeded and chopped red bell pepper	4 slices Canadian bacon, chopped
1½ cups whole milk	¼ teaspoon salt
6 eggs	¼ teaspoon ground black pepper

1. Preheat the oven to 350°F. Heat the oil in a medium skillet over medium-high heat. Add the broccoli and bell pepper and cook, stirring frequently, for 6 minutes, or until the broccoli is slightly tender. Remove from the skillet and set aside.

2. In a large bowl, whisk together the milk and eggs. Gently stir in the quinoa. Stir in the broccoli mixture, cheese, Canadian bacon, salt, and black pepper.

3. Coat a 12-cup muffin pan with cooking spray and pour ¼ to ⅓ cup of the mixture into each of 4 muffin cups. Bake for 25 minutes, or until the eggs are firm and a fork inserted in the center comes out clean. Let cool for 15 minutes, then remove from the pan. Refrigerate for up to 3 days, or freeze for up to 2 months.

PER SERVING: 388 calories 35 g protein, 16 g carbohydrates, 6 g sugar, 20 g total fat, 7.5 g saturated fat, 2 g fiber, 907 mg sodium

FRENCH TOAST WITH STRAWBERRY TOPPING

■ Serves 2
PREP TIME: **10 minutes**
TOTAL TIME: **20 minutes**

⅓ cup fresh orange juice

2 teaspoons honey

½ pint strawberries, sliced (about 1 cup)

2 teaspoons canola oil

2 eggs, lightly beaten

¼ cup fat-free milk

½ teaspoon vanilla extract

¼ teaspoon ground cinnamon

4 slices 100% whole multigrain bread

1. In a saucepan, combine the orange juice and honey over medium-high heat. Bring to a simmer, whisking to dissolve the honey. Reduce the heat and stir in the strawberries. Cook for 1 minute to soften the strawberries. Remove from the heat and set aside.

2. Heat the oil in a large nonstick skillet over medium-high heat. In a shallow bowl, combine the eggs, milk, vanilla, and cinnamon. Whisk until smooth. Dip the bread slices into the egg mixture, turning once. Place the bread in the pan and cook 2 to 2½ minutes per side, until golden. Serve with the strawberry topping.

PER SERVING: 354 calories, 16 g protein, 47 g carbohydrates, 21 g sugar, 12 g total fat, 2 g saturated fat, 10 g fiber, 359 mg sodium

MAKE IT AHEAD

Double the recipe, cool the toast, and then freeze in resealable plastic bags. Cool the strawberry sauce and refrigerate in an airtight container for up to a week. To serve, reheat the toast on a piece of aluminum foil in a toaster oven. If desired, reheat the strawberry sauce in a microwaveable dish for about 1 minute on medium power.

FRUIT AND SPICE CUT OATMEAL

Serves 4
PREP TIME: 10 minutes
TOTAL TIME: 40 minutes

1   cup steel-cut oats
⅛ teaspoon salt
1   large tart apple, cored and chopped
1   large pear, cored and chopped
¼ cup dried figs, chopped
1   tablespoon maple syrup

1   teaspoon pumpkin pie spice
½ teaspoon ground ginger
½ cup fat-free milk
1   cup pomegranate seeds
½ cup sliced almonds

1. In a medium saucepan, bring 3 cups water to a boil. Stir in the oats and salt and bring to a bare simmer. Cook for 15 minutes, stirring occasionally.

2. Stir in the apple, pear, figs, syrup, pumpkin pie spice, and ginger. Return to a bare simmer and cook, covered, for 15 minutes longer, or until the oats are tender but still have a slight bite to them.

3. Spoon the oatmeal into 4 bowls, drizzle each with 2 tablespoons milk, and top with ¼ cup pomegranate seeds and 2 tablespoons almonds.

PER SERVING: 372 calories, 11 g protein, 59 g carbohydrates, 21 g sugar, 9 g total fat, 1 g saturated fat, 10 g fiber, 98 mg sodium

HUMMUS, TOMATO, AND SPINACH BREAKFAST MUFFIN

Serves 1
PREP TIME: 3 minutes
TOTAL TIME: 10 minutes

2   teaspoons olive oil
1   egg
1   whole wheat or multigrain English muffin, split

3   tablespoons prepared hummus
1   thick tomato slice
    Baby spinach leaves

1. Heat the oil in a small skillet over medium heat. Add the egg and cook, turning once, for about 3 minutes, until the white is set and the yolk is firm.

2. Meanwhile, toast the muffin. Spread the hummus on the bottom half of the muffin. Top with the tomato, some spinach leaves, the egg, and the top of the English muffin.

PER SERVING: 375 calories, 16 g protein, 35 g carbohydrates, 6 g sugar, 20 g total fat, 4 g saturated fat, 8 g fiber, 500 mg sodium

IRISH OATS QUICK BREAD

■ Serves 6
PREP TIME: **20 minutes**
TOTAL TIME: **1 hour 5 minutes**

1¾ cups whole wheat flour
½ cup rolled oats + 1 tablespoon for topping
2 tablespoons ground flaxseed
1 teaspoon baking soda

⅛ teaspoon salt
1 egg
1 tablespoon honey
1 cup + 2 tablespoons low-fat buttermilk

1. Preheat the oven to 375°F. Lightly coat an 8 x 5 x 3-inch loaf pan with cooking spray.

2. In a large mixing bowl, combine the flour, ½ cup oats, flaxseed, baking soda, and salt.

3. In a medium bowl, beat the egg and honey with a fork until smooth. Add the buttermilk and stir to mix. Add the wet ingredients to the dry ingredients and stir just until combined. Transfer to the prepared pan and sprinkle with 1 tablespoon oats.

3. Bake for about 45 minutes, or until a wooden pick comes out clean. Turn out onto a rack and let cool. Serve warm or cold.

PER SERVING: 200 calories, 9 g protein, 36 g carbohydrates, 5 g sugar, 3 g total fat, 1 g saturated fat, 5 g fiber, 304 mg sodium

MAKE IT AHEAD

Freeze cooled slices individually in aluminum foil. Thaw in a toaster oven.

MAKE IT DIFFERENT

Add ¼ cup raisins or dried cranberries with the buttermilk.

MEDITERRANEAN SCRAMBLE

Serves 1
PREP TIME: 5 minutes
TOTAL TIME: 10 minutes

2 eggs

1 tablespoon water or milk

1 teaspoon olive oil

½ cup coarsely chopped baby spinach

⅓ cup chopped tomato

⅓ cup rinsed and drained canned white beans

2 tablespoons feta cheese

1 tablespoon kalamata olives, coarsely chopped

1. In a small bowl, whisk the eggs together with the water or milk.

2. Heat the oil in a nonstick skillet over medium-high heat. Add the eggs and scramble with the spinach, tomato, beans, feta, and olives for about 4 minutes, or until the eggs are set.

PER SERVING: 404 calories, 23 g protein, 25 g carbohydrates, 3 g sugar, 24 g total fat, 7 g saturated fat, 6 g fiber, 705 mg sodium

MUESLI WITH DRIED FRUIT AND WALNUTS

Serves 8
PREP TIME: 10 minutes
TOTAL TIME: 30 minutes

4 cups regular or steel-cut oats

½ cup chopped walnuts

⅓ cup chopped dried apricots

⅓ cup coarsely chopped dried apples

⅓ cup dried cherries

¼ cup ground flaxseed

1. Preheat the oven to 375°F.

2. Spread the oats evenly on a rimmed baking sheet and bake, stirring occasionally, for 10 minutes. Stir in the walnuts and bake for 7 to 10 minutes longer, or until lightly browned. Scrape into a large bowl and let cool.

3. Stir in the apricots, apples, cherries, and flaxseed. Refrigerate the muesli in a tightly sealed container.

PER SERVING: 279 calories, 9 g protein, 41 g carbohydrates, 10 g sugar, 9 g total fat, 1 g saturated fat, 7 g fiber, 25 mg sodium

MAKE IT QUICKER

This version of dry muesli is a simpler version of granola. If you prefer, you can skip toasting the oats altogether and instead simply toast the walnuts in a dry skillet.

NUTTY CHOCO-BANANA OATMEAL

Serves 1
PREP TIME: **5 minutes**
TOTAL TIME: **5 minutes**

1¼ cups unsweetened soy milk or whole milk
½ cup rolled oats
½ small ripe banana, mashed

1 tablespoon unsweetened cocoa powder
1 tablespoon walnuts
1 teaspoon ground flaxseeds

1. In a medium microwaveable bowl, combine the soy milk or milk, oats, banana, and cocoa. Microwave on high power for 60 to 90 seconds. Stir and microwave for 30 to 60 seconds longer, or until the oats are soft.

2. Remove from the microwave and stir in the walnuts and flaxseeds.

PER SERVING: 392 calories, 21 g protein, 50 g carbohydrates, 8 g sugar, 15 g total fat, 1.5 g saturated fat, 13 g fiber, 40 mg sodium

PEACH SMOOTHIE

Serves 2
PREP TIME: **5 minutes**
TOTAL TIME: **5 minutes**

2 cups whole milk
2 cups frozen sliced peaches
1 banana

2 tablespoons almond butter
¼ teaspoon ground cinnamon
Ice cubes (optional)

In a blender, combine the milk, peaches, banana, almond butter, and cinnamon. Blend until smooth and creamy. Add a few ice cubes, if desired, and blend again.

PER SERVING: 348 calories, 13 g protein, 42 g carbohydrates, 32 g sugar, 17 g total fat, 6 g saturated fat, 5 g fiber, 142 mg sodium

PINEAPPLE-STRAWBERRY SMOOTHIE

■ Serves 1
PREP TIME: **5 minutes**
TOTAL TIME: **5 minutes**

1 cup frozen strawberries

¾ cup fat-free plain yogurt

½ cup unsweetened pineapple chunks (with juice)

¼ cup plain unsweetened almond milk

In a blender, combine the strawberries, yogurt, pineapple (including juice), and almond milk. Blend until smooth and creamy.

PER SERVING: 212 calories, 9 g protein, 48 g carbohydrates, 35 g sugar, 1 g total fat, 0 g saturated fat, 4 g fiber, 150 mg sodium

PUMPKIN SPICE OATS

■ Serves 1
PREP TIME: **5 minutes**
TOTAL TIME: **15 minutes**

⅓ cup rolled oats

⅔ cup milk

¼ cup pumpkin puree

1 teaspoon almond butter

¼ teaspoon pumpkin pie spice + more for sprinkling

⅛ teaspoon salt

2 tablespoons plain Greek yogurt

2 tablespoons chopped toasted pecans

1. In a small saucepan, whisk the oats, milk, pumpkin puree, almond butter, pumpkin pie spice, and salt. Cook over high heat until the mixture comes to a boil. Reduce the heat to medium-low and simmer for 7 to 10 minutes, or until the oats are soft and thick.

2. Remove from the heat and top with the yogurt, a pinch of pumpkin pie spice, and the pecans.

PER SERVING: 382 calories, 15 g protein, 35 g carbohydrates, 13 g sugar, 21 g total fat, 5.5 g saturated fat, 7 g fiber, 384 mg sodium.

MAKE IT QUICKER

Oatmeal can easily be made in the microwave. Use a larger microwaveable bowl than you think you'll need, since the high power can cause the oats and milk to boil over. Combine the oats and milk, microwave on high power for 60 to 90 seconds, stir, and microwave for 30 to 60 seconds longer, until the oats are soft. Stir in the remaining ingredients in step 1, then proceed.

SCRAMBLED EGGS WITH SPINACH, TOMATOES, AND CANADIAN BACON

■ Serves 2
PREP TIME: **5 minutes**
TOTAL TIME: **10 minutes**

6 eggs

½ teaspoon Cajun seasoning

1 teaspoon extra-virgin olive oil

2 slices (2 ounces) Canadian bacon, chopped

2 cups packed baby spinach leaves, chopped

½ cup grape or cherry tomatoes, chopped

Ground black pepper

4 slices multigrain toast

1. In a small bowl, combine the eggs and Cajun seasoning. Beat with a fork until smooth.

2. Heat the oil in a nonstick skillet over medium heat. Add the bacon, spinach, and tomatoes. Cook, stirring, for about 2 minutes, or until the spinach is wilted.

3. Add the egg mixture. Cook, stirring, for about 2 minutes, or until the eggs are set. Season to taste with the pepper.

4. Place the eggs on 2 serving plates and serve with the toast.

PER SERVING: 390 calories, 30 g protein, 26 g carbohydrates, 2 g sugar, 20 g total fat, 6 g saturated fat, 7 g fiber, 880 mg sodium

VEGETABLE QUICHE

Serves 4
PREP TIME: 15 minutes
TOTAL TIME: 60 minutes

1   premade or store-bought unbaked pie crust (9-inch)

1   teaspoons extra-virgin olive oil

½   medium onion, chopped

1   large carrot, finely chopped

½   large red bell pepper, seeded and diced

4   ounces sliced cremini (baby bella) mushrooms

4   eggs

¾   teaspoon dry mustard

⅓   cup chopped fresh parsley

¼   cup (1 ounce) shredded low-fat extra-sharp Cheddar cheese

Hot-pepper sauce (optional)

1. Preheat the oven to 350°F.

2. Roll the pie dough out on a lightly floured surface, and transfer to a pie plate. Trim the edges, if necessary, to overhang by ½ inch. Tuck under the extra dough and crimp the edges of the crust all around the edge.

3. Heat the oil in a large nonstick skillet over medium-high heat. Add the onion, carrot, pepper, and mushrooms and cook, stirring occasionally, for 5 minutes, or until the vegetables are soft.

4. In a large bowl, whisk together the eggs, mustard, and parsley. Add the Cheddar and the cooked vegetables and stir just to combine. Pour into the prepared pie crust.

5. Bake for 35 minutes, or until the quiche is set and lightly browned. Let it sit for 5 minutes before cutting into 4 wedges. Serve with hot-pepper sauce (if using).

PER SERVING: 390 calories, 11 g protein, 36 g carbohydrates, 6 g sugar, 22 g total fat, 8.5 g saturated fat, 3 g fiber, 385 mg sodium

MAKE IT AHEAD

For instant breakfasts, bake the quiche on a weekend or weeknight. Cool the quiche completely. Cover tightly with plastic wrap and refrigerate for up to 5 days. Quiche can be eaten at room temperature or placed on a microwaveable plate, covered with waxed paper, and cooked on medium power for 1 to 2 minutes (per serving), or until warmed.

RECIPES
Lunches and Dinners

Vegetarian Dishes

BROCCOLI, MUSHROOM, AND TOFU STIR-FRY WITH WALNUTS*
(page 271)

CURRIED BLACK-BEAN-AND-CORN BURGER
OVER QUINOA SALAD* (page 272)

GREEK VEGETABLE SANDWICHES* (page 273)

HEARTY LENTIL-QUINOA BOWL (page 274)

PINTO BEANS AND PASTA IN TOMATO-BASIL SAUCE* (page 275)

Poultry Dishes

BEAN AND TURKEY CHILI* (page 276)

ARROZ CON POLLO* (page 277)

CHICKEN AND RICE SALAD WITH PECANS* (page 278)

CHICKEN GYROS WITH YOGURT-CUCUMBER SAUCE* (page 279)

CRUNCHY SESAME CHICKEN AND BULGUR BOWL* (page 280)

ORANGE CHICKEN-AND-BROCCOLI STIR-FRY* (page 281)

OVEN-FRIED ROSEMARY CHICKEN BREASTS
WITH FARRO AND ASPARAGUS* (page 282)

TURKEY MEAT LOAF WITH ROASTED VEGETABLES* (page 283)

TURKEY-AND-RED-CABBAGE-SLAW SANDWICH* (page 284)

Meat Dishes

BRAISED BEEF WITH MUSHROOMS AND ZOODLES (page 285)

PORK TENDER WRAP IN A CORN TORTILLA* (page 286)

ROSEMARY-ROASTED BABY POTATOES AND CARROTS
WITH SIRLOIN* (page 287)

SAGE-ROASTED PORK TENDERLOIN WITH STUFFED
ACORN SQUASH* (page 288)

Seafood Dishes

BROILED MUSTARD SALMON WITH ROASTED BROCCOLI
AND MILLET (page 289)

GRILLED SARDINES OVER WILTED ARUGULA (page 290)

GRILLED TROUT WITH CHIVE AND DILL SAUCE* (page 291)

LEMON-SALMON TABBOULEH (page 292)

MAHI, MANGO, AND AVOCADO QUESADILLAS* (page 293)

PISTACHIO-CRUSTED WILD SALMON* (page 294)

ROASTED ARCTIC CHAR, CARROTS, AND LEEKS WITH PENNE*
(page 295)

SESAME SCALLOP SKEWERS WITH BABY BOK CHOY
AND GREEN TEA RICE* (page 296)

SEVEN-VEGETABLE COUSCOUS WITH BLACK COD (page 297)

SHELLFISH SCAMPI OVER CAULIFLOWER "RICE"* (page 298)

TUNA STEAKS WITH MILLET AND NECTARINE SALSA
(page 299)

WILD SALMON WITH SWISS CHARD AND COUSCOUS*
(page 300)

*Recipes are from the 21-day meal plan. The other recipes can be swapped into the meal plans or used to create your own meals.

VEGETARIAN DISHES

BROCCOLI, MUSHROOM, AND TOFU STIR-FRY WITH WALNUTS

■ Serves 4
PREP TIME: 10 minutes
TOTAL TIME: 50 minutes

12–14 ounces firm tofu

1 cup quinoa

3 teaspoons canola oil

8 ounces sliced cremini (baby bella) mushrooms

4 cups broccoli florets

1 bunch scallions, thinly sliced

1 large clove garlic, minced

1 tablespoon soy sauce

⅓ cup chopped walnuts

1. Place the tofu on a paper towel–lined plate and top with a cutting board or large plate. Place several canned goods on the board to weigh it down. Let the tofu rest for 30 minutes while the water is squeezed out.

2. Meanwhile, cook the quinoa according to package directions. Remove from the heat and set aside.

3. Heat 1 teaspoon of the oil in a wok or large skillet over medium-high heat. Add the mushrooms. Cover and cook for about 1 minute, or until the mushrooms start to sizzle. Stir and re-cover. Continue cooking for about 4 minutes, or until the mushrooms give off their liquid.

4. Add the broccoli, scallions, and garlic. Cover and cook for about 2 minutes, or until the broccoli is bright green. Remove the mushrooms and broccoli to a plate.

5. Set the skillet back on medium-high heat. Heat the remaining 2 teaspoons oil. Cut the tofu into small cubes (discard the water) and add it to the pan. Cook for about 5 minutes, stirring constantly, until golden.

6. Return the broccoli mixture to the skillet. Add the soy sauce. Cook, stirring, for 2 minutes to blend the flavors.

7. Sprinkle on the walnuts. Serve each portion with ¾ cup quinoa.

PER SERVING: 371 calories, 19 g protein, 40 g carbohydrates, 4 g sugar, 16 g total fat, 2 g saturated fat, 8 g fiber, 257 mg sodium

MAKE IT AHEAD

To have pressed and drained tofu on hand, cut the block into 6 slices. Arrange on a small baking sheet without touching. Freeze overnight or until solid. Pack in a resealable plastic freezer bag. To thaw, place the desired number of tofu slices on a microwaveable dish. Cover with waxed paper. Cook on medium-low power for about 2 minutes, or until thawed. With clean hands, squeeze each slice like a sponge to release the water.

CURRIED BLACK-BEAN-AND-CORN BURGER OVER QUINOA SALAD

■ Serves 1

PREP TIME: **10 minutes**

TOTAL TIME: **25 minutes**

½ cup black beans

1 egg, lightly beaten

¼ teaspoon curry power

⅛ teaspoon onion powder

⅛ teaspoon salt

⅛ teaspoon ground black pepper

¼ cup corn kernels

2 teaspoons olive oil

1 teaspoon apple-cider vinegar

¼ teaspoon minced garlic

½ cup chopped cucumber

⅓ cup seeded and chopped red bell pepper

⅓ cup cooked quinoa

1. If using canned beans, rinse and drain before using. In a medium bowl, mash the beans. Mix in the egg, curry powder, onion powder, salt, and black pepper. Stir in the corn and form the mixture into a patty.

2. In a small skillet over medium heat, heat 1 teaspoon of the oil. Cook the burger for 12 minutes, turning once, until golden on both sides.

3. Meanwhile, in a small bowl, whisk together the remaining 1 teaspoon oil, the vinegar, and garlic. Add the cucumber, bell pepper, and quinoa. Gently toss to coat. Serve the burger over the salad.

PER SERVING: 387 calories, 18 g protein, 46 g carbohydrates, 7 g sugar, 16 g total fat, 3 g saturated fat, 11 g fiber, 836 mg sodium

GREEK VEGETABLE SANDWICHES

■ Serves 4
PREP TIME: 10 minutes
TOTAL TIME: 20 minutes

2 small eggplants (8 ounces each),
  each cut into 8 slices

1 red onion, cut into 4 slices

1 red bell pepper, seeded
  and cut into 4 sections

4 ounces halloumi or feta cheese,
  cut into 4 equal-size planks

1 tablespoon extra-virgin olive oil

¼ teaspoon salt

¼ teaspoon ground black pepper

1 can (15 ounces) cannellini beans,
  drained and rinsed

1 tablespoon fresh lemon juice or white
  wine vinegar

1 teaspoon chopped fresh rosemary or
  ¼ teaspoon dried

2 multigrain submarine rolls (3 ounces
  each), halved lengthwise

2 roma tomatoes, sliced lengthwise

8 leaves romaine

1. Coat a grill rack with cooking spray, then preheat.

2. Lightly brush the eggplant, onion, bell pepper, and halloumi or feta with the oil, then sprinkle with the salt and black pepper. Grill the onion and bell pepper for 6 to 7 minutes per side, until they are tender and well marked. A few minutes after adding the onions, place the eggplant on the grill and cook 4 to 5 minutes per side, until they are tender and well marked. Near the end of grilling, add the cheese planks and grill about 2 minutes per side, until well marked. Separate the onion slices into rings and slice the peppers into strips. Set all aside.

3. In a small bowl, combine the beans, lemon juice or vinegar, and rosemary. Mash lightly with a fork until combined.

4. Grill the rolls, cut side down, for about 45 seconds, until lightly toasted. Spread the cut halves with the bean mixture and top each with one-quarter of the tomato slices, 4 eggplant slices, one-quarter of the onion rings and pepper strips, 1 plank of cheese, and 2 romaine leaves to serve as the top "bun."

PER SERVING: 344 calories, 16 g protein, 44 g carbohydrates, 11 g sugar, 16 g total fat, 6.5 g saturated fat, 10 g fiber, 971 mg sodium

MAKE IT AHEAD

The eggplant, onion, bell pepper, and cheese can all be grilled, cooled, and refrigerated in a tightly sealed container for up to 5 days. The bean mixture can also be refrigerated for up to 5 days. To make the sandwiches, pick up the recipe at step 4.

HEARTY LENTIL-QUINOA BOWL

■ Serves 1

PREP TIME: **5 minutes**

TOTAL TIME: **30 minutes**

1 teaspoon olive oil

¼ cup shredded carrot

¼ cup finely chopped onion

¼ cup brown lentils

1 clove garlic, minced

¼ teaspoon salt

¼ teaspoon ground cumin

¼ teaspoon turmeric (optional)

¼ cup quinoa

1. In a medium saucepan over medium heat, warm the oil. Add the carrot and onion and cook for 5 minutes, or until soft and golden. Add the lentils, garlic, salt, cumin, and turmeric (if using) and stir for 1 minute, until fragrant.

2. Add 1 cup water. Bring to a boil, cover, reduce the heat, and simmer for 10 minutes, until the lentils begin to soften.

3. Stir in the quinoa, cover again, and simmer for about 10 minutes longer, until the lentils and quinoa are tender.

PER SERVING: 399 calories, 19 g protein, 64 g carbohydrates, 6 g sugar, 8 g total fat, 1 g saturated fat, 19 g fiber, 618 mg sodium

PINTO BEANS AND PASTA IN TOMATO-BASIL SAUCE

■ Serves 4
PREP TIME: **8 minutes**
TOTAL TIME: **30 minutes**

8 ounces whole grain or whole wheat pasta such as rotini, penne, or farfalle

1 tablespoon extra-virgin oil

1 medium onion, sliced

2 large cloves garlic, thinly sliced

1 small zucchini (6 ounces), cut into ¼-inch chunks

¼ teaspoon salt

¼ teaspoon ground black pepper

1 can (14½ ounces) diced tomatoes (with juice)

1 can (15 ounces) pinto beans, drained and rinsed

2 tablespoons ground flaxseed

2 tablespoons chopped fresh basil

¼ cup freshly grated Parmesan cheese or nutritional yeast

1. Prepare the pasta according to package directions.

2. Meanwhile, warm the oil in a large nonstick skillet over medium heat. Add the onion and garlic and cook, stirring often, for about 5 minutes, until tender. Add the zucchini and sprinkle with the salt and pepper. Stir to blend well with the onion.

3. Add the tomatoes with juice and bring to a simmer. Cook, uncovered, stirring occasionally, for 6 to 8 minutes, until the zucchini is tender. Add the beans and flaxseed. Cover and cook 2 to 3 minutes, just until heated through. Stir in the basil. Serve with the pasta, sprinkled with 1 tablespoon Parmesan or nutritional yeast.

PER SERVING: 378 calories, 17 g protein, 63 g carbohydrates, 6 g sugars, 8 g fat, 2 g saturated fat, 11 g fiber, 694 mg sodium

MAKE IT AHEAD

The beans can be refrigerated in a tightly sealed container for up to 1 week or frozen for up to 1 month.

MAKE IT DIFFERENT

Using nutritional yeast instead of Parmesan cheese keeps this dish vegan. Found in the natural foods section of most grocery stores, nutritional yeast has a cheesy, nutty taste. Look for the flakes, and don't confuse it with brewer's yeast, which is sometimes labeled as a nutritional additive.

POULTRY DISHES

BEAN AND TURKEY CHILI

▓ Serves 6
PREP TIME: **10 minutes**
TOTAL TIME: **40 minutes**

1 tablespoon extra-virgin olive oil

1 onion, chopped

1 green bell pepper, seeded and chopped

2 cloves garlic, minced

1 jalapeño pepper, stemmed, seeded, and minced (wear plastic gloves when handling)

1 tablespoon dried oregano

1 tablespoon chili powder

1 pound ground turkey

1 can (28 ounces) diced tomatoes (with juice)

1 can (15 ounces) tomato sauce

½ cup bulgur

2 cans (15 ounces each) red kidney beans, drained and rinsed

½ cup plain Greek yogurt or sour cream

6 tablespoons pumpkin seeds

Hot-pepper sauce (optional)

1. Warm the oil in a Dutch oven or large pot over medium heat. Add the onion, bell pepper, garlic, jalapeño, oregano, and chili powder. Cook, stirring occasionally, for 5 minutes, or until softened. Add the turkey and cook, stirring to break up the turkey, for 5 minutes, or until the turkey is no longer pink.

2. Add the tomatoes (with juice), tomato sauce, and 2 cups water. Increase the heat to medium-high and bring to a simmer. Stir in the bulgur and kidney beans. Reduce the heat to medium and simmer for 15 minutes, or until thickened.

3. Spoon into bowls and top each portion with 1 tablespoon of the yogurt or sour cream, 1 tablespoon of the pepitas, and hot-pepper sauce (if using).

PER SERVING: 379 calories, 27 g protein, 40 carbohydrates, 11 g sugar, 13 g total fat, 3 g saturated fat, 10 g fiber, 975 mg sodium

MAKE IT DIFFERENT

Feel free to change up the beans in this recipe: Opt for pinto, black, navy, cannellini, or great Northern beans. Terrific low-fat chili toppers and add-ons include any low-fat shredded cheese, lime wedges, chopped fresh cilantro, chopped fresh parsley, and shredded carrots.

ARROZ CON POLLO

■ Serves 4
PREP TIME: 10 minutes
TOTAL TIME: 1 hour

1 pound boneless, skinless chicken thighs, cut into ½-inch-wide strips
¼ teaspoon salt
¼ teaspoon ground black pepper
3 teaspoons olive oil
1 large onion, chopped
1 red bell pepper, seeded and chopped
2 cloves garlic, minced

1 cup brown rice
2 teaspoons ground cumin
1 can (14½ ounces) diced tomatoes (with juice)
2 cups reduced-sodium chicken broth
1½ cups frozen shelled edamame or peas
Crushed red-pepper flakes

1. Sprinkle the chicken with ⅛ teaspoon of the salt and ⅛ teaspoon of the black pepper. Heat 2 teaspoons of the oil in a large pot over medium-high heat. Add the chicken and cook for about 2 minutes per side, until browned. Transfer to a plate and set aside.

2. Return the pot to the stove and add the onion, bell pepper, and garlic. Cook, stirring occasionally, for about 4 minutes, until the vegetables start to soften. Stir in the rice, cumin, the remaining ⅛ teaspoon salt, and the remaining ⅛ teaspoon black pepper. Cook, stirring, for 1 minute.

3. Add the reserved chicken, tomatoes (with juice), and broth. Bring to a boil, reduce the heat to medium-low, cover, and simmer for about 35 minutes, until the liquid has been absorbed and the rice is tender.

4. Stir in the edamame or peas. Cook for 2 minutes, or until heated through. Remove from the heat and let stand for 5 minutes. Serve with red-pepper flakes at the table.

PER SERVING: 388 calories, 36 g protein, 34 g carbohydrates, 8 g sugar, 12 g total fat, 2 g saturated fat, 6 g fiber, 522 mg sodium

MAKE IT AHEAD

Many main dishes cooked in a sauce taste as good as freshly cooked, if not better, when they are reheated. If you like, you can make this dish on a weekend afternoon, cool it, and refrigerate it in a tightly sealed container for up to 5 days. To reheat, transfer to a pot and reheat gently over medium heat. Stir in a few tablespoons of water, if needed, to loosen the sauce.

CHICKEN AND RICE SALAD WITH PECANS

■ Serves 2

PREP TIME: **10 minutes**

TOTAL TIME: **10 minutes**

⅓ cup plain Greek yogurt

1 teaspoon grated orange zest

3 tablespoons fresh orange juice

¼ teaspoon salt

¼ teaspoon black pepper

1½ cups chopped cooked boneless, skinless chicken

1 cup cooked brown basmati rice

4 scallions, sliced

1 rib celery with leaves, minced

3 tablespoons chopped pecans

2 cups torn red romaine lettuce leaves

In a large bowl, whisk together the yogurt, orange zest, orange juice, salt, and pepper. Add the chicken, rice, scallions, celery, and pecans and toss well. Serve on a bed of lettuce.

PER SERVING: 405 calories, 40 g protein, 31 g carbohydrates, 7 g sugar, 14 g total fat, 3 g saturated fat, 4 g fiber, 416 mg sodium

MAKE IT QUICKER

This salad goes from refrigerator to plate in less than 10 minutes thanks to already-cooked chicken and rice. Use a rotisserie chicken or grill an extra chicken breast on a previous evening. For the rice, many brands offer cooked rice in the freezer or packaged foods sections of the grocery stores—check labels to ensure there are no ingredients other than rice.

CHICKEN GYROS WITH YOGURT-CUCUMBER SAUCE

■ Serves 2
PREP TIME: 15 minutes
TOTAL TIME: 35 minutes

8 ounces boneless, skinless chicken breast halves

1 teaspoon extra-virgin olive oil

½ teaspoon dried oregano

⅛ teaspoon ground black pepper

2 multigrain pitas

½ cup chopped romaine lettuce

1 plum tomato, chopped

¼ small red onion, thinly sliced

2 tablespoons kalamata olives, sliced

½ cup plain Greek yogurt

¼ cucumber, peeled, seeded, and grated, excess liquid squeezed out

1 small clove garlic, minced

1. Coat a grill pan with cooking spray and heat over medium-high heat. In a bowl, combine the chicken, oil, oregano, and pepper. Place on the pan and grill for 5 to 6 minutes per side, or until a thermometer inserted into the thickest portion registers 165°F and the juices run clear. Transfer to a cutting board, let rest for 5 minutes, and cut into thin slices.

2. Toast the pitas. Cut into half-moons. With the tip of a knife, open each half to make a pocket. Fill each pita half with equal amounts of romaine, tomato, onion, olives, and chicken.

3. In a small bowl, combine the yogurt, cucumber, and garlic. Spoon over the chicken.

PER SERVING: 399 calories, 35 g protein, 33 g carbohydrates, 5 g sugar, 15 g total fat, 4 g saturated fat, 5 g fiber, 717 mg sodium

CRUNCHY SESAME CHICKEN AND BULGUR BOWL

Serves 1
PREP TIME: **10 minutes**
TOTAL TIME: **10 minutes**

1 tablespoon rice vinegar

1½ teaspoons toasted sesame oil

½ clove garlic, minced

½ teaspoon soy sauce

3 ounces skinless grilled or rotisserie chicken breast

1 cup coarsely chopped baby spinach

⅔ cup cooked bulgur

1 carrot, shredded

1 scallion, chopped

1 tablespoon chopped roasted salted peanuts

1. In a small bowl, whisk together the vinegar, oil, garlic, and soy sauce.

2. Using a fork, shred the chicken. Transfer to a medium bowl. Add the spinach, bulgur, carrot, scallion, and peanuts. Gently toss to combine. Drizzle with the dressing and toss to coat.

PER SERVING: 395 calories, 35 g protein, 33 g carbohydrates, 4 g sugar, 15 g total fat, 2.5 g saturated fat, 9 g fiber, 313 mg sodium

ORANGE CHICKEN-AND-BROCCOLI STIR-FRY

■ Serves 4
PREP TIME: **15 minutes**
TOTAL TIME: **30 minutes**

6 ounces soba noodles

1½ pounds broccoli (whole stalks)

⅓ cup fresh orange juice

1 tablespoon soy sauce

2 teaspoons cornstarch

2 teaspoons canola or peanut oil

1 pound chicken tenders, trimmed and cut into 1-inch pieces

3 scallions, sliced

3 large cloves garlic, minced

1 tablespoon minced fresh ginger

⅓ cup reduced-sodium chicken broth

1 red bell pepper, seeded and thinly sliced

1 navel orange, cut into small chunks

2 teaspoons toasted sesame oil

1 teaspoon toasted sesame seeds

1. Prepare the soba noodles according to package directions. Set aside.

2. Trim and discard any tough part on the bottom of the broccoli stems. Cut the stems into thin slices and the florets into bite-size pieces.

3. In a small bowl, combine the orange juice, soy sauce, and cornstarch. Stir until blended. Set aside.

4. Heat the canola or peanut oil in a wok or large nonstick skillet over high heat. Add the chicken and cook, stirring frequently, for 2 to 3 minutes, or until opaque. Add the scallions, garlic, and ginger. Stir to combine. With a slotted spoon, remove the chicken to a plate.

5. Add the broth and broccoli to the mixture in the wok and reduce the heat to medium. Cover and cook for 2 minutes. Increase the heat to high and add the bell pepper. Cook, stirring frequently, for 2 minutes, or until the broth evaporates and the vegetables are crisp-tender.

6. Stir the sauce and add it to the wok along with the chicken. Cook, stirring constantly, for 1 to 2 minutes, or until the sauce thickens and the chicken is hot. Stir in the orange, sesame oil, and sesame seeds. Divide among 4 bowls with the soba noodles.

PER SERVING: 404 calories, 39 g protein, 55 g carbohydrates, 9 g sugar, 7 g total fat, 1 g saturated fat, 6 g fiber, 671 mg sodium

MAKE IT AHEAD

Because of the high heat involved, stir-fries come together in a flash. Have everything chopped and ready to go before you begin to cook—do it earlier in the week, and you've just shaved 15 minutes of prep time from tonight's dinner.

OVEN-FRIED ROSEMARY CHICKEN BREASTS WITH FARRO AND ASPARAGUS

■ Serves 4

PREP TIME: **10 minutes**

TOTAL TIME: **25 minutes**

2 cups reduced-sodium chicken broth or water

1 cup pearled farro

4 boneless, skinless chicken breasts (about 5 ounces each)

1 tablespoon dried rosemary, crumbled

1 tablespoon ground flaxseed

4 teaspoons extra-virgin olive oil

1 large clove garlic, minced

¼ teaspoon salt

¼ teaspoon ground black pepper

1 pound asparagus, trimmed

1 tablespoon balsamic vinegar

1. Preheat the oven to 475°F and arrange racks in the top and bottom thirds of the oven.

2. Bring the chicken broth or water to a boil in a medium saucepan. Add the farro, lower the heat, and simmer for 15 to 20 minutes, until the grains are al dente,.

3. Meanwhile, make several shallow, diagonal cuts into the smoother, rounder side of each chicken breast. In a small bowl, combine the rosemary, flaxseed, 3 teaspoons of the oil, the garlic, and ⅛ teaspoon of the salt and ⅛ teaspoon of the pepper. Rub the mixture onto all sides of the chicken.

4. Arrange the asparagus on a small baking sheet and toss with the remaining 1 teaspoon oil, the remaining ⅛ teaspoon salt, and the remaining ⅛ teaspoon pepper.

5. Place an ovenproof skillet over high heat. Coat with cooking spray. Place the chicken, cut side down, in the skillet. Cover and cook for 5 minutes. Uncover, flip the chicken, and slide the skillet into the preheated oven on the lower rack. Put the asparagus on the top rack.

6. Bake the asparagus for 10 to 15 minutes, until golden brown in spots. Remove from the oven and drizzle with the vinegar. Bake the chicken for 10 minutes, or until a thermometer inserted in the thickest portion registers 165°F and the juices run clear. Allow to rest for 5 minutes before cutting diagonally into slices. Divide among 4 plates, with equal portions of the asparagus and farro.

PER SERVING: 385 calories, 34 g protein, 41 g carbohydrates, 2 g sugar, 10 g total fat, 2 g saturated fat, 7 g fiber, 240 mg sodium

MAKE IT LAST

Extra cooked chicken may be wrapped tightly and refrigerated for up to 3 days. Use it to garnish a main dish salad or in a sandwich or wrap.

TURKEY MEAT LOAF
WITH ROASTED VEGETABLES

■ Serves 6
PREP TIME: **20 minutes**
TOTAL TIME: **2 hours**

8 ounces sweet potato (1 small), well-scrubbed but not peeled, cut into ¼-inch cubes

2 slices multigrain bread

1½ cups rolled oats

2 tablespoons ground flaxseed

½ cup milk

1 pound Brussels sprouts, trimmed and halved

½ pound carrots, cut into 1-inch pieces

½ pound parsnips, cut into 1-inch pieces

4 teaspoons olive oil

1 teaspoon salt

1 teaspoon ground black pepper

1 pound ground turkey

1 small onion, chopped

½ cup tomato puree

¼ cup chopped fresh parsley

1. Preheat the oven to 350°F. Coat a rimmed baking sheet with cooking spray.

2. Place the sweet potato in a small saucepan with enough water to cover by 2 inches. Bring to a boil and cook for 5 to 6 minutes, until fork-tender but still firm. Drain and let cool for 5 minutes.

3. Meanwhile, place the bread into the bowl of a food processor. Pulse into bread crumbs. Transfer to a bowl and stir in the oats, flaxseed, and milk. Let stand for 5 minutes, or until the oats are softened.

4. In a medium bowl, toss together the Brussels sprouts, carrots, parsnips, oil, ½ teaspoon of the salt, and ½ teaspoon of the pepper. Set aside.

5. In a large bowl, combine the turkey, sweet potato, bread crumb mixture, onion, 3 tablespoons of the tomato puree, parsley, the remaining ½ teaspoon salt, and the remaining ½ teaspoon pepper. Transfer the mixture to the prepared baking sheet and form into a 9 x 4-inch loaf. Spread the top with the remaining 5 tablespoons tomato puree. Scatter the vegetables evenly around the meat loaf.

6. Bake for about 1 hour, until a thermometer inserted into the thickest part of the loaf registers 165°F and the juices run clear. Remove from the oven and let stand for 10 minutes before cutting into 12 slices and serving with the vegetables.

PER SERVING: 389 calories, 25 g protein, 47 g carbohydrates, 11 g sugar, 13 g total fat, 2.5 g saturated fat, 11 g fiber, 638 mg sodium

MAKE IT LAST

To save time and work, double the recipe and bake 2 meat loaves. Tightly wrap leftover meat loaf slices and refrigerate for up to 3 days, or freeze for up to 1 month. Use in sandwiches or salads.

TURKEY-AND-RED-CABBAGE-SLAW SANDWICH

▓ Serves 1
PREP TIME: 5 minutes
TOTAL TIME: 10 minutes

¼ cup mayonnaise

1 tablespoon ketchup

1 tablespoon dill pickle relish

⅛ teaspoon onion powder

Pinch of garlic powder

Pinch of salt

2 teaspoons white wine vinegar

1 teaspoon canola or olive oil

½ teaspoon dried thyme

¼ teaspoon ground black pepper

½ cup finely shredded red cabbage

1 small carrot, grated

2 slices seeded rye bread

2 ounces thinly sliced roasted turkey breast

1. In a small bowl, mix together the mayonnaise, ketchup, relish, onion powder, garlic powder, and salt. Set aside.

2. In a medium bowl, whisk the vinegar, canola or olive oil, thyme, and pepper. Add the cabbage and carrot. Toss to coat.

3. Toast the bread. Spread 1 slice with 1 tablespoon of the mayonnaise mixture. Top with the turkey and slaw. Top with the second slice of bread. Serve right away.

PER SERVING: 380 calories, 24 g protein, 38 g carbohydrates, 6 g sugar, 15 g total fat, 2 g saturated fat, 6 g fiber, 651 mg sodium

MAKE IT AHEAD

The slaw can be refrigerated in a tightly sealed container for up to 3 days before making the sandwich. For a brown-bag lunch that won't get soggy, pack the slaw in an airtight container or a resealable plastic bag and top the sandwich with it just before eating. Extra mayonnaise spread can be stored in the refrigerator for up to 2 weeks.

MEAT DISHES

BRAISED BEEF WITH MUSHROOMS AND ZOODLES

■ Serves 6
PREP TIME: **15 minutes**
TOTAL TIME: **2 hours 10 minutes**

¼ ounce (2 tablespoons) dried porcini or shiitake mushrooms

½ cup boiling water

2 pounds boneless beef stew meat, cut into 1½-inch cubes

½ teaspoon salt

¼ teaspoon ground black pepper

2 tablespoons olive oil

4 cups (10 ounces) cremini (baby bella) mushrooms, quartered

1 onion, chopped

1 clove garlic, minced

2 tablespoons whole wheat flour

1¼ cups dry red wine or reduced-sodium beef broth

½ teaspoon dried thyme or oregano

3 zucchini (about 1½ pounds)

1. Preheat the oven to 350°F.

2. In a small bowl, soak the dried mushrooms in the boiling water for about 20 minutes, until softened. Using tongs, pluck out the mushrooms and reserve the water. Trim away any dirty sections from the mushrooms and chop any large pieces. Set aside.

3. Meanwhile, season the meat with the salt and pepper. Heat the oil in a large, ovenproof pot over medium-high heat. Working in batches, add the meat and cook for 12 to 15 minutes, until browned, removing pieces to a plate as they are done.

4. Reduce the heat to medium and add the fresh mushrooms, rehydrated mushrooms, onion, and garlic. Cook, stirring, for 2 minutes. Return the meat to the pot, sprinkle with the flour, and cook, stirring, for 1 minute. Carefully pour in the mushroom soaking liquid, leaving behind any grit that has settled to the bottom of the bowl. Add the wine or broth and ½ cup water. If the mixture is too thick, add up to ½ cup more water. Bring to a boil and add the thyme or oregano. Cover and bake for about 1½ hours, until the meat is tender.

5. Meanwhile, spiralize the zucchini with a spiralizer or vegetable peeler; you should have about 6 cups. When the meat is done, distribute the zoodles among 6 bowls and top with the hot meat and a bit of the braising liquid.

PER SERVING: 415 calories, 29 g protein, 11 g carbohydrates, 4 g sugar, 24 g total fat, 8 g saturated fat, 2 g fiber, 268 mg sodium

PORK TENDER WRAP IN A CORN TORTILLA

■ Serves 1
PREP TIME: **5 minutes**
TOTAL TIME: **10 minutes**

2   corn tortillas (6-inch diameter)

8   thin slices (about 3 ounces) roasted pork tenderloin, cut into strips

2   thin slices red onion, separated into rings

2   leaves red oak leaf lettuce, shredded

¼   avocado, peeled, pitted, and sliced

2   tablespoons shredded Cheddar cheese

2   tablespoons jarred salsa

1. Place the tortillas on a microwaveable plate. Cover with waxed paper or a damp paper towel and microwave on medium power for 30 seconds, or until hot and steaming.

2. On each tortilla, arrange half the pork, onion rings, lettuce, avocado, Cheddar, and salsa on top. Roll up into wraps.

PER SERVING: 378 calories, 31 g protein, 29 g carbohydrates, 2 g sugar, 15 g total fat, 4.5 g saturated fat, 6 g fiber, 251 mg sodium

MAKE IT QUICKER

Use leftover pork from Sage-Roasted Pork Tenderloin with Stuffed Acorn Squash (page 288) for this wrap.

ROSEMARY-ROASTED BABY POTATOES AND CARROTS WITH SIRLOIN

■ Serves 1
PREP TIME: **5 minutes**
TOTAL TIME: **35 minutes**

¾ cup halved baby potatoes

1 cup baby carrots

2 teaspoons olive oil

½ teaspoon dried rosemary

¼ teaspoon salt

¼ teaspoon ground black pepper

4 ounces sirloin steak

½ teaspoon balsamic vinegar

1. Preheat the oven to 375°F.

2. On a baking sheet, toss the potatoes and carrots with 1 teaspoon of the oil, the rosemary, ⅛ teaspoon of the salt, and ⅛ teaspoon of the pepper. Roast for 20 minutes, or until tender.

3. Meanwhile, heat the remaining 1 teaspoon oil in an ovenproof skillet over medium-high heat. Sprinkle the steak with the remaining ⅛ teaspoon salt and pepper and place in the hot skillet. Sear for 3 to 4 minutes, or until it develops a crust on the bottom.

4. Remove the potatoes and carrots from the oven, turn the oven to broil with a rack 6 inches from the heat source. Flip the steak and place the skillet under the broiler for 4 minutes (for medium). Remove from the oven and let rest for 5 minutes. Drizzle with the vinegar and serve with the carrots and potatoes.

PER SERVING: 397 calories, 29 g protein, 36 g carbohydrates, 7 g sugar, 14 g total fat, 3 g saturated fat, 5 g fiber, 715 mg sodium

SAGE-ROASTED PORK TENDERLOIN WITH STUFFED ACORN SQUASH

■ Serves 4
PREP TIME: **10 minutes**
TOTAL TIME: **1 hour 10 minutes**

2	acorn squash, halved and seeded		2	tablespoon pine nuts
2	teaspoons olive oil		2	tablespoons dried cranberries
¼	teaspoon salt		2	cloves garlic, minced
¼	teaspoon ground black pepper		1	teaspoon dried thyme
1½	cups reduced-sodium chicken broth or water		1	pound pork tenderloin, trimmed
¾	cup bulgur		1	tablespoon crumbled dried sage

1. Preheat oven to 450°F.

2. Set the squash, cut side up, on a baking sheet. Rub the flesh with 1 teaspoon of the oil and sprinkle with ⅛ teaspoon of the salt and ⅛ teaspoon of the pepper. Cover with aluminum foil and roast for 30 minutes.

3. Meanwhile, in a medium saucepan, combine the broth or water and bulgur. Bring to a boil, cover, and reduce the heat to medium-low. Simmer for 12 to 15 minutes, until tender. Strain out any liquid. Add the pine nuts, cranberries, garlic, and thyme, mixing well to combine.

4. Rub the pork with the remaining 1 teaspoon oil and sprinkle evenly with the remaining ⅛ teaspoon salt and the remaining ⅛ teaspoon pepper. Press the sage evenly over the roast so it sticks.

5. Remove the baking sheet from the oven and uncover the squash. Using tongs or potholders, carefully arrange the squash so there's room to lay down the pork. Divide the bulgur among the 4 halves, mounding, as necessary.

6. Roast for 15 to 20 minutes, or until a thermometer inserted in the center registers 145°F and the juices run clear. Let stand 10 minutes before slicing. Serve with the squash.

PER SERVING: 393 calories, 32 g protein, 50 g carbohydrates, 8 g sugar, 9 g total fat, 2 g saturated fat, 10 g fiber, 248 mg sodium

MAKE IT AHEAD

Roast 2 tenderloins at the same time to have lean cooked pork on hand for brown-bag sandwiches. Or, add the cooked pork to quick weeknight stir-fries or soups. Cool the tenderloin and then wrap it tightly in plastic wrap before refrigerating.

SEAFOOD DISHES

BROILED MUSTARD SALMON WITH ROASTED BROCCOLI AND MILLET

■ Serves 1
PREP TIME: **5 minutes**
TOTAL TIME: **35 minutes**

1½ cups broccoli florets
1½ teaspoons olive oil
 1 clove garlic, minced
 ¼ teaspoon salt
 ¼ teaspoon ground black pepper
   or crushed red-pepper flakes

½ teaspoon Dijon mustard
½ teaspoon balsamic vinegar
¼ teaspoon dried oregano
5 ounces wild salmon fillet
½ cup cooked millet

1. Preheat the oven to 375°F.

2. On a baking sheet, toss the broccoli with the oil, half of the garlic, the salt, and pepper. Spread out on the baking sheet and bake for 20 minutes, until the broccoli begins to brown and turn tender.

3. In a small bowl, combine the mustard, vinegar, oregano, and remaining garlic. Spread onto the flesh of the salmon.

4. Turn the oven to broil with the rack 6 inches from the heat source. Turn the broccoli and add the salmon, skin side down, on the baking sheet. Broil for 6 to 7 minutes, or until the salmon is opaque and flakes easily with a fork. Serve the salmon with the broccoli and the millet.

PER SERVING: 406 calories, 35 g protein, 29 g carbohydrates, 1 g sugar, 17 g total fat, 2.5 g saturated fat, 5 g fiber, 736 mg sodium

GRILLED SARDINES OVER WILTED ARUGULA

■ Serves 4
PREP TIME: **15 minutes**
TOTAL TIME: **40 minutes**

4 teaspoons olive oil

12 fresh sardines, cleaned, or 4 cans (4.4 ounces each)

2 tablespoons fresh lemon juice

1 pound baby gold potatoes, quartered

¼ teaspoon ground black pepper

1 pint grape or cherry tomatoes, halved

1 clove garlic, minced

8 cups baby arugula

1 tablespoon balsamic vinegar

1. Preheat a grill pan over medium-high heat. Brush with 1 teaspoon of the oil.

2. If using fresh sardines, grill them for 10 minutes, turning once, or until the fish flakes easily. If using canned sardines, grill them for 3 to 4 minutes until heated through, turning once. Transfer to a plate, drizzle with 1 tablespoon of the lemon juice, and cover to keep warm.

3. Coat the potatoes with 1 teaspoon of the oil and place on the grill pan. Cover and grill, turning occasionally, for 8 to 10 minutes, or until browned and tender. Transfer to a bowl and toss with the remaining 1 tablespoon lemon juice and the pepper. Cover to keep warm.

4. Meanwhile, heat the remaining 2 teaspoons oil in a large nonstick skillet over medium-high heat. Add the tomatoes and garlic and cook for 3 minutes, or until the tomatoes are softened. Add the arugula and vinegar. Cook for 1 minute, stirring, or until just wilted. Divide among 4 plates and serve with one-quarter of the potatoes and sardines.

PER SERVING: 399 calories, 32 g protein, 27 g carbohydrates, 5 g sugar, 19 g total fat, 4 g saturated fat, 4 g fiber, 1,093 mg sodium

GRILLED TROUT WITH CHIVE AND DILL SAUCE

■ Serves 4
PREP TIME: **10 minutes**
TOTAL TIME: **1 hour 10 minutes**

3   cups reduced-sodium chicken broth

1   cup wild rice

3   teaspoons olive oil

1   cup frozen peas, thawed

1   tablespoon finely minced chives

1   tablespoon finely minced fresh dill
    or 1 teaspoon dried

1   teaspoon coarse-grain mustard

4   farmed rainbow trout fillets
    (5 ounces each), skin on

¼   teaspoon salt

¼   teaspoon ground black pepper

1   recipe Spinach and Orange Salad with
    Honey-Mustard Dressing (page 304)

1. In a medium saucepan, bring 2¼ cups of the broth to a boil. Stir in the rice, cover, reduce the heat, and simmer for 45 minutes, or until the rice is tender. Remove from the heat and let sit for 10 minutes. Stir in 1 teaspoon of the oil and the peas.

2. Meanwhile, coat a grill rack or grill pan with cooking spray. Preheat.

3. In a medium skillet, combine the remaining ¾ cup broth, the chives, dill, and mustard. Bring to a boil over high heat, whisking frequently. Continue to boil and whisk for about 3 minutes, or until the sauce has been reduced to half its volume. Keep warm over very low heat.

4. Rub the remaining 2 teaspoons oil over the surface of each fillet and sprinkle the flesh with the salt and pepper. Set on the grill rack, skin side down, and cook for 4 to 5 minutes per side, or until the fish is opaque.

5. Transfer the fish to 4 plates alongside the rice. Drizzle with the sauce. Serve with the salad.

PER SERVING (WITH SALAD): 347 calories, 35 g protein, 20 g carbohydrates, 9 g sugars, 14 g fat, 2 g saturated fat, 5 g fiber, 766 mg sodium

LEMON-SALMON TABBOULEH

Serves 2
PREP TIME: **10 minutes**
TOTAL TIME: **10 minutes**

1½ tablespoons olive oil

3 tablespoons fresh lemon juice

1 clove garlic, minced

¼ teaspoon ground cumin

¼ teaspoon salt

¼ teaspoon ground black pepper

2 cups cooked bulgur

1 can (6 ounces) boneless, skinless wild-caught salmon, drained

1 cup chopped cucumber

1 cup chopped tomato

½ cup chopped fresh parsley

2 tablespoons chopped fresh mint

6 pitted kalamata olives, chopped

In a medium bowl, whisk together the oil, lemon juice, garlic, cumin, salt, and pepper. Add the bulgur, salmon, cucumber, tomato, parsley, mint, and olives. Gently toss to coat.

PER SERVING: 392 calories, 23 g protein, 43 g carbohydrates, 4 g sugar, 16 g total fat, 2 g saturated fat, 11 g fiber, 777 mg sodium

MAHI, MANGO, AND AVOCADO QUESADILLAS

■ Serves 4
PREP TIME: **10 minutes**
TOTAL TIME: **30 minutes**

1 tablespoon olive oil

2 fillets (6 ounces each) mahi mahi or other firm white fish, such as halibut

¼ teaspoon salt

¼ teaspoon ground black pepper

4 whole wheat tortillas (8-inch diameter)

½ cup shredded Monterey Jack cheese

1 mango, sliced

1 avocado, peeled, pitted, and sliced

1 cup shredded baby spinach leaves

2 tablespoons chopped fresh cilantro

Olive or canola oil in a mister

1. Heat the oil in a large nonstick skillet over medium heat. Season the fish with the salt and pepper. Cook the fish for 3 minutes, flip, and cook for 3 to 4 minutes longer, until just opaque. Remove from the heat and transfer the fish to a plate. Flake the fish with a fork and wipe out the skillet.

2. Sprinkle the lower half of each tortilla with 1 tablespoon of the cheese. Top with one-fourth of the fish, mango, avocado, and spinach. Top each with ½ tablespoon of the cilantro and another 1 tablespoon cheese. Fold the top half of each tortilla over the filling to form a half-moon. Mist one side of the tortillas with olive or canola oil.

3. Return the skillet to medium heat. Add 1 or 2 quesadillas and cook for 3 to 4 minutes on each side, until lightly browned and the filling is hot. Transfer to a cutting board. Let stand 1 minute. Cut each into 4 wedges. Repeat with the remaining quesadillas.

PER SERVING: 395 calories, 25 g protein, 38 g carbohydrates, 11 g sugar, 17 g total fat, 5 g saturated fat, 7 g fiber, 629 mg sodium

MAKE IT DIFFERENT

In season, replace the mango with a ripe peach, nectarine, or apricot.

PISTACHIO-CRUSTED WILD SALMON

■ Serves 4
PREP TIME: **10 minutes**
TOTAL TIME: **30 minutes**

1½ pounds green beans, trimmed

8 ounces frozen pearl onions, thawed

4 teaspoons olive oil

1 teaspoon salt

1 teaspoon ground black pepper

2 teaspoons Dijon mustard

1½ pounds skinless wild salmon fillet

½ cup shelled pistachios, ground or finely chopped

1. Preheat the oven to 425°F. Spray a large rimmed baking sheet with cooking spray.

2. Add the green beans and onions. Drizzle with 1 tablespoon of the oil, sprinkle with ½ teaspoon of the salt and ½ teaspoon of the pepper, and toss to coat.

3. In a small bowl, mix the mustard and the remaining 1 teaspoon oil, ½ teaspoon salt, and ½ teaspoon pepper. Brush over top of the fish. Put the pistachios on a plate and press the top of the fish into the nuts. Place the fish, plain side down, onto the baking sheet. Roast for 15 to 20 minutes, until the fish flakes and the beans and onions are tender.

PER SERVING: 408 calories, 39 g protein, 18 g carbohydrates, 8 g sugar, 20 g total fat, 3 g saturated fat, 6 g fiber, 782 mg sodium

ROASTED ARCTIC CHAR, CARROTS, AND LEEKS WITH PENNE

■ Serves 4
PREP TIME: **10 minutes**
TOTAL TIME: **1 hour**

1½ pounds leeks (white and light green parts only)

3 carrots, thinly sliced

¼ cup reduced-sodium chicken or vegetable broth

3 teaspoons olive oil

2 teaspoons dried thyme

½ teaspoon ground black pepper

1 pound skinless arctic char or wild salmon fillet

½ teaspoon salt

2 cups (8 ounces) whole wheat penne

1. Preheat the oven to 400°F.

2. Halve the leeks lengthwise and cut into 2-inch lengths. Transfer to a large bowl of cool water and swish to rinse completely. With a slotted spoon, lift the leeks out of the water and place with the carrots in a 13 x 9-inch baking dish. Add the chicken or vegetable broth, 2 teaspoons of the oil, the thyme, and ¼ teaspoon of the pepper. Cover with foil and bake for 15 minutes.

3. Add the fish to the baking dish, drizzle with the remaining 1 teaspoon oil, and sprinkle with the salt and the remaining ¼ teaspoon pepper. Cover and bake for 30 minutes, or until the fish is opaque and the vegetables are tender.

4. Meanwhile, prepare the pasta according to package directions. Place the penne in a large serving bowl. Break the fish into bite-size pieces and add to the penne with the vegetables and pan juices.

PER SERVING: 402 calories, 29 g protein, 44 g carbohydrates, 6 g sugar, 12 g total fat, 1.5 g saturated fat, 6 g fiber, 399 mg sodium

SESAME SCALLOP SKEWERS WITH BABY BOK CHOY AND GREEN TEA RICE

■ Serves 4
PREP TIME: **10 minutes**
TOTAL TIME: **1 hour 15 minutes**

4½ cups hot water

1 cup brown basmati rice

6 scallions, whites finely chopped and greens thinly sliced

2 teaspoons soy sauce

2 teaspoons toasted sesame oil

2 teaspoons grated fresh ginger

2 cloves garlic, minced

16 sea scallops (about 1 pound), side muscle removed

8 heads baby bok choy, halved lengthwise

4 teaspoons black or white sesame seeds

4 teaspoons matcha (green tea) powder

¼ teaspoon salt

2 cups shelled frozen edamame, thawed

1. In a medium saucepan, bring 2½ cups of the water to a boil and add the rice. Reduce the heat, cover, and simmer for 50 minutes, or until the rice is tender and the water is absorbed. Remove from the heat and let stand, covered, for 10 minutes.

2. Meanwhile, in a large resealable plastic storage bag, combine the scallion whites, soy sauce, oil, ginger, and garlic. Add the scallops, seal the bag, and toss gently to coat. Refrigerate for 15 minutes.

3. Preheat the broiler. Coat a broiler rack with cooking spray.

4. Drain the scallops in a sieve set over a bowl. Thread the scallops horizontally through their sides, leaving the flat ends exposed, onto 4 bamboo skewers (6 to 8 inches long). Place the skewers on the prepared rack and set into the broiler pan.

5. Brush the bok choy on both sides with the marinade. Arrange on the broiler pan. Sprinkle the scallops and bok choy with 2 teaspoons of the sesame seeds.

6. Broil 4 inches from the heat for 2 minutes. Turn the skewers and the bok choy over and broil for 2 minutes longer, or until the scallops are opaque and the bok choy is wilted.

7. In a small bowl, mix the matcha with the salt. Add the remaining 2 cups hot water, whisking until dissolved, about 1 minute.

8. Stir the edamame, scallion greens, and the remaining 2 teaspoons sesame seeds into the rice. Divide among 4 bowls, mounding in the center. Pour the matcha mixture around the rice. Top with 1 scallop skewer and a quarter of the bok choy.

PER SERVING: 370 calories, 21 g protein, 49 g carbohydrates, 6 g sugar, 11 g total fat, 1 g saturated fat, 8 g fiber, 640 mg sodium

SEVEN-VEGETABLE COUSCOUS WITH BLACK COD

■ Serves 4
PREP TIME: **20 minutes**
TOTAL TIME: **55 minutes**

2 teaspoons olive oil

1 onion, finely chopped

1 pound butternut squash or pumpkin, cut into 1-inch cubes

3 carrots, cut into 1-inch pieces

2 parsnips, cut into 1-inch pieces

1 turnip, cut into 1-inch cubes

1 red bell pepper, seeded and cut into 1-inch pieces

2 cups reduced-sodium chicken broth

1 teaspoon ground ginger

½ teaspoon ground allspice

¼ teaspoon salt

2 teaspoons ground cinnamon

2 cups chopped kale or Swiss chard leaves

½ cup chopped fresh parsley

1¼ pounds black cod (sablefish), cut into 2-inch chunks

1 cup whole wheat couscous

1. Heat the oil in a large pot or Dutch oven over medium heat. Add the onion and cook for 4 minutes, until softened. Add the squash or pumpkin, carrots, parsnips, turnip, pepper, broth, ginger, allspice, salt, and cinnamon. Bring to a boil. Reduce to a simmer, cover, and cook for about 25 minutes, or until the vegetables are tender.

2. Stir in the kale or chard and parsley. Nestle the fish into the vegetables, cover, and simmer for 5 to 7 minutes, or until the fish is cooked through.

2. Meanwhile, prepare the couscous according to package directions.

3. Spoon the fish and vegetables over ⅓-cup servings of couscous.

PER SERVING: 405 calories, 22 g protein, 45 g carbohydrates, 7 g sugar, 17 g total fat, 3.5 g saturated fat, 9g fiber, 251 mg sodium

SHELLFISH SCAMPI OVER CAULIFLOWER "RICE"

⬛ Serves 4
PREP TIME: **20 minutes**
TOTAL TIME: **45 minutes**

1   small head cauliflower (about 1¾ pounds), trimmed and cored

½   cup no-salt-added chicken or vegetable broth, or water

½   cup finely chopped fresh parsley

4   cloves garlic, minced

1   pound baby spinach, kale, or dandelion greens, coarsely chopped

1   tablespoon olive oil

1   tablespoon unsalted butter

1   pound jumbo shrimp, peeled and deveined

1   pound mussels, debearded (discard any that are open)

8   scallions, trimmed and cut into ½-inch pieces

Juice of 1 lemon

3   tablespoons dry white wine

¼   teaspoon ground black pepper or crushed red-pepper flakes

1. Place the cauliflower in a food processor and pulse about 20 times, until it's finely chopped to roughly the size of rice grains. Do not overprocess. (Alternatively, halve the head of cauliflower and grate each half on the large holes of a box grater.) You should have 4 to 5 cups of cauliflower "rice" total.

2. In a large skillet over medium heat, bring ¼ cup of the broth or water to a simmer. Add the cauliflower and cook, stirring, for about 5 minutes, or until tender. Sprinkle with 2 tablespoons of the parsley, transfer to a plate or bowl, and cover to keep warm. Wipe out the skillet.

3. Return the skillet to medium heat and add the remaining ¼ cup broth or water. When warm, add half the garlic and cook for 1 minute. Add the spinach, kale, or dandelion greens in handfuls, cover, and cook, tossing occasionally, until all the greens are in the skillet. Cover and cook for 4 to 8 minutes, until wilted. Transfer the greens to a bowl or plate and cover to keep warm. Wipe out the skillet.

4. Warm the oil and butter in the skillet over medium-high heat. Add the shrimp and mussels, cover, and cook for 2 minutes, or until the shrimp start to turn pink.

5. Flip the shrimp. Add the scallions and the remaining garlic. Cook for 1 minute, or until fragrant. Add the lemon juice, wine, and black or red pepper and bring to a brisk simmer. Cover and simmer for 2 minutes, or until the shrimp are opaque and the mussels open. Discard any mussels that do not open. Sprinkle with the remaining 6 tablespoons parsley and serve with the cauliflower "rice" and garlicky greens.

PER SERVING: 293 calories, 27 g protein, 27 g carbohydrates, 4 g sugar, 9 g total fat, 3 g saturated fat, 9 g fiber, 974 mg sodium

MAKE IT AHEAD

Cauliflower rice freezes well. Make a double batch and store it in a freezer-safe storage bag or container. Thaw on the counter for 15 minutes before using, or warm it in the microwave for 30 seconds to 1 minute.

TUNA STEAKS WITH MILLET AND NECTARINE SALSA

■ Serves 4
PREP TIME: 10 minutes
TOTAL TIME: 30 minutes

¾ cup millet

1 cup chopped ripe nectarines or peaches

¼ cup finely chopped red onion

¼ cup seeded and chopped bell pepper

2 tablespoons chopped fresh cilantro

Juice of 1 lime

½–1 jalapeño pepper, stemmed, seeded, and finely chopped (wear plastic gloves when handling)

1 clove garlic, thinly sliced

½ teaspoon salt

½ teaspoon ground black pepper

1 tablespoon olive oil

4 yellowfin (ahi) tuna steaks (4 ounces each)

1. Bring 1½ cups water to a boil in a small saucepan. Add the millet, cover, reduce the heat to medium-low, and simmer for about 20 minutes, until the water is absorbed.

2. Meanwhile, in a small bowl, combine the nectarines or peaches, onion, bell pepper, cilantro, lime juice, jalapeño, garlic, ¼ teaspoon of the salt, and ¼ teaspoon of the black pepper. Set aside for the flavors to meld.

3. Heat the oil in a large nonstick skillet over medium-high heat. Pat the fish dry with paper towels and sprinkle with the remaining ¼ teaspoon salt and ¼ teaspoon black pepper. Sear in the skillet for 2 minutes per side, until a nice crust forms and the fish is still slightly pink in the center. Remove to a plate. Spoon the nectarine or peach mixture over the hot fish and serve with the millet.

PER SERVING: 393 calories, 35 g protein, 50 g carbohydrates, 11 g sugar, 6 g total fat, 1 g saturated fat, 7 g fiber, 353 mg sodium

MAKE IT DIFFERENT

Mango can replace the nectarines or peaches. Scallions can replace the red onion. Any whole grain can replace the millet.

MAKE IT AHEAD

Millet stores beautifully in the fridge. In an airtight container, it can keep for up to 4 days. Make it ahead, and this dinner will come together in a flash.

WILD SALMON WITH SWISS CHARD AND COUSCOUS

■ Serves 4
PREP TIME: **10 minutes**
TOTAL TIME: **30 minutes**

1 pound Swiss chard (stalks and leaves), thinly sliced

4 scallions, thinly sliced

2 cloves garlic, minced

½ teaspoon salt

1 tablespoon lemon zest

4 skinless wild salmon fillets (5 ounces each), about 1½ inches thick

½ lemon

¼ teaspoon ground black pepper

1 cup whole wheat couscous

Crushed red-pepper flakes (optional)

1. In a large deep nonstick skillet, place the chard, ¼ cup water, scallions, garlic, and salt. Cover and cook over high heat for about 4 minutes, or until the mixture boils. Use tongs to toss the chard in the pan. Add the lemon zest. Reduce the heat to medium. Cover and continue cooking for about 2 minutes, or until the leaves are wilted.

2. Set the salmon fillets on top of the chard mixture, adding up to ¼ cup more water, if needed. Squeeze the lemon over the fillets and sprinkle with the black pepper. Cover and cook over medium-high heat for 10 to 12 minutes, or until the salmon is opaque.

3. Prepare the couscous according to package directions.

4. Remove the salmon to 4 plates. Spoon one-fourth of the couscous next to each fillet. Increase the heat to high and cook off any remaining liquid. Spoon the chard next to the fillet on each plate. Sprinkle with red-pepper flakes (if using).

PER SERVING: 402 calories, 38 g protein, 44 g carbohydrates, 3 g sugar, 10 g total fat, 1.5 g saturated fat, 8 g fiber, 603 mg sodium

MAKE IT LAST

Individual portions of leftover refrigerated steamed salmon with chard can be used for a quick brown-bag lunch salad. Replace the couscous with ½ cup cooked brown rice or other cooked whole grain per serving.

RECIPES
Salads

Some of these salads are hearty enough to be a meal on their own (about 400 calories), while others are lighter and should be combined with other dishes to create 400-calorie meals.

ASIAN EDAMAME AND CARROT SALAD (page 302)

ASPARAGUS AND BARLEY SALAD WITH DILL DRESSING*
(page 302)

FAST AND FRESH SALAD* (page 303)

ROASTED VEGGIE AND COUSCOUS SALAD WITH FETA DRESSING*
(page 303)

SPINACH AND ORANGE SALAD WITH HONEY-MUSTARD
DRESSING* (page 304)

TANGY MEDITERRANEAN TUNA SALAD* (page 304)

WARM COUSCOUS AND BEAN SALAD* (page 305)

*Recipes are from the 21-day meal plan. The other recipes can be swapped into the meal plans or used to create your own meals.

ASIAN EDAMAME AND CARROT SALAD

■ Serves 1
PREP TIME: **5 minutes**
TOTAL TIME: **5 minutes**

2 teaspoons toasted sesame oil

2 teaspoons rice vinegar

½ teaspoon grated fresh ginger

   Pinch of salt

½ cup shelled frozen edamame

⅓ cup shredded carrot

1 scallion, chopped

In a small bowl, whisk together the oil, vinegar, ginger, and salt. Add the edamame, carrot, and scallion. Gently toss to coat.

PER SERVING: 201 calories, 9 g protein, 14 g carbohydrates, 3 g sugar, 12 g total fat, 1.5 g saturated fat, 5 g fiber, 203 mg sodium

ASPARAGUS AND BARLEY SALAD WITH DILL DRESSING

■ Serves 4
PREP TIME: **10 minutes**
TOTAL TIME: **60 minutes**

1 pound asparagus, tough ends trimmed and cut diagonally into 2-inch pieces

1 cup unpearled barley

1 cup plain yogurt

¼ cup chopped fresh dill

3 tablespoons fresh lemon juice

1 tablespoon extra-virgin olive oil

2 cloves garlic, minced

½ teaspoon salt

½ teaspoon ground black pepper

4 scallions, thinly sliced

1. Bring 4 cups water to a boil in a covered large saucepan over high heat. Add the asparagus. Cook, stirring often, for 3 to 5 minutes, or until crisp-tender. With a skimmer or slotted spoon, lift the asparagus to a colander and rinse briefly under cold running water. Drain. Cover and refrigerate until ready to assemble the salad.

2. To the asparagus water, add the barley and return to a boil. Reduce the heat to low, cover, and simmer for about 35 minutes, or until the barley is tender. Drain in a colander and let stand, tossing occasionally, for about 15 minutes, or until lukewarm.

3. In a large salad bowl, combine the yogurt, dill, lemon juice, oil, garlic, salt, and pepper. Add the scallions, asparagus, and barley and toss gently to mix well. Cover and chill until ready to serve.

PER SERVING: 265 calories, 11 g protein, 44 g carbohydrates, 6 g sugar, 7 g total fat, 2 g saturated fat, 11 g fiber, 335 mg sodium

FAST AND FRESH SALAD

■ Serves 4
PREP TIME: **5 minutes**
TOTAL TIME: **5 minutes**

1 tablespoon extra-virgin olive oil

2 teaspoons red wine vinegar or white wine vinegar

¼ teaspoon salt

1 bag (10 ounces) prewashed salad greens, preferably with carrots and radicchio

1 cup grape tomatoes

3 scallions, sliced

Ground black pepper

In a large bowl, whisk together the oil, vinegar, and salt. Add the greens, tomatoes, and scallions. Toss to coat. Season to taste with the pepper.

PER SERVING: 53 calories, 1 g protein, 5 g carbohydrates, 3 g sugar, 4 g total fat, 0.5 g saturated fat, 2 g fiber, 132 mg sodium

ROASTED VEGGIE AND COUSCOUS SALAD WITH FETA DRESSING

■ Serves 4
PREP TIME: **15 minutes**
TOTAL TIME: **25 minutes**

2 red or orange bell peppers, each sliced into 8 pieces

1 large red onion, cut into chunks

1 zucchini, halved lengthwise and cut into bite-size pieces

1 pint cherry or grape tomatoes

2 tablespoons olive oil

1 can (15 ounces) chickpeas, drained and rinsed

2 cups reduced-sodium chicken or vegetable broth

1 cup whole wheat couscous

3 tablespoons red wine vinegar

Juice of 1 lemon

2 cloves garlic, minced

1 teaspoon dried oregano

⅓ cup crumbled feta cheese

1. Preheat the oven to 400°F.

2. On a baking sheet, toss the peppers, onion, zucchini, and tomatoes with 1 tablespoon of the oil. Bake for 10 minutes, toss, and add the chickpeas. Bake for 10 minutes longer, or until the vegetables are golden and tender.

3. Meanwhile, in a medium saucepan, bring the broth to a boil. Add the couscous, cover, and remove from the heat. Allow to sit for 5 to 10 minutes, or until all the liquid is absorbed.

4. In a small bowl, whisk together the vinegar, lemon juice, the remaining 1 tablespoon oil, the garlic, and oregano. Whisk in the feta.

5. In a large bowl, toss the chickpea mixture with the couscous and drizzle with the dressing. Toss to combine.

PER SERVING: 406 calories, 17 g protein, 61 g carbohydrates, 9 g sugar, 13 g total fat, 3 g saturated fat, 12 g fiber, 381 mg sodium

SPINACH AND ORANGE SALAD WITH HONEY-MUSTARD DRESSING

Serves 4
PREP TIME: 10 minutes
TOTAL TIME: 10 minutes

1 tablespoon flaxseed oil or extra-virgin olive oil

1 tablespoon red wine vinegar or white wine vinegar

1 tablespoon honey

1 teaspoon Dijon mustard

8 cups torn spinach leaves

1 navel orange, cut into chunks

2 tablespoons chopped walnuts

In a large bowl, whisk the oil, vinegar, honey, and mustard. Add the spinach and orange. Toss to coat. Transfer to 4 salad plates and sprinkle with the walnuts.

PER SERVING: 100 calories, 2 g protein, 13 g carbohydrates, 7 g sugar, 6 g total fat, 1 g saturated fat, 4 g fiber, 120 mg sodium

TANGY MEDITERRANEAN TUNA SALAD

Serves 2
PREP TIME: 10 minutes
TOTAL TIME: 10 minutes

3 tablespoons red wine vinegar

1 tablespoon olive oil

1 teaspoon Dijon mustard

1 small clove garlic, minced

1 can (5 ounces) water-packed tuna, drained

1 can (15 ounces) no-salt-added chickpeas, drained and rinsed

¼ cup kalamata or green olives, sliced

4 cups coarsely chopped romaine lettuce

In a medium bowl, whisk together the vinegar, oil, mustard, and garlic. Add the tuna, chickpeas, and olives and gently toss. Serve over the romaine.

PER SERVING: 408 calories, 23 g protein, 32 g carbohydrates, 2 g sugar, 20 g total fat, 2.5 g saturated fat, 8 g fiber, 967 mg sodium

WARM COUSCOUS AND BEAN SALAD

■ Serves 4
PREP TIME: 15 minutes
TOTAL TIME: 25 minutes

¾ cup whole wheat couscous

½ cup canned red kidney beans, rinsed and drained

1 stalk broccoli, peeled and chopped (about 4 ounces)

½ green bell pepper, seeded and chopped

½ red onion, thinly sliced

¼ cup crumbled feta cheese

2 tablespoons thinly sliced fresh basil

2 tablespoons fresh lemon juice or white wine vinegar

1 tablespoon extra-virgin olive oil

¼ teaspoon ground black pepper

⅛ teaspoon salt

1. Bring 1¼ cups water to a boil in a medium saucepan over medium-high heat. Stir in the couscous. Return to a boil, reduce the heat to low, cover, and simmer for 2 minutes. Remove from the heat and let stand, covered, for 5 minutes. Fluff with a fork and cool, uncovered, for 5 minutes longer.

2. Meanwhile, in a large bowl, combine the beans, broccoli, bell pepper, onion, feta, and basil. Add the couscous and toss well. In a small bowl, combine the lemon juice or vinegar, oil, black pepper, and salt. Pour over the couscous and toss well.

PER SERVING: 236 calories, 10 g protein, 38 g carbohydrates, 3 g sugar, 6 g total fat, 2 g saturated fat, 8 g fiber, 190 mg sodium

MAKE IT LAST

This salad is great for brown-bag lunches. It can be refrigerated in a tightly sealed container for up to 5 days.

RECIPES
Soups

Soups are a perfect side dish for a meal, or they can take center stage. With calorie counts ranging from 185 to around 320, you can pair them with a salad, side dishes, or even an entrée for a 400-calorie meal. Or, adjust the serving size and enjoy one as a snack.

CREOLE CAULIFLOWER SOUP* (page 307)

CURRIED LENTIL AND SPINACH SOUP* (page 308)

MEDITERRANEAN SEAFOOD SOUP* (page 309)

MUSHROOM, BEEF, AND BARLEY SOUP* (page 310)

PASTA E FAGIOLE* (page 311)

PUMPKIN BISQUE* (page 312)

*Recipes are from the 21-day meal plan. The other recipes can be swapped into the meal plans or used to create your own meals.

CREOLE CAULIFLOWER SOUP

Serves 4
PREP TIME: **15 minutes**
TOTAL TIME: **55 minutes**

1 tablespoon canola oil

2 teaspoons salt-free Creole or Cajun seasoning

1 medium onion, halved and sliced

2 cloves garlic, minced

1 quart reduced-sodium chicken broth

1 head cauliflower, cut into small florets

1 pound medium shrimp, peeled and deveined

4 ounces mustard greens, thinly sliced

1. Warm the oil in large saucepan over medium heat. Stir in the seasoning and reduce the heat to medium-low. Add the onion and garlic. Cook, stirring occasionally, for about 8 minutes, until the onion is soft and translucent.

2. Add the broth and cauliflower. Bring to a boil. Reduce the heat and simmer, covered, for 25 minutes, or until cooked through.

3. Add the shrimp and cook for about 5 minutes, until pink and opaque. Stir in the mustard greens and cook for about 2 minutes, just until wilted.

PER SERVING: 208 calories, 24 g protein, 16 g carbohydrates, 5 g sugar, 7 g total fat, 1 g saturated fat, 4 g fiber, 765 mg sodium

MAKE IT LAST

The cooled soup can be refrigerated in a tightly sealed container for up to 5 days. Reheat and add additional water, if needed, to thin the soup.

CURRIED LENTIL AND SPINACH SOUP

Serves 6
PREP TIME: **15 minutes**
TOTAL TIME: **55 minutes**

1 tablespoon extra-virgin olive oil

1 large onion, chopped

3 cloves garlic, minced

1 tablespoon curry powder

1 tablespoon minced fresh ginger

4 cups reduced-sodium chicken broth

2 cups dried lentils

1 package (6 ounces) baby spinach

2 tablespoons white wine vinegar or red wine vinegar

¼ teaspoon salt

½ teaspoon ground black pepper

6 tablespoons plain yogurt

1. Heat the oil in a large heavy soup pot over medium-high heat. Add the onion and garlic and cook, stirring frequently, for about 10 minutes, until golden. Stir in the curry powder and ginger.

2. Add the broth, 4 cups water, and the lentils. Bring to a boil, reduce the heat to medium-low, and simmer, uncovered, for about 25 minutes, until the lentils are tender.

3. Transfer 2 cups of the soup to the bowl of a food processor or a blender. Process until smooth and return to the saucepan. Add the spinach, vinegar, salt, and pepper. Simmer for about 5 minutes, until heated through.

4. Ladle the soup into 6 bowls. Top each serving with 1 tablespoon yogurt.

PER SERVING: 321 calories, 22 g protein, 48 g carbohydrates, 3 g sugar, 6 g total fat, 2 g saturated fat, 22 g fiber, 206 mg sodium

MAKE IT AHEAD

Cool the soup and refrigerate it in a tightly sealed container for up to 1 week, or freeze for up to 1 month.

MEDITERRANEAN SEAFOOD SOUP

■ Serves 4
PREP TIME: **10 minutes**
TOTAL TIME: **35 minutes**

1 tablespoon extra-virgin olive oil

½ medium onion, chopped

½ medium red or yellow bell pepper, seeded and chopped

2 cloves garlic, minced

1 can (14½ ounces) reduced-sodium chicken broth

½ cup no-salt-added canned diced tomatoes (with juice)

2 tablespoons white wine vinegar

8 littleneck clams

8 ounces sea scallops

8 ounces medium shrimp, peeled and deveined

2 tablespoons finely chopped flat-leaf parsley (optional)

8 slices (½ inch thick) French bread, toasted

1. In a large pot, combine the oil, onion, pepper, and garlic. Cook over medium heat, stirring occasionally, for 5 minutes, or until softened. Add the broth, 1 cup water, the tomatoes (with juice), and vinegar. Cover and bring almost to a boil. Reduce the heat and simmer for 10 minutes.

3. Add the clams. Cover and cook over medium-high heat for 5 minutes, or until most of the clams open. Stir in the scallops and shrimp. Cover and cook for about 5 minutes, or until the scallops and shrimp are opaque. Discard any unopened clams. Stir in the parsley, if desired. Serve with the French bread for dipping.

PER SERVING: 348 calories, 27 g protein, 45 g carbohydrates, 4 g sugar, 6 g total fat, 1 g saturated fat, 2 g fiber, 1,087 mg sodium

MAKE IT AHEAD

The cooled soup can be refrigerated in a tightly sealed container for up to 3 days.

MUSHROOM, BEEF, AND BARLEY SOUP

Serves 4
PREP TIME: **25 minutes**
TOTAL TIME: **2 hours 5 minutes**

1 tablespoon extra-virgin olive oil

8 ounces well-trimmed lean boneless beef top round, cut into ¼-inch cubes

2 medium onions, halved and thinly sliced

3 cloves garlic, minced

¼ teaspoon salt

¼ teaspoon ground black pepper

½ teaspoon dried thyme, crumbled

1 pound cremini (baby bella) mushrooms, sliced

2 ribs celery with some leaves, thinly sliced

2 medium carrots, sliced

1 medium turnip, halved lengthwise and sliced

3 cups reduced-sodium beef broth

½ cup unpearled barley

Minced fresh parsley or dill (optional)

1. Heat the oil in a Dutch oven or a large heavy saucepan over medium heat. Add the beef cubes. Lightly brown the beef until the liquid evaporates. Add the onions and garlic and cook for 3 to 5 minutes, or until the onions soften. Add the salt, pepper, and thyme and cook for 1 minute. Add the mushrooms and cook for 3 minutes, or until the mushrooms begin to soften. Add the celery, carrots, and turnip and stir for 2 minutes. Add 3 cups water and the broth. Reduce the heat if necessary and simmer for 30 minutes.

2. Stir in the barley and simmer for about 45 minutes longer, or until the barley is soft. Sprinkle with fresh parsley or dill, if using.

PER SERVING: 276 calories, 22 g protein, 33 g carbohydrates, 8 g sugar, 7 g fat, 2 g saturated fat, 7 g fiber, 598 mg sodium

MAKE IT AHEAD

The cooled soup can be refrigerated in a tightly sealed container for up to 1 week or frozen for up to 1 month.

PASTA E FAGIOLE

▓ Serves 4
PREP TIME: **10 minutes**
TOTAL TIME: **30 minutes**

2 teaspoons extra-virgin olive oil

1 small onion, chopped

2 cloves garlic, chopped

4 cups reduced-sodium vegetable broth

1 can (15 ounces) no-salt-added diced tomatoes (with juice)

½ teaspoon dried oregano

1 can (15 ounces) no-salt-added kidney beans, rinsed and drained

½ cup (2 ounces) whole wheat macaroni or other small pasta

½ pound Swiss chard leaves or spinach leaves, coarsely chopped

¼ teaspoon salt

1. Warm the oil in a pot set over medium heat. Add the onion and garlic. Cook, stirring occasionally, for 3 to 5 minutes, or until the onion is soft.

2. Add the broth, tomatoes (with juice), oregano, beans, and pasta. Cook, stirring occasionally, for 15 minutes, or until the pasta is cooked. Add the Swiss chard or spinach and salt. Cook, stirring occasionally, for 2 to 3 minutes, or until the chard or spinach is wilted. Divide evenly among 4 plates.

PER SERVING: 200 calories, 10 g protein, 35 g carbohydrates, 6 g sugar, 3 g total fat, 0 g saturated fat, 10 g fiber, 430 mg sodium

MAKE IT AHEAD

The cooled soup can be refrigerated in a tightly sealed container for up to 5 days.

PUMPKIN BISQUE

■ Serves 4
PREP TIME: **20 minutes**
TOTAL TIME: **40 minutes**

2 teaspoons olive oil

2 onions, chopped

1 large red bell pepper, seeded and chopped

1 potato, peeled and diced

1 tablespoon minced garlic

1 tablespoon fresh oregano or 1 teaspoon dried

4 cups reduced-sodium vegetable broth

1 can (15 ounces) pumpkin puree

½ teaspoon salt

½ teaspoon freshly ground black pepper

½ cup roasted unsalted pumpkin seeds

2 teaspoons balsamic vinegar

1. Heat the oil in a large pot or Dutch oven over medium-high heat. Add the onions, bell pepper, potato, garlic, and oregano.

2. Cook, stirring occasionally, for 5 minutes, or until the onion is softened. Add the broth, pumpkin, salt, and black pepper. Simmer for 10 minutes, or until the potato is very tender.

3. Transfer the soup to a blender (in batches, if necessary). Process until smooth.

4. Return the soup to the pot. If necessary, add water to thin to desired consistency. Reheat, if needed.

5. Ladle into 4 bowls and top each with 2 tablespoons of pumpkin seeds. Drizzle lightly with the balsamic vinegar.

PER SERVING: 185 calories, 5 g protein, 32 g carbohydrates, 8 g sugar, 5 g total fat, 1 g saturated fat, 8 g fiber, 442 mg sodium

RECORDS

Sides

These side dishes range from about 75 to about 165 calories, so you'll need to combine them with other dishes for a 400-calorie meal. Or, increase your portion size and enjoy them as a 200-calorie snack.

BAKED APPLES AND SWEET POTATOES* (page 314)

CRUNCHY CHINESE SLAW* (page 314)

GLAZED BRUSSELS SPROUTS WITH CRANBERRIES AND WALNUTS (page 315)

ROASTED BROCCOLI AND CAULIFLOWER* (page 315)

SKILLET GREEN BEANS WITH RED ONIONS AND TOMATOES (page 316)

STIR-FRIED CURLY KALE* (page 317)

SWEET-AND-SOUR RED CABBAGE* (page 318)

*Recipes are from the 21-day meal plan. The other recipes can be swapped into the meal plans or used to create your own meals.

BAKED APPLES AND SWEET POTATOES

▨ Serves 4
PREP TIME: **5 minutes**
TOTAL TIME: **25 minutes**

- 2 tart red apples, cored and quartered
- 1 large sweet potato, scrubbed and thickly sliced
- ¼ cup apple juice
- 1 tablespoon raisins
- ½ teaspoon ground cinnamon

Preheat the oven to 400°F. In an 8 x 8-inch baking dish, toss together the apples, sweet potato, apple juice, raisins, and cinnamon. Cover with foil and bake for 20 to 25 minutes, or until the sweet potato is soft. Divide evenly among 4 plates and serve warm.

PER SERVING: 91 calories, 1 g protein, 23 g carbohydrates, 14 g sugar, 0 g total fat, 0 g saturated fat, 3 g fiber, 20 mg sodium

CRUNCHY CHINESE SLAW

▨ Serves 4
PREP TIME: **15 minutes**
TOTAL TIME: **15 minutes**

- 2 tablespoons rice wine vinegar or white wine vinegar
- 2 teaspoons reduced-sodium soy sauce
- 1 teaspoon grated fresh ginger
- 2 teaspoons toasted sesame oil
- ½ head Chinese or Savoy cabbage, shredded
- 2 carrots, shredded
- 3 scallions, sliced
- ½ red bell pepper, seeded and cut into slivers
- 2 tablespoons chopped fresh cilantro
- 2 teaspoons toasted sesame seeds

In a large bowl, combine the vinegar, soy sauce, ginger, and oil. Add the cabbage, carrots, scallions, pepper, and cilantro. Toss to coat. Spoon into 4 bowls, and sprinkle each serving with sesame seeds.

PER SERVING: 76 calories, 2 g protein, 11 g carbohydrates, 5 g sugar, 3 g total fat, 0.5 g saturated fat, 4 g fiber, 137 mg sodium

GLAZED BRUSSELS SPROUTS WITH CRANBERRIES AND WALNUTS

■ Serves 4
PREP TIME: 5 minutes
TOTAL TIME: 15 minutes

1   pound Brussels sprouts, halved
½   cup vegetable broth or water
1   tablespoon honey
2   tablespoons fresh cranberries

1   teaspoon olive oil
⅛   teaspoon salt
    Ground black pepper
1   tablespoon chopped walnuts

1. In a skillet, combine the Brussels sprouts, broth or water, honey, cranberries, oil, and salt. Stir to mix. Cover and set over medium-high heat. Cook, stirring occasionally, for about 8 minutes, or until the sprouts are crisp-tender and glazed. Add scant amounts of water, if needed, if the bottom of the skillet is browning too fast.

2. Season to taste with pepper. Divide evenly among 4 plates and sprinkle with the walnuts.

PER SERVING: 90 calories, 5 g protein, 15 g carbohydrates, 7 g sugar, 3 g total fat, 0.5 g saturated fat, 5 g fiber, 491 mg sodium

ROASTED BROCCOLI AND CAULIFLOWER

■ Serves 4
PREP TIME: 10 minutes
TOTAL TIME: 30 minutes

2   pounds broccoli, cut into florets
2   pounds cauliflower, cut into florets
1   tablespoon extra-virgin olive oil

⅛   teaspoon salt
⅛   teaspoon ground black pepper
2   teaspoons lemon zest

1. Preheat the oven to 450°F. Coat a large baking sheet with cooking spray.

2. In a large bowl, combine the broccoli and cauliflower. Toss with the oil, salt, and pepper. Spread evenly on the prepared baking sheet. Roast, stirring occasionally, for about 20 minutes, until tender-crisp and slightly browned. Return to the bowl and toss with the lemon zest.

PER SERVING: 166 calories, 11 g protein, 27 g carbohydrates, 8 g sugar, 5 g total fat, 1 g saturated fat, 11 g fiber, 216 mg sodium

MAKE IT AHEAD

The roasted broccoli and cauliflower can be cooled and refrigerated in an airtight container for up to 3 days. To reheat, place on a microwaveable dish, cover with waxed paper, and cook on medium-high power for about 3 minutes, or until heated through.

SKILLET GREEN BEANS WITH RED ONIONS AND TOMATOES

■ Serves 4
PREP TIME: **15 minutes**
TOTAL TIME: **35 minutes**

1 pound green beans, trimmed and cut in half

1 tablespoon extra-virgin olive oil

1 medium red onion, thinly sliced

1 red bell pepper, seeded and sliced

2 cloves garlic, cut into thin slivers

⅛ teaspoon salt

⅛ teaspoon ground black pepper

1 pint grape tomatoes, halved

1. Bring ½-inch water to a boil in a large deep skillet over high heat. Add the green beans, cover, and cook for 6 to 8 minutes, until tender. Drain and set aside.

2. Dry the skillet. Heat the oil in the same skillet over medium heat. Stir in the onion, bell pepper, garlic, salt, and black pepper. Cook for 6 minutes, stirring often, until tender. Add the tomatoes. Toss well and add 1 tablespoon water. Cook for 2 to 3 minutes, stirring often, until the tomatoes start to collapse.

3. Return the beans to the skillet. Toss for 1 minute, until heated through. Serve hot or at room temperature.

PER SERVING: 108 calories, 4 g protein, 17 g carbohydrates, 9 g sugar, 4 g total fat, 1 g saturated fat, 5 g fiber, 87 mg sodium

STIR-FRIED CURLY KALE

■ Serves 4
PREP TIME: **5 minutes**
TOTAL TIME: **15 minutes**

1 tablespoon extra-virgin olive oil

2 cloves garlic, minced

1 pound kale leaves, chopped or torn into small pieces

⅛ teaspoon salt

Salt and ground black pepper

1. In a large skillet or large pot set over low heat, place the oil and garlic. Cook for about 3 minutes, or until the garlic is softened. Do not brown. Increase the heat to high.

2. Add half the kale to the pan and toss with tongs. Cover for about 1 minute, or until the leaves start to wilt. Add the remaining kale. Toss and cover for 1 minute. Uncover and cook, tossing, for about 2 minutes, or until the leaves are wilted, brightly colored, and glossy. Season to taste with salt and pepper.

PER SERVING: 89 calories, 5 g protein, 10 g carbohydrates, 0 g sugar, 5 g total fat, 1 g saturated fat, 2 g fiber, 116 mg sodium

MAKE IT AHEAD

Double the recipe, then cool and refrigerate the leftovers in a tightly sealed container. For an instant cooked dark green veggie, heat in the microwave, covered, on medium-high power, for about 90 seconds.

MAKE IT QUICKER

Bagged prewashed trimmed kale is sold in many supermarkets.

MAKE IT DIFFERENT

Collards, Swiss chard, mustard greens, or turnip greens may replace the kale.

SWEET-AND-SOUR RED CABBAGE

■ Serves 4
PREP TIME: **5 minutes**
TOTAL TIME: **40 minutes**

2 teaspoons canola oil

½ medium onion, chopped

8 ounces red cabbage, shredded (4 cups)

1 can (15 ounces) sliced beets, rinsed, drained, and cut into sticks

2 tablespoons red wine vinegar

1 tablespoon honey

2 bay leaves

Ground black pepper

1. In a large pot set over medium-low heat, place the oil and onion. Cook for about 3 minutes, or until the onion softens. Add the cabbage, beets, vinegar, honey, and bay leaves. Cook, stirring, for 2 minutes, or until sizzling. Reduce the heat to medium-low.

2. Cover and cook, stirring occasionally, for 30 minutes, or until the cabbage is very tender. Remove and discard the bay leaves. Season to taste with pepper.

PER SERVING: 93 calories, 2 g protein, 18 g carbohydrates, 13 g sugar, 3 g total fat, 0.5 g saturated fat, 3 g fiber, 222 mg sodium

RECIPES
Snacks

Here are a variety of 200-calorie snacks or desserts. You could also use these to create 400-calorie meals by combining two of them.

BEAN-AND-OLIVE BRUSCHETTA* (page 320)

BLACK BEAN DIP WITH BABY CARROTS* (page 320)

BROCCOLI SPEARS WITH ASIAN PEANUT SAUCE* (page 321)

CARAMELIZED ONION AND LENTIL SPREAD* (page 322)

SALSA FRESCA AND CHIPS* (page 323)

SEAFOOD ANTIPASTO* (page 324)

SPICED SWEET POTATO CHIPS* (page 325)

SPICY TOMATO-PARMESAN BITES* (page 325)

*Recipes are from the 21-day meal plan. The other recipes can be swapped into the meal plans or used to create your own meals.

BEAN-AND-OLIVE BRUSCHETTA

■ Serves 4
PREP TIME: **10 minutes**
TOTAL TIME: **14 minutes**

½ cup quartered cherry tomatoes
1 tablespoon extra-virgin olive oil
1 clove garlic, crushed
⅛ teaspoon ground black pepper

1 can (15.5 ounces) no-salt-added pinto beans, drained and rinsed
2 tablespoons chopped parsley
4 kalamata olives, sliced
4 slices crusty whole grain bread

1. In a medium bowl, combine the tomatoes, oil, garlic, and pepper. Stir vigorously until the tomatoes release their juices. Add the beans, parsley, and olives.

2. Toast or grill the bread until lightly brown and crisp. Top with the bean mixture and any juices. Cut in half and serve.

PER SERVING: 195 calories, 9 g protein, 27 g carbohydrates, 2 g sugar, 6 g total fat, 1 g saturated fat, 6 g fiber, 166 mg sodium

BLACK BEAN DIP WITH BABY CARROTS

■ Serves 2
PREP TIME: **5 minutes**
TOTAL TIME: **5 minutes**

1 can (15 ounces) reduced-sodium black beans, drained and rinsed
½ cup chopped tomato
1 tablespoon fresh lime juice
1 tablespoon chopped fresh cilantro

2 teaspoons flaxseed oil or extra-virgin olive oil
½ teaspoon ground cumin
   Hot-pepper sauce (optional)
2 cups baby carrots

1. Reserve ¼ cup of the beans. In a small mixing bowl, combine the remaining beans, tomato, lime juice, cilantro, oil, cumin, and a few dashes of hot-pepper sauce (if using). With a potato masher, squash the mixture into a paste. Add a few teaspoons of water, if needed, to make a softer mixture.

2. Stir in the reserved beans. Eat with baby carrots for dipping.

PER SERVING: 175 calories, 7 g protein, 32 g carbohydrates, 9 g sugar, 5 g total fat, 0.5 g saturated fat, 11 g fiber, 396 mg sodium

MAKE IT AHEAD

Refrigerate the dip in a tightly sealed container for up to 1 week, or freeze for up to 1 month.

BROCCOLI SPEARS WITH ASIAN PEANUT SAUCE

Serves 4
PREP TIME: 10 minutes
TOTAL TIME: 13 minutes

1 pound broccoli

⅓ cup smooth or chunky natural peanut butter

3 tablespoons rice wine vinegar or white wine vinegar

1½ teaspoons reduced-sodium soy sauce

1 teaspoon honey

2 cloves garlic, minced

2 teaspoons Asian chile sauce (optional)

2–3 tablespoons hot water (optional)

1. Cut the broccoli into long spears. Fill a large bowl with ice cubes and water to cover. Bring a large saucepan of salted water to a boil. Add the broccoli spears and cook for about 3 minutes, just until bright green and slightly tender. Drain and immediately transfer the broccoli to the cold water to stop the cooking. When cool, drain well and blot dry.

2. In a medium bowl, combine the peanut butter, vinegar, soy sauce, honey, garlic, and chile sauce (if using). Whisk together, adding hot water, if necessary, to make a sauce. Serve with the broccoli spears.

PER SERVING: 173 calories, 9 g protein, 14 g carbohydrates, 5 g sugar, 11 g total fat, 2 g saturated fat, 4 g fiber, 209 mg sodium

MAKE IT AHEAD

Refrigerate the cooled broccoli in a resealable plastic storage bag for up to 3 days. Refrigerate the dip in a tightly sealed container for up to 1 week.

MAKE IT DIFFERENT

Cauliflower or turnips can replace the broccoli.

CARAMELIZED ONION AND LENTIL SPREAD

■ Serves 8
PREP TIME: **10 minutes**
TOTAL TIME: **1 hour**

3 onions, diced

1 tablespoon extra-virgin olive oil

½ teaspoon dried sage

½ cup dry lentils

2 teaspoons red wine vinegar or balsamic vinegar

½ teaspoon ground black pepper

¼ teaspoon salt

2 tablespoons chopped fresh parsley

16 multigrain crispbreads

1. In a medium heavy-bottomed saucepan, combine the onions, 3 tablespoons water, oil, and sage. Cook over medium heat, stirring occasionally, for about 15 minutes, or until the onions are just golden.

2. Add the lentils and an additional 1½ cups water. Cover and cook, stirring occasionally, over very low heat for about 30 minutes, or until the lentils are very tender.

3. Stir in the vinegar, pepper, and salt and cook, uncovered, over medium heat, about 5 minutes, until thickened to a compote. Remove from the heat, add the parsley, and let cool.

4. Serve it spread on the crispbreads.

PER SERVING: 194 calories, 7 g protein, 34 g carbohydrates, 3 g sugar, 4 g total fat, 1 g saturated fat, 7 g fiber, 256 mg sodium

MAKE IT AHEAD

Cool the spread and refrigerate in a tightly sealed container for up to 1 week, or freeze for up to 1 month.

MAKE IT DIFFERENT

This pâté-like spread is also great on whole wheat pita chips or with broccoli spears for dipping.

SALSA FRESCA AND CHIPS

■ Serves 8

PREP TIME: 10 minutes

TOTAL TIME: 10 minutes

4 large ripe tomatoes, finely chopped

½ cup minced onion

½ cup chopped cilantro

2 jalapeño or serrano chile peppers, stemmed, seeded, and minced (wear plastic gloves when handling), or more to taste

1 tablespoon fresh lime juice or red wine vinegar

2 cloves garlic, minced

½ teaspoon salt

10 ounces tortilla chips

In a large bowl, combine the tomatoes, onion, cilantro, chile peppers, lime juice or vinegar, garlic, and salt. Stir to mix. Serve right away or let stand for at least 30 minutes to allow the flavors to blend. Serve with the tortilla chips.

PER SERVING: 200 calories, 3 g protein, 29 g carbohydrates, 3 g sugar, 8 g total fat, 1 g saturated fat, 3 g fiber, 259 mg sodium

MAKE IT AHEAD

The salsa can be refrigerated in an airtight container for up to 1 week.

SEAFOOD ANTIPASTO

■ Serves 6
PREP TIME: **5 minutes**
TOTAL TIME: **10 minutes**

1   fennel bulb
1   tablespoon balsamic vinegar
1   tablespoon extra-virgin olive oil
¼   red or yellow bell pepper, seeded and
    thinly sliced
¼   small red onion, thinly sliced

1   can (4.375 ounces) water-packed
    sardines, drained and patted dry
1   can (6 ounces) whole baby clams, drained
    and rinsed
    Ground black pepper
6½ -inch-thick slices (4 ounces each) whole
    wheat baguette, toasted

1. Thinly slice the fennel bulb, reserving the fronds for garnish.

2. In a bowl, combine the vinegar and oil. Whisk to blend. Add the fennel bulb, bell pepper, onion, sardines, and clams. Toss gently. Season to taste with black pepper. Serve garnished with the reserved fennel fronds and with the baguette.

PER SERVING: 211 calories, 14 g protein, 22 g carbohydrates, 4 g sugar, 8 g total fat, 1 g saturated fat, 2 g fiber, 765 mg sodium

MAKE IT AHEAD

Refrigerate the antipasto in a tightly covered container for up to 3 days.

MAKE IT DIFFERENT

Replace the fennel with 4 sliced ribs celery and the fennel fronds with celery leaves.

SPICED SWEET POTATO CHIPS

■ Serves 2
PREP TIME: **5 minutes**
TOTAL TIME: **20 minutes**

1 sweet potato (12 ounces), well-scrubbed but not peeled

½ teaspoon ground cumin

½ teaspoon kosher salt

¼ teaspoon chili powder

¼ cup sour cream

1 tablespoon fresh lime juice

1. Heat the oven to 375°F. Coat 2 baking sheets with cooking spray.

2. Cut the potato into very thin slices. Arrange the slices on the sheets in a single layer. Lightly coat the slices with cooking spray. Bake for 7 minutes, or until the potato starts to brown. Remove the pans from the oven and turn the slices. Return to the oven and bake for 7 to 10 minutes, or until browned. Remove the potatoes to a large tray. Allow to cool for 10 minutes.

3. Meanwhile, in a small bowl, combine the cumin, salt, and chili powder. In another bowl, mix the sour cream and lime juice. Sprinkle the cumin mixture over the chips and toss well.

4. Serve with the sour cream for dipping.

PER SERVING: 205 calories, 4 g protein, 37 g carbohydrates, 12 g sugar, 5 g total fat, 3 g saturated fat, 6 g fiber, 561 mg sodium

MAKE IT LAST

Refrigerate the chips in a tightly sealed storage container for up to 5 days.

SPICY TOMATO-PARMESAN BITES

■ Serves 4
PREP TIME: **5 minutes**
TOTAL TIME: **10 minutes**

¼ cup extra-virgin olive oil

2 tablespoons fresh lime juice

½ jalapeño pepper, stemmed, seeded, and minced (wear plastic gloves when handling)

1 teaspoon honey

1 clove garlic, minced

Pinch of salt

4 thin slices (½ ounce each) Parmesan cheese, halved

16 cherry tomatoes

1. In a small bowl, combine the oil, lime juice, jalapeño, honey, garlic, and salt.

2. Using a toothpick, skewer half a chunk of cheese between 2 cherry tomatoes. Set on a plate. Repeat with the remaining tomatoes and Parmesan. Drizzle with the dressing.

PER SERVING: 203 calories, 6 g protein, 6 g carbohydrates, 4 g sugar, 18 g total fat, 4.5 g saturated fat, 1 g fiber, 261 mg sodium

RECIPES

Treats

The delicious treats come in around 200 calories or less. For the lighter ones, check out the meal plans for other foods to pair them with for a 200-calorie indulgence.

BAKED PEARS WITH CREAMY LEMON SAUCE* (page 327)

BALSAMIC STRAWBERRIES WITH PISTACHIOS AND CHOCOLATE* (page 327)

BLUEBERRY-RICOTTA SUNDAE* (page 328)

CHOCOLATE-PEANUT BUTTER BROWNIES (page 329)

CREAMY TROPICAL FRUIT MEDLEY* (page 330)

DARK CHOCOLATE-RASPBERRY PATTIES* (page 330)

DOUBLE CHOCOLATE PUDDING* (page 331)

STRAWBERRY SORBET* (page 331)

WARM GLAZED ORANGES WITH WALNUTS* (page 332)

*Recipes are from the 21-day meal plan. The other recipes can be swapped into the meal plans or used to create your own meals.

BAKED PEARS WITH CREAMY LEMON SAUCE

■ Serves 4
PREP TIME: 5 minutes
TOTAL TIME: 30 minutes

5 teaspoons honey
1 teaspoon canola oil
4 large ripe pears, halved and cored

1 cup 0% plain Greek yogurt
1 tablespoon fresh lemon juice
2 teaspoons lemon zest

1. Preheat the oven to 375°F.

2. In a 13 x 9-inch glass baking dish, combine 2 teaspoons of the honey, 2 tablespoons water, and the oil. Stir well with a fork. Place the pears in the baking dish, folding the mixture until coated. Turn the pears cut side up, making sure that some of the honey mixture is in the cavities. Bake for 15 to 20 minutes, or until the pears are very tender when pierced with a fork. Remove from the oven and let to cool in the pan for about 10 minutes.

3. In a small bowl, combine the yogurt, lemon juice, lemon zest, and the remaining 3 teaspoons honey and whisk until smooth.

4. Transfer 2 pear halves to each of 4 dessert dishes, and spoon some of the pan juices over the top. Dollop ¼ cup of the yogurt over each.

PER SERVING: 200 calories, 6 g protein, 45 g carbohydrates, 32 g sugar, 2 g total fat, 0 g saturated fat, 7 g fiber, 24 mg sodium

MAKE IT AHEAD

Double the recipe. Cool the leftover pears and refrigerate with the cooking sauce in a tightly sealed container for up to 1 week.

BALSAMIC STRAWBERRIES WITH PISTACHIOS AND CHOCOLATE

■ Serves 1
PREP TIME: 5 minutes
TOTAL TIME: 15 minutes

¾ cup sliced strawberries
1½ teaspoons balsamic vinegar
1 tablespoon plain Greek yogurt

½ ounce dark chocolate, chopped
1 tablespoon shelled pistachios, coarsely chopped

1. In a small bowl, toss the strawberries with the vinegar. Let sit for 10 minutes.

2. Top with the yogurt, chocolate, and pistachios.

PER SERVING: 182 calories, 4 g protein, 22 g carbohydrates, 15 g sugar, 9 g total fat, 3.5 g saturated fat, 4 g fiber, 43 mg sodium

BLUEBERRY-RICOTTA SUNDAE

■ Serves 4
PREP TIME: **8 minutes**
TOTAL TIME: **1 hour 5 minutes**

2   cups blueberries
1   tablespoon honey
1   teaspoon cornstarch
2   teaspoons fresh lime juice

½   cup part-skim ricotta cheese
½   cup 0% plain Greek yogurt
1½ teaspoons vanilla extract
     Dash of ground cinnamon

1. In a small saucepan, combine the blueberries, honey, cornstarch, and lime juice. Cook, stirring, over medium-high heat for 5 minutes, or until the sauce thickens slightly. Transfer to a large bowl, cover, and refrigerate for at least 1 hour until chilled.

2. In a blender or food processor, combine the ricotta, yogurt, vanilla, and cinnamon. Process until smooth. Spoon into 4 dessert bowls and top with the blueberry sauce.

PER SERVING: 140 calories, 7 g protein, 18 g carbohydrates, 12 g sugar, 5 g total fat, 2 g saturated fat, 3 g fiber, 51 mg sodium

MAKE IT DIFFERENT

Replace the blueberries with strawberries or raspberries.

CHOCOLATE-PEANUT BUTTER BROWNIES

▣ Serves 24
PREP TIME: **15 minutes**
TOTAL TIME: **1 hour 45 minutes**

1   cup whole wheat pastry flour
¾   cup unsweetened cocoa powder
½   teaspoon baking powder
⅛   teaspoon salt
¼   cup butter, softened

2   ounces low-fat cream cheese, softened
¾   cup sugar
3   eggs
1   tablespoon vanilla extract
½   cup natural peanut butter

1. Preheat the oven to 350°F. Coat a 13 x 9-inch baking pan with nonstick spray.

2. In a medium bowl, combine the flour, cocoa, baking powder, and salt.

3. In a large mixing bowl, combine the butter, cream cheese, and sugar. With an electric mixer on medium speed, beat for 2 to 3 minutes, or until smooth. Add the eggs, one at a time, beating until smooth after each addition. Stir in the vanilla.

4. Reduce the mixer speed to low. Gradually add the flour mixture, beating just to combine. Pour the batter into the prepared pan.

5. Microwave the peanut butter in a small bowl until slightly melted, 20 to 30 seconds. Dollop evenly over the top of the brownie batter, and swirl peanut butter into the batter with a knife.

6. Bake for about 30 minutes, or until a wooden pick inserted in the center comes out with just a few moist crumbs. Be careful not to overbake, or brownies will be dry.

PER SERVING: 114 calories, 3 g protein, 13 g carbohydrates, 7 g sugar, 6 g total fat, 2 g saturated fat, 2 g fiber, 43 mg sodium

CREAMY TROPICAL FRUIT MEDLEY

▦ Serves 8
PREP TIME: 20 minutes
TOTAL TIME: 20 minutes

3   tablespoons chopped fresh mint
2   tablespoons honey
2   cups 0% plain Greek yogurt
¼   cup unsweetened coconut flakes
½   small honeydew, cubed

½   cantaloupe, cubed
1   pint strawberries, hulled and halved
2   cups fresh pineapple chunks
½   cup sliced almonds

1. In a large bowl, combine the mint, honey, and 1 tablespoon water. Stir and use the spoon to lightly crush the mint. Stir in the yogurt and coconut.

2. Add the honeydew, cantaloupe, strawberries, and pineapple and gently toss to combine. Top with the almonds just before serving.

PER SERVING: 166 calories, 8 g protein, 25 g carbohydrates, 20 g sugar, 5 g total fat, 2 g saturated fat, 3 g fiber, 40 mg sodium

DARK CHOCOLATE-RASPBERRY PATTIES

▦ Serves 6
PREP TIME: 5 minutes
TOTAL TIME: 1 hour 5 minutes

4   ounces dark chocolate
½   teaspoon vanilla extract

6   ounces raspberries

1. Line a baking sheet with parchment paper or a silicone baking mat.

2. In a small, heavy saucepan, melt the chocolate, over very low heat, stirring frequently. (Or microwave on low power for about 90 seconds, stirring frequently.) Stir in the vanilla.

3. Spoon the chocolate onto the prepared pan to create twelve 2-inch circles. Press 1 or 2 raspberries into each circle. Refrigerate for about 1 hour, or until the chocolate is set.

PER SERVING: 100 calories, 2 g protein, 13 g carbohydrates, 8 g sugar, 7 g total fat, 4.5 g saturated fat, 4 g fiber, 0 mg sodium

DOUBLE CHOCOLATE PUDDING

■ Serves 6
PREP TIME: **10 minutes**
TOTAL TIME: **22 minutes**

6 tablespoons unsweetened cocoa powder
¼ cup sugar
2 tablespoons cornstarch
1 teaspoon instant coffee powder

2 cups fat-free milk
1 ounce unsweetened chocolate, finely chopped
2 teaspoons vanilla extract

1. In a medium saucepan, whisk together the cocoa, sugar, cornstarch, and coffee powder until blended. Gradually whisk in the milk.

2. Cook over medium heat, stirring constantly, for 10 minutes, or until the pudding thickens and comes to a boil. Reduce the heat to low and add the unsweetened chocolate. Cook, stirring constantly, for 1 minute, until the chocolate melts. Remove from the heat and stir in the vanilla. Pour the pudding into 6 custard cups. Serve warm.

PER SERVING: 119 calories, 18 g carbohydrates, 13 g sugar, 2 g fiber, 4 g total fat, 2 g saturated fat, 4 g protein, 35 mg sodium

MAKE IT AHEAD

Allow to pudding cool, cover with plastic wrap and refrigerate for at least 2 hours. Serve cold.

STRAWBERRY SORBET

■ Serves 4
PREP TIME: **10 minutes**
TOTAL TIME: **10 minutes**

1 pound frozen strawberries
½ cup 0% plain yogurt or silken tofu

1 tablespoon honey

In a food processor, process the strawberries, yogurt or tofu, and honey until creamy, stopping to scrape down the sides of the bowl, as needed. If the fruit doesn't break down completely, gradually add cold water, as needed, a tablespoon or two at a time, being careful not to process the sorbet into liquid. Serve immediately or freeze.

PER SERVING: 71 calories, 3 g protein, 16 g carbohydrates, 11 g sugar, 0 g total fat, 0 g saturated fat, 2 g fiber, 13 mg sodium

MAKE IT AHEAD

To serve later, allow 10 to 15 minutes for the sorbet to soften at room temperature.

MAKE IT DIFFERENT

Replace the strawberries with frozen peaches, mangoes, or mixed berries.

WARM GLAZED ORANGES WITH WALNUTS

■ Serves 4
PREP TIME: 10 minutes
TOTAL TIME: 13 minutes

4 navel oranges

4 teaspoons honey

1 teaspoon canola oil

¼ cup chopped walnuts

1. Grate the zest from 2 of the oranges into a large nonstick skillet. Add the honey, 1 tablespoon water, and the oil. Set over medium-high heat.

2. Peel the oranges and slice into rounds. Place in the skillet and cook, shaking the pan occasionally, for 3 minutes, or until the oranges are glazed.

3. Spoon the oranges and pan juices onto 4 dessert plates. Sprinkle with the walnuts.

PER SERVING: 148 calories, 2 g protein, 24 g carbohydrates, 18 g sugar, 6 g total fat, 0.5 g saturated fat, 4 g fiber, 2 mg sodium

MAKE IT AHEAD

The oranges are also delicious at room temperature. Pack the oranges and walnuts separately for a brown-bag snack.

Chapter 24

Overcoming Obstacles

It's easy to start exercising. Millions of people do it every January 1st, but around about February, most of them have dropped out. I don't want you to join this constantly frustrated club full of dropouts. Instead, I want you to find the continual motivation you need to just keep on doing it. That way, you can avoid the torture of having to keep starting over as well as the guilt that comes every time you backslide into sedentary living.

In this chapter, you'll find my best advice for overcoming the most common obstacles and excuses to maintaining a walking habit for life.

EXCUSE BUSTER #1: SURVIVE SHIN PAIN

Shin pain is one of the most common problems both new and experienced walkers encounter. In most cases, the pain is not a result of an injury but due to deconditioned muscles. This muscle group, which includes a muscle called the anterior tibialis, is responsible for pulling your toes up as you walk. Remember proper walking technique? You land on your heel. Well, it's your shin muscles that keep your toes off the ground as you land and minimize

impact by preventing your foot from slapping to the ground too quickly. Every step you take, they kick into action.

If you've been walking in the past, you may or may not have experienced shin pain. Your shins don't have to work as hard during a casual stroll, when you're landing more flat-footed. But when you turn up the tempo on your walks, your shins might start screaming. The faster you move, the more steps you take, which makes your shins work harder than they are used to.

The good news is that as your shins become conditioned, you'll have less pain.

And by the way, I'm not talking about "shin splints" as many people incorrectly refer to this more-common pain. Shin splits, or medial tibial stress syndrome as it's technically known, is inflammation of the muscles, tendons, and bone tissue around your tibia (the big bone that you can feel on the inside of your lower leg). This type of injury typically occurs along the inner border of the tibia, where muscles attach to the bone. The area tends to be painful to the touch, and the pain usually doesn't ease when you stop moving. Shin splints are more common in high-impact activities like running.

The shin pain walkers usually experience, on the other hand, is more central, right in the front of the shins, and eases when you slow down or stop. Usually, the area isn't painful to the touch. It's more like the discomfort or burning you get when you've done lots and lots of crunches or leg lifts. Not an injury, per se.

For On-the-Spot Relief

Try the following tactics to reduce shin pain when it strikes.

Increase your warmup time. Taking a little longer to get up to fast speeds increases blood flow to these muscles and makes them more flexible, which may minimize pain. Also, try the Dynamic Warmup on page 48. Some of the moves specifically target this area.

Check your shoes. Worn out, thick-heeled, or stiff shoes may contribute to shin pain. If any of these describes your footwear, make a trip to that athletic store and try on some new sneaks to see if they make a difference.

Shorten your steps. Overstriding can provoke pain because it adds impact, and your shins have to work harder to lift your toes. (For more on how and why to shorten your stride, see page 73.)

Tighten your butt. This helps in two ways. You can't reach your leg far out in front of you when you're squeezing, so you'll achieve that shorter stride mentioned above. It also works as a diversionary tactic. While you're focusing on the butt squeeze, you'll pay less attention to your shins.

Slow down. If adjusting your technique doesn't help, take your speed down just a notch. For many people, this may be enough to ease the ache so you can keep going. Also, pay attention to your push-off with your rear leg. Try to keep your toes on the ground as long as possible to open up the angle of your foot and ankle . . . and provide a little stretch for your shins.

Stop and stretch. If you still feel pain after slowing down, stop and loosen up your shins by pointing and flexing your feet and rotating them like you're drawing circles with your toes. (You can additionally do some of the stretches on the next page, and then ease back into walking.)

Chill out. Icing your shins after a walk may help to alleviate more intense pain.

And remember, shin pain usually resolves in a week or two, once your shins get in shape. But it can return temporarily if you turn up the intensity of your walks and challenge your shins to get fitter. In the meantime, you may be able to speed up the conditioning with the stretches and strength moves below.

If pain persists for more than 2 weeks, or the pain intensifies, see your doctor or other health-care professional.

To Prevent Shin Pain

You may be able to avoid shin pain altogether, or at least minimize it, by doing the following stretches during or after a walk. Do all of them or choose the one or two that give you the best stretch. Hold each stretch for 10 to 30 seconds, and aim to do a total of 1 to 2 minutes of stretches for each shin. You can do these stretches with sneakers on, but you'll get a better stretch if you do them barefoot.

Toe tuck—Place your right foot behind you with the top of your toes on the floor. Press your toes, the top of your foot, and your ankle down toward the floor until you feel a stretch in your shin. Hold for 10 to 15 seconds, and repeat once or twice with each foot.

Assisted toe tuck—Stand with your left leg crossed in front of your right. Point the toes of your left foot so the tops of your toes are on the floor. Bend your right knee slightly so that it gently presses into your left calf until you feel a stretch in your left shin and the top of your left foot. Hold for 10 to 15 seconds, and repeat once or twice with each foot.

Seated knee lift—Sit on the floor or ground (if you're outside, you'll want to do this on grass to protect your knees) with your legs bent underneath you so you're sitting on your heels and the tops of your feet are on the floor. You can do this with or without shoes. Place your right hand on the floor beside you for balance. Slowly lift your right knee off of the floor, assisting with your left hand. Lift until you

feel a stretch in your shin. Hold for 10 to 15 seconds, and repeat once or twice with each foot.

Strengthen Your Shins

To speed up shin conditioning, you can add these three shin strengtheners to your routine. (Don't do all of the moves on the same day.)

Heel walk—During your warmups, cooldowns, or anytime, walk around on your heels to strengthen your shins. Start with just a few seconds and gradually build up to about a minute at a time. You can do this daily.

Double toe tap—While sitting with your feet flat on the floor, lift your toes off the floor and then lift the balls of your feet off the floor in two separate steps.

Lower in two steps also: First place the balls of your feet back on the floor, keeping your toes lifted. Then lower your toes. Do 1 to 3 sets of 8 to 12 reps. You can do this daily.

Toe pull—Attach a resistance band around a sturdy piece of furniture or a railing. Sit on the floor with your right leg straight and your left one bent. Loop the band around your right foot. Flex your right foot, pulling your toes toward you and against the band. Slowly release, but only to neutral position. Don't point your toes, otherwise the band will slip off. Do 1 to 3 sets of 8 to 12 reps. You can do this 2 or 3 days a week.

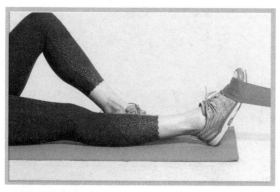

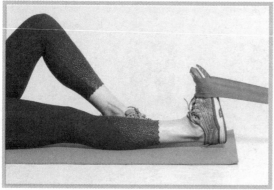

EXCUSE BUSTER #2: FIND ENOUGH TIME

"I don't have time" may be *the* all-time excuse—and I don't mean just for exercising. By the way, I'm not immune to it either. "Crazy busy" is one of my popular refrains when friends and family ask how things are going. And it hasn't changed since I left my working-in-an-office full-time job for more flexible freelance hours. I really hate to admit this, but my husband was right. Instead of having more free time, I simply filled up the time that used to be spent commuting or sitting in meetings with other stuff, some of it useful and productive—more exercise, volunteering, and more time with friends—but too much of it, like Facebook or game apps, not!

I'm telling you this so you know that I get it. I'm right there with you using these very strategies to keep myself on track, too. So, don't hate me when I tell you that most of us aren't as busy as we think, and we have more time than we think. Yes, I'm calling myself out on this, too. (Now, this doesn't apply to you if you're working two or three jobs to make ends meet while raising kids or caring for other family members. God bless you if you are! And I'm so proud of you for still taking steps to do something good for your health. Do "what you can when you can," sage advice from Carla Birnberg, a favorite blogger of mine.)

So, let's start tackling this no-time obstacle.

There are a lot of time-management programs, tools, and books available—but we all still seem to have no time, so what does that say? The only thing I'm going to say about time management is that you need to be aware of where you are currently spending your time if you want to change it.

This is one reason your activity log (page 38) is such a valuable resource. It will help you to see how you are spending your time. Use your log to see if there are activities that maybe you should cut back on, such as watching TV, checking e-mail every 15 minutes, socializing around food, and so on. Then, replace those activities with some walking.

Another strategy is to combine some of those sedentary activities with more active ones. Watch

TV while you walk on a treadmill. Stand up and march in place or walk around as you check e-mail on your phone. Socialize with friends or family by taking a walk in the park, playing golf (even the mini kind), or going ice-skating.

If you think you've squeezed all the time you can out of your activity log, try refining the practice using another useful tool. Toggl.com is a Web site and app that you can use to track your time. (I'm sure there are many others, too.) You can color code things so it's easy to see how much time you're spending on certain activities related to work, family time, volunteering, chores, social media, or whatever categories you are interested in tracking.

Writing your workouts down in your calendar and treating them like other appointments can also help. This was the strategy that really helped Rebecca (see page 70) to finally make exercise a part of her life. When she did, she found that she had more energy (a 33 percent boost when she was tested), and she actually felt like she had more time once she started walking. "It's amazing how exercise gives you back the time you spent in having more energy to accomplish things. I'm much more productive, and my mind is much clearer and organized when I walk regularly."

And remember how those neuropathways in your brain can form around repeated thoughts and feelings (page 20)? If you keep telling yourself that you don't have time to take a walk, eventually that becomes your reality. So, start telling yourself: "I have time to take a walk. Exercise is important. I'll make the time." Keep saying it over and over again, and it will become a self-fulfilling prophecy.

EXCUSE BUSTER #3: BEAT BAD WEATHER

In the northeast area of the United States, the amount of walking that people do decreases by 50 to 65 percent in the winter months, according to research.[1] No wonder so many of us dread slipping on shorts come spring and summer. We really need to get over this weather thing!

Here's my adopted philosophy from the British on weather: "There's no such thing as bad weather, only bad clothing." With a few exceptions (for example, slick, frigid, or icy conditions that are unsafe), it holds true. I mean, think about people who climb Everest. They withstand subzero temperatures and hurricane-force winds. But they survive, in large part, because of their gear.

So maybe some snow and temperatures in the teens aren't looking so bad now?

The key to scratching weather off of your obstacles list is to invest in some good-quality gear. For

Walk Your Way Past Inertia

Sometimes, you have to use tough love, and just force yourself to do it. When you do, you might be surprised at the result. That's what happened to me one day when I begrudgingly went for a walk. It was one of those days (since this is a tip, I won't clutter it up with details). I was in a really crabby mood. Despite knowing that taking a walk would help, I didn't feel like walking. But, I went because I was on a "streak." I immediately opened Facebook to distract myself. When my hands got cold, I shoved my phone in my pocket and finally looked up. Overhead were the most brilliant cloud patterns painted in blues, purples, and pinks from the setting sun. One looked like a giant flower in the sky with the sun as its center. It was breathtaking, and I instantly felt more relaxed and very thankful that I had forced myself to take a walk.

most conditions, layering is the key. So, let's start with that.

Base layer—This is what's up against your skin. Think of the thermal underwear you wore as a kid, but now it looks more stylish. The goal of this layer is to keep you dry. To do that, you want a top, bottom, and underwear that are made from a wicking fabric such as a synthetic polyester. So, when you start sweating, the fabric pulls the moisture away from your skin so it can evaporate more easily. Wet skin will make you feel colder. The worst base layer is cotton, because it stays wet and keeps moisture on your skin. There are different thicknesses of base layers, depending on conditions. You may want a thinner layer for cool spring or fall days, and a thicker one for winter. Some are also designed so you can wear them on their own when it's not too cold. And, in addition to wicking away moisture, some base layers also offer insulation, which is the primary job of the next layer. Many brands have their own specially-designed fabrics, like Patagonia's Capilene. They are usually made of synthetic polyester, silk, or wool blends. Some are lightweight, while others are heavier weight for colder climates.

Middle layer—As its name implies, you generally wear this layer on top of your base layer and under an outer layer in more extreme conditions. The purpose of this layer is to keep you warm, so it is often made of synthetic fleece like Polartec or wool such as SmartWool or merino wool. Again, you will find different thicknesses for different conditions. The fabrics for this layer also tend to be moisture wicking to carry the sweat from your base layer farther away from your body. You could wear your old college sweatshirt, but it will be bulkier and won't wick away sweat, so you may get colder.

Top layer—This is your outermost layer, the one between you and the elements. In choosing this layer, you need to consider the elements you will be facing. For rainy areas, it's worth investing in a waterproof fabric like Gore-Tex that will keep even heavy rains out while still allowing moisture that's inside, like sweat, to evaporate. Many brands have their own line such as the North Face's DryVent or Marmot's MemBrain. There are also water-resistant jackets and pants. They make it harder for rain and snow to seep in, but eventually they will. In a pinch, a department store rain poncho or garbage bag can offer some protection, and it may be an option if rainy weather is infrequent in your area. If you live

BUST THIS CRAZY EXCUSE

People used to believe that the body had a set number of heartbeats, and once your body used them up, you died. A great excuse for not exercising . . . since your heart beats faster and you're using more beats, right? Wrong! When you exercise and become more fit, your resting heart rate decreases. So, even if you rev up your heart rate for an hour a day with high-intensity walking, you'd actually be using up fewer heart beats over time. Here's how it works.

If your resting heart rate were 70 beats per minute (bpm), your heart would beat 100,800 times a day. Now, if you started exercising and lowered your resting heart rate to 60 bpm, and did an hour of intense walking in which your heart rate was at 140 bpm (probably more than most could do), you'd log 94,800 beats a day. So, you'd actually save 6,000 heartbeats a day by exercising!

in a particularly cold region, select dark colors for your outer layers, because they absorb sunlight to keep you warmer.

When choosing your layers, dress for temperature about 10 degrees higher than outside, since you'll be generating some of your own heat. Wear a thin, moisture-wicking pair of gloves underneath heavier gloves. That way, if your hands get sweaty, you can remove the outer layer without exposing your skin. And, if icy air bothers you, wrap a scarf over your mouth to warm the air as you inhale.

For those in southern areas, or wherever summers run hot, you may be dealing with the exact opposite—too much heat and humidity. In this case, the fewer layers, the better. You'll also want to choose synthetic, moisture-wicking fabrics instead of cotton, which stays damp and can cause chafing. It's best to keep your clothes loose-fitting, lightweight, and light-colored to reflect the sun.

Even more important than clothing in hot weather is your walking technique. When temperatures start to rise, shorten and slow down your walks until you acclimate. You should also avoid walking during midday, when temperatures are at their peak. The coolest times are usually early morning or late evening. Another option is to choose shady walking routes, where temperatures may feel up to 25° cooler.

For all weather conditions, stay hydrated and listen to your body. If you're not feeling well, stop exercising and go inside.

How to Motivate Yourself through Any Storm

In addition to wearing the right gear, use these strategies to make walking fun. This way, you'll want to get out and do it—even if the weather is crummy!

Book it. Nope, I'm not talking about speeding up this time. If you love to read or have a desire to

Walk Your Way to Get Noticed

No matter what the weather is, if you're walking at dawn, dusk, or nighttime, wear reflective gear, so motorists can see you. The more reflective you are, the sooner you'll be seen, especially if some of the reflective material is on moving body parts like your arms and legs.

read more, combine literature with walking and start a walking book club. Pick a book and meet weekly to walk and talk about a few chapters at a time, instead of cramming to read it all at once. Or, you can select an article of interest, such as work–life balance, if you're all working moms. Since walking improves brain function, you may find your discussions livelier than if you were sitting around someone's living room—and you'll burn instead of consume calories.

Add a friend. A common motivation strategy is to walk with a friend, but what if you don't go at the same pace or one of you prefers longer walks than the other? Instead of giving up the camaraderie or sacrificing a good workout, simply arrange to meet at the appropriate time. For instance, you can do a hard-core, 30-minute walk, and have a friend meet you at the end for an easier 30-minute walk-and-talk. "Solo walks are nice, but walking with a friend is happiness for the soul," said test panelist Jenny Hughes. "Everything seems brighter when with a friend! It helps to encourage you, makes walking distances seem easier, and makes time go faster."

Take an art walk. No museum required. Instead, create your own work of art as you walk. Use a smartphone app like MapMyWalk, which creates a color outline of your route as you go. You can even design your route first to match a design and then follow it—others have used GPS to create routes shaped like guitars, robots, and even messages like "Will you marry me?" (Check out sample images on their Facebook page or go to Pinterest to find other GPS creations.) Give it a try, and post your picture online when you're done—maybe you'll inspire your friends.

Make walking truly app-ealing. MapMyWalk (mapmywalk.com) is the free app I use the most, and the one that most test panelists used. Why? It's easy. You get data on exactly what you did—how far you went, for how long, and at what pace. You can see progress over time and compare walks. I often try to beat my time on my regular routes. You can share your walks with others and even compete with each other, like test panelist Kim (page 17) and her sister do.

- If you're not motivated by data, there are other free apps that may inspire you more. Charity Miles (charitymiles.org) allows you to raise money for a cause of your choice. There are more than a dozen charities—including Habitat for Humanity, Autism Speaks, Wounded Warrior Project, and Pencils of Promise—from which to choose. They'll donate 25 cents for every mile you walk. The more you walk, the more you help.

- Become an integral part of a spy thriller with The Walk—Fitness Tracker and Game ($4.99; thewalkgame.com). It's like an interactive audiobook. As you walk, you unlock audio clips that tell you the story, and you're the instigator of the action for 500 miles.

- Virtual Walk (virtual-walk.com) is a free app that will turn your neighborhood walk into a trek through Central Park or the Grand Canyon, complete with photos and history. But you have to cover the real-life distances in between landmarks to unlock them.

Go on a family outing. Turn your walk into a scavenger hunt to entice your kids and spouse to join you. For a high-tech version, try geocaching (free; geocaching.com). You pick a geocache in your area (or anywhere, they are hidden all over the world) and use your GPS to find it. It's both a physical and mental workout as you navigate to the location and then search to find the geocache container. For more ideas, see "Walk Your Way to Make It a Family Affair," page 61.

EXCUSE BUSTER #4: GET MORE SLEEP

This isn't an obvious obstacle, but if you're frustrated with your results, you might want to look at your sleep habits. It seems like almost every day there is a new study revealing the detrimental effects of getting fewer than 7 to 8 hours of sleep a night. Besides making you groggy, grumpy, and more accident-prone, a lack of sleep can be a serious saboteur of your weight-loss efforts. When you're sleep deprived, your body produces less stay-young growth hormone, which maintains your muscles, and more of the stress hormone cortisol, which contributes to belly fat. Lack of sleep also affects hunger and satiety hormones, thus spurring on your appetite, preventing you from feeling satisfied when you eat, and increasing cravings. Finally, it messes with your metabolism, priming your body to store, instead of burn, fat.

So, if you're not getting enough sleep, make going to bed earlier one of your goals and ask your family to hold you accountable. If you have trouble falling asleep, eliminate stimulating activities like watching TV or being on your phone or computer during the hour or two preceding bedtime. And in the evening, dim the lights to help your body get into sleep mode (but when it's time for sleep, make sure your room is dark).

PROFILE: Jackie Harth, 37

Lost 14.2 pounds & 10.25 inches

Jackie didn't have a very high opinion of walking in the beginning. "I thought it was time consuming and not enjoyable," she admitted. But she was intrigued by the possibilities, and she needed a kick-start so she signed up.

It didn't take long for Jackie to notice that walking gave her more. "It used to take me a long time to get motivated to get things done during the day," she explained. "Now, when I walk in the morning, I get home, have a cup of coffee, and get to work, throwing a load of laundry in right away or vacuuming first thing instead of sitting down and watching TV."

There were still more than a few days where it was a struggle for Jackie to lace up her sneakers, but pushing through helped to reinforce why she was doing this. "One day, I was cranky and felt like being lazy," she said. "But I realized that if I did that, I would probably just sit at home and eat. So, instead, I forced myself to walk. In doing so, I (1) avoided overeating and (2) released the stress that had built up." When she needed an extra push, she enlisted the aid of her husband, telling him to nag her at a specific time until she went for a walk. "I would be angry at him for the first 5 minutes, but then I was thankful, because my body would feel good getting out and stretching, and I'd usually walk for 45 to 60 minutes."

Jackie also struggled with the strength training until she stopped trying to do it at home and personalized the program to her needs. She joined some friends for a twice-a-week BodyPump class instead. "Being in a class setting motivates me more, and we all text each other to see who's going."

Despite thinking that walking wouldn't burn enough calories to lose weight, Jackie shed 14 pounds and 10¼ inches. And, while she was right about walking toning her legs (she lost 1¼ inches off her thighs), she discovered that it also helped her lose 2½ inches off of her waist and 2 inches off of her hips.

BEFORE

AFTER

Acknowledgments

Writing a book is a lot like walking a marathon. You take it one step at a time. You build up gradually. And, you require *a lot* of support along the way. I am profoundly grateful to everyone who helped to make this book possible.

To the team at Rodale: Anne Egan for your belief in the project; Alisa Bowman for your guidance and reassurance; Allyson Machate for your skillful and speedy editing; Sabrina Mastronardo and Leah Polakoff for your quick research assistance; Christina Gaugler for your creativity; Juli Roberts, Jennifer Kushnier, and Amy Fritch, of the Rodale test kitchen, for your culinary and nutrition know-how; Tammy Strunk for your assistance with our test panel; and the photo team: Mitch Mandel, Matt Rainey, Troy Schnyder, Nikki Weber, Colleen Kubrick, and Pam Simpson.

To the test panel: Kim Bray, Barbara Breisch, Marybeth Dreisbach, Eileen Gradwell, Jackie Harth, Denise Heberling, Jenny Hughes, Karen Malley, Rebecca Owens, Umberto Piscina, Kathy Rack, Sue Schoch, Gwen Shields, Sue Snyder, Andrew Stanten, and Janet Starner. My utmost thanks for sharing your experiences.

To my fellow walking coach, Lee Scott, for generously sharing your time and knowledge. And, to Wayne Westcott, PhD, for all of your guidance in all things fitness.

And to my family: My husband Andrew, who's always believed in me even when I haven't; my kids Jacob and Mia, whose hugs make everything better; and my parents, Gary and Rosalie Toth, who are always ready to pitch in and help at a moment's notice. Thank you for putting up with me! I love you all!

Hugs,
Michele

Endnotes

· · ➤➤➤ ⦗⦗⦗ · ·

CHAPTER 1

1   Julie Deardorff, "Why Walking Is Not Exercise," *Chicago Tribune*, April, 14, 2011. www
    .chicagotribune.com/chi-walking-is-it-exercise-20110414-story.html

2   "Walking Is Not Exercise—But It May Still Be the Best Form of Exercise We Know," Braindiet.com.
    www.braindiet.com/walking-is-not-exercise-but-it-may-still-the-best-form-of-exercise-we-know

3   "Walking Is Not Exercise," Slobody. www.vimeo.com/172410006

4   https://www.surgeongeneral.gov/library/calls/walking-and-walkable-communities/

5   Victoria A. Catenacci, et al. "Physical Activity Patterns in the National Weight Control Registry,"
    Obesity (Silver Spring), January 2008; 16(1):153–61. www.ncbi.nlm.nih.gov/pmc/articles
    /PMC4578963/

6   "NWCR Facts," National Weight Control Registry. www.nwcr.ws/research/default.htm

7   S. Garnier et al., "Is Practice Rate Rather Than Exercise Intensity More Important in Health
    Benefits of Moderately Obese Postmenopausal Women?" *Annals of Physical and Rehabilitation
    Medicine,* June 2015; 58(3):119–25. www.ncbi.nlm.nih.gov/pubmed/26004812

8   Victoria A. Catenacci et al., "Physical Activity Patterns Using Accelerometry in the National
    Weight Control Registry," *Obesity,* June 2011; 19(6):1163–170. https://www.ncbi.nlm.nih.gov
    /pmc/articles/PMC4560526/

CHAPTER 2

1   K. C. Heesch, "Physical Activity, Walking, and Quality of Life in Women with Depressive
    Symptoms," *American Journal of Preventive Medicine,* March 2015; 48(3):281–91. www
    .scientificamerican.com/article/regular-walking-can-help-ease-depression

2   James A. Blumenthal et al., "Exercise and Pharmacotherapy in the Treatment of Major Depressive
    Disorder," *Psychosomatic Medicine,* 2007; Sept.–Oct. 69(7):587–96. www.ncbi
    .nlm.nih.gov/pmc/articles/PMC2702700

3   Jorge Mota-Pereira et al., "Moderate Exercise Improves Depression Parameters in Treatment-
    Resistant Patients with Major Depressive Disorder," *Journal of Psychiatric Research,* August 2011;
    45(8):1005–1011. www.walkboston.org/sites/default/files/Moderate%20exercise%20improves
    %20depression%20parameters%20in%20treatment-resistant%20patients%20with
    %20major%20depressive%20disorder.pdf

4   Sharon G. Curhan et al., "Body Mass Index, Waist Circumference, Physical Activity, and Risk of
    Hearing Loss in Women," *American Journal of Medicine,* December 2013; 126(12):1142.e1–1142.
    e8. www.amjmed.com/article/S0002-9343(13)00673-6/fulltext

5   Kirk I. Erickson et al., "Exercise Training Increases Size of Hippocampus and Improves Memory," *Proceedings of the National Academy of Sciences,* February 15, 2011; 108(7):3017–22. www.ncbi.nlm.nih.gov/pmc/articles /PMC3041121

6   Joe Verghese et al., "Motoric Cognitive Risk Syndrome," *Neurology,* December 9, 2014; 83(24):2278–284. www .neurology.org/content/early/2014/07/16/WNL.0000000000000717.short?sid=20996e9a-9642-4870-b1fe -c7f1926407fc

7   K. I. Erickson et al., "Physical Activity Predicts Gray Matter Volume Late in Adulthood," *Neurology,* October 19, 2010; 75(16):1415–422. www.ncbi.nlm.nih.gov/pmc/articles/PMC3039208

8   Larissa Ledochowski et al., "Accute Effects of Brisk Walking on Sugary Snack Cravings in Overweight People, Affect and Responses to a Manipulated Stress Situation and to a Sugary Snack Cue: A Crossover Study," *PLOS One,* March 11, 2015; 10(3):e0119278. www.journals.plos.org/plosone/article?id=10.1371/journal.pone.0119278

9   Jose Maria Huerta et al., "Physical Activity and Risk of Cerebrovascular Disease in the European Prospective Investigation into Cancer and Nutrition-Spain Study," *Stroke,* December 24, 2012; 44(1):111–18. www.stroke .ahajournals.org/content/44/1/111

10 K. L. Moreau et al., "Increasing Daily Walking Lowers Blood Pressure in Postmenopausal Women," *Medicine and Science in Sports and Exercise,* November 2001; 33(11):1825–831. www.ncbi.nlm.nih.gov/pubmed/11689731

11 M. Hamer and Y. Chida, "Walking and Primary Prevention: A Meta-Analysis of Prospective Cohort Studies," *British Journal of Sports Medicine,* April 2008; 42(4):238–43. www.ncbi.nlm.nih.gov/pubmed/18048441

12 A. Emaus and I. Thune, "Physical Activity and Lung Cancer Prevention," *Recent Results in Cancer Research,* 2011; 186:101-133. www.ncbi.nlm.nih.gov/pubmed/21113762

13 Cristobal Esteban et al., "Influence of Changes in Physical Activity on Frequency of Hospitalization in Chronic Obstructive Pulmonary Disease," *Respirology,* April 2014; 19(3):330–38. www.onlinelibrary.wiley.com/doi /10.1111/resp.12239/abstract

14 Michelle D. Holmes et al., "Physical Activity and Survival after Breast Cancer Diagnosis," *Journal of the American Medical Association,* May 25, 2005; 293(20):2479–486. www.jamanetwork.com/journals/jama/fullarticle/200955

15 D. Feskanich et al., "Walking and Leisure-Time Activity and Risk of Hip Fracture in Postmenopausal Women," *Journal of the American Medical Association,* November 13, 2002; 288(18):2300–306. www.ncbi.nlm.nih.gov /pubmed/12425707

16 D. D. Dunlop et al., "Physical Activity Minimum Threshold Predicting Improved Function in Adults with Lower Limb Symptoms," *Arthritis Care and Research,* December 28, 2016; doi: 10.1002/acr.23181. www.ncbi.nlm.nih .gov/pubmed/28029748

17 Steven C. Moore et al., "Leisure Time Physical Activity of Moderate to Vigorous Intensity and Mortality: A Large Pooled Cohort Analysis," *PLOS Medicine,* November 2012; 9(11):e1001335. www.plos.org/plosmedicine/article ?id=10.1371/journal.pmed.1001335

18 Elizabeth V. Menshikova et al., "Effects of Exercise on Mitochondrial Content and Function in Aging Human Skeletal Muscle," *Journals of Gerontology Series A: Biological Sciences and Medical Sciences,* June 2006; 61(6):534–40. www.ncbi.nlm.nih.gov/pmc/articles/PMC1540458

19 Jason L. Talanian et al., "Two Weeks of High-Intensity Aerobic Interval Training Increases the Capacity for Fat Oxidation during Exercise in Women," *Journal of Applied Physiology,* April 1, 2007; 102(4):1439–47. www.jap .physiology.org/content/102/4/1439

20 Christie Y. Jeon et al., "Physical Activity of Moderate Intensity and Risk of Type 2 Diabetes," *Diabetes Care,* March 2007; 30(3):744–52. www.care.diabetesjournals.org/content/30/3/744.long

21 Cris A. Slentz et al., "Effects of Exercise Training Alone vs a Combined Exercise and Nutritional Lifestyle Intervention on Glucose Homeostasis in Prediabetic Individuals: A Randomised Controlled Trial," *Diabetologia,* October 2016; 59(10):2088–2098. www.link.springer.com/article/10.1007%2Fs00125-016-4051-z

22 Y. Okubo et al., "Walking Can Be More Effective Than Balance Training in Fall Prevention among Community-Dwelling Older Adults," *Geriatrics & Gerontology International,* January 2016; 16(1):118–25. www.ncbi.nlm.nih.gov/pubmed/25613322

23 Justin D. Crane, "Exercise-Stimulated Interleukin-15 Is Controlled by AMPK and Regulates Skin Metabolism and Aging," *Aging Cell,* August 2015; 14(4):625–34. www.ncbi.nlm.nih.gov/pmc/articles/PMC4531076

24 M. Hagner-Derengowska et al., "The Effect of a 10-Week Nordic Walking Training Program on the Level of GH and LH in Elderly Women," *Climacteric,* 2015;18(6):835–40. https://www.ncbi.nlm.nih.gov/pubmed/26406397

25 Romain Barres et al., "Acute Exercise Remodels Promoter Methylation in Human Skeletal Muscle," *Cell Metabolism,* March 7, 2012; 15(3):405–11. www.cell.com/cell-metabolism/abstract/S1550-4131(12)00005-8

26 Tina Ronn et al., "A Six Months Exercise Intervention Influences the Genome-Wide DNA Methylation Pattern in Human Adipose Tissue," *PLOS Genetics,* June 27, 2013; 9(6):e1003572. www.ncbi.nlm.nih.gov/pmc/articles/PMC3694844

27 Qibin Qi et al., "Television Watching, Leisure-Time Physical Activity and the Genetic Predisposition in Relation to Body Mass Index in Women and Men," *Circulation,* October 9, 2012; 126(15):1821–827. www.ncbi.nlm.nih.gov/pmc/articles/PMC3667660

28 Hudson Reddon et al., "Physical Activity and Genetic Predisposition to Obesity in a Multiethnic Longitudinal Study," *Scientific Reports,* January 4, 2016; 6:18672. www.ncbi.nlm.nih.gov/pmc/articles/PMC4698633

29 Eli Puterman et al., "The Power of Exercise: Buffering the Effect of Chronic Stress on Telomere Length," *PLOS One,* May 26, 2010; 5(5):e10837. www.ncbi.nlm.nih.gov/pmc/articles/PMC2877102

CHAPTER 3

1 D. K. White et al., "Trajectories of Gait Speed Predict Mortality in Well-Functioning Older Adults: The Health, Aging, and Body Composition Study," *Journals of Gerontology Series A: Biological Sciences and Medical Sciences,* April 2013; 68(4):456–64. ncbi.nlm.nih.gov/pubmed/23051974

2 Deirdre A. Roberson et al., "Negative Perceptions of Aging and Decline in Walking Speed: A Self-Fulfilling Prophecy," *PLOS One,* April 29, 2015; 10(4):e0123260. www.ncbi.nlm.nih.gov/pmc/articles/PMC4414532

3 Jason Duvall and Raymond De Young, "Some Strategies for Sustaining a Walking Routine: Insights from Experienced Walkers," *Journal of Physical Activity and Health,* 2013; 10:10–18. www.naspspa.org/AcuCustom/Sitename/Documents/DocumentItem/02_duvall_JPAH_20110050-eja.pdf

4 Vanessa M. Patrick and Henrik Hagtvedt, " 'I Don't' versus 'I Can't': When Empowered Refusal Motives Goal-Directed Behavior," *Journal of Consumer Research,* August 1, 2012; 39(2):371–81. www.academic.oup.com/jcr/article/39/2/371/1797950/I-Don-t-versus-I-Can-t-When-Empowered-Refusal

5 Carolina O. C. Werle et al., "Is It Fun or Exercise? The Framing of Physical Activity Biases Subsequent Snacking," *Marketing Letters,* December 2015; 26(4):691–702. www.link.springer.com/article/10.1007/s11002-014-9301-6

6 Loretta DiPietro et al., "Three 15-min Bouts of Moderate Postmeal Walking Significantly Improves 24-h Glycemic Control in Older People at Risk for Impaired Glucose Tolerance," *Diabetes Care,* October 2013; 36(10):3262–268. www.care.diabetesjournals.org/content/36/10/3262

CHAPTER 5

1 Jeffrey Conrath Miller and Ziatan Krizan, "Walking Facilitates Positive Affect (Even When Expecting the Opposite)," *Emotion,* August 2016; 16(5):775–85. www.psycnet.apa.org/psycinfo/2016-19953-001

2 B. C. Focht, "Brief Walks in Outdoor and Laboratory Environments: Effects on Affective Responses, Enjoyment, and Intentions to Walk for Exercise," *Research Quarterly for Exercise and Sport,* September 2009; 80(3):611–20. https://www.ncbi.nlm.nih.gov/pubmed/19791648

3 J. Barton and J. Pretty, "What Is the Best Dose of Nature and Green Exercise for Improving Mental Health? A Multi-Study Analysis, *Environmental Science and Technology,* May 15, 2010; 44(10): 3497–455. https://www.ncbi.nlm.nih.gov/pubmed/20337470

4 J. Michalak et al., "How We Walk Affects What We Remember: Gait Modifications through Biofeedback Change Negative Affective Memory Bias," *Journal of Behavior Therapy and Experimental Psychiatry,* March 2015; 46: 121–25. https://www.ncbi.nlm.nih.gov/pubmed/25310681

CHAPTER 6

1 J. J. Duncan et al., "Women Walking for Health and Fitness. How Much Is Enough?" *Journal of the American Medical Association,* December 18, 1991; 266(23):3295–299. www.jamanetwork.com/journals/jama/article-abstract/393937

2 Werner W. K. Hoeger et al., "One-Mile Step Count at Walking and Running Speeds," *American College of Sports Medicine's Health and Fitness Journal,* January/February 2008; 12(1):14–19. www.journals.lww.com/acsm-health fitness/Abstract/2008/01000/ONE_MILE_STEP_COUNT_AT_WALKING_AND_RUNNING_SPEEDS .7.aspx

CHAPTER 7

1 K. Karstoft, "The Effects of Free-Living Interval-Walking Training on Glycemic Control, Body Composition, and Physical Fitness in Type 2 Diabetic Patients: A Randomized, Controlled Trial," *Diabetes Care,* February 2013; 36(2):22836. www.ncbi.nlm.nih.gov/pubmed/23002086

2 Larissa Ledochowski et al., "Accute Effects of Brisk Walking on Sugary Snack Cravings in Overweight People, Affect and Responses to a Manipulated Stress Situation and to a Sugary Snack Cue: A Crossover Study," *PLOS One,* March 11, 2015; 10(3):e0119278. www.journals.plos.org/plosone/article?id=10.1371/journal.pone.0119278

CHAPTER 8

1 Brian A. Irving et al., "Effect of Exercise Training Intensity on Abdominal Visceral Fat and Body composition," *Medicine and Sciences in Sports and Exercise,* November 2008; 40(11):1863–872. www.ncbi.nlm.nih.gov/pmc /articles/PMC2730190

CHAPTER 9

1 Barbara J. Jefferis et al., "Protective Effect of Time Spent Walking on Risk of Stroke in Older Men," *Stroke,* January 2014; 45(1):194–99. www.stroke.ahajournals.org/content/early/2013/11/14/STROKEAHA.113.002246

2 Dena M. Bravata et al., "Using Pedometers to Increase Physical Activity and Improve Health: A Systematic Review," *Journal of the American Medical Association,* November 21, 2007; 298(19):2296–304. www.jamanetwork .com/journals/jama/article-abstract/209526

CHAPTER 15

1 K. Karstoft et al., "The Effects of Interval- vs. Continuous Exercise on Excess Post-Exercise Oxygen Consumption and Substrate Oxidation Rates in Subjects with Type 2 Diabetes," *Metabolism,* September 2016; 65(9):1316–325. www.ncbi.nlm.nih.gov/pubmed/27506739

CHAPTER 16

1 K. Karstoft, "The Effects of Free-Living Interval-Walking Training on Glycemic Control, Body Composition, and Physical Fitness in Type 2 Diabetic Patients: A Randomized, Controlled Trial," *Diabetes Care,* February 2013; 36(2):228–36. www.ncbi.nlm.nih.gov/pmc/articles/PMC3554285

CHAPTER 17

1 Andrea D. Smith et al. Physical Activity and Incident Type 2 Diabetes Mellitus: A Systematic Review and Dose–Response Meta-analysis of Prospective Cohort Studies. *Diabetologia*, 2016; doi: 10.1007/s00125-016-4079-0.

2 Stoyan Dimitrov et al, Inflammation and Exercise: Inhibition of Monocytic Intracellular TNF Production by Acute exercise via β2-adrenergic Activation. *Brain, Behavior, and Immunity*, 2016; doi: 10.1016/j.bbi.2016.12.017.

CHAPTER 21

1 Ami R. Zota et al., "Recent Fast Food Consumption and Bisphenol A and Phthalates Exposures among the U.S. Population in NHANES, 2003–2010," *Environmental Health Perspectives,* October 2016; 124(10):1521–528. www.ehp.niehs.nih.gov/15-10803

2 Xia Wang et al., "Fruit and Vegetable Consumption and Mortality from All Causes, Cardiovascular Disease, and Cancer: Systematic Review and Dose-Response Meta-Analysis of Prospective Cohort Studies," *British Medical Journal,* July 29, 2014; 349:bmj.g4490. www.bmj.com/content/349/bmj.g4490

3 Quanhe Yang et al., "Added Sugar Intake and Cardiovascular Diseases Mortality among US Adults," *Journal of the American Medical Association Internal Medicine,* April 2014; 174(4):516–24. www.jamanetwork.com/journals/jamainternalmedicine/fullarticle/1819573

4 Shana J. Kim et al., "Effects of Dietary Pulse Consumption on Body Weight: A Systematic Review and Meta-Analysis of Randomized Controlled Trials," *American Journal of Clinical Nutrition,* 2016; 103:1213–223. www.ajcn.nutrition.org/content/103/5/1213.full.pdf+html

5 Marlene D. Kristensen et al., "Meals Based on Vegetable Protein Sources (Beans and Peas) Are More Satiating Than Meals Based on Animal Protein Sources (Veal and Pork)—A Randomized Cross-Over Meal Test Study," *Food and Nutrition Research,* 2016; 60:32634. www.ncbi.nlm.nih.gov/pmc/articles/PMC5073301

6 Hongyu Wu et al., "Association between Dietary Whole Grain Intake and Risk of Mortality: Two Large Perspective Studies in US Men and Women," *Journal of the American Medical Association Internal Medicine,* March 2015; 175(3):373–84. www.jamanetwork.com/journals/jamainternalmedicine/fullarticle/2087877

7 Rebecca S. Mozaffarian et al., "Identifying Whole Grain Foods: A Comparison of Different Approaches for Selecting More Healthful Whole Grain Products," *Public Health Nutrition,* December 2013; 16(12):2255264. www.ncbi.nlm.nih.gov/pmc/articles/PMC4486284

8 Ameneh Madjd et al., "Beneficial Effects of Replacing Diet Beverages with Water on Type 2 Diabetic Obese Women Following a Hypo-Energetic Diet: A Randomized, 24-Week Clinical Trial," *Diabetes, Obesity, and Metabolism,* January 2017; 19(1):125–32. www.onlinelibrary.wiley.com/doi/10.1111/dom.12793/full

CHAPTER 24

1 Catherine B. Chan and Daniel A. Ryan, "Assessing the Effects of Weather Conditions on Physical Activity Participation Using Objective Measures," *International Journal of Environmental Research and Public Health,* October 2009; 6(10):2639–654. ncbi.nlm.nih.gov/pmc/articles/PMC2790098

Index

·‚·ᐳᐳᐳ ᐸᐸᐸ‚·‚

Underscored page references indicate sidebar/table references. **Boldface** references indicate photographs.

Listen, Lose & Love Every Step

I wish I could be with you for every walk, but it's just not physically possible.

That's where the *Walk Your Way to Better Health* MP3 player comes in. You just clip this handy device to your shirt, pop in your earbuds, and press play. Let me do the rest. It comes fully loaded with 8 different walking routines—4½ hours worth, in all:

- Track 1   Introduction
- Track 2   45-Minute Moderate Walk
- Track 3   30-Minute Brisk Walk
- Track 4   40-Minute Fast Walk
- Track 5   20-Minute Fat Burning Interval 1
- Track 6   20-Minute Fat Burning Interval 2
- Track 7   40-Minute Fat Burning Interval 3
- Track 8   25-Minute Get Fast Interval Walk
- Track 9   25-Minute Firm Up Walk
- Track 10   Cooldown

No matter which track you listen to, you can take me with you on every single walk. Even better, each routine is set to music that automatically helps you to walk at the right pace.

If you already have the MP3 player, then just use the track that best fits your Walk Your Way to Better Health goals. If you don't already have the player, you can order it from RodaleStore.com.

Happy walking!